Praise

"*Crybaby* depicts obstacles of
Along the way, a triumph of the soul emerges."

— JESSICA ZUCKER, author of
I Had a Miscarriage: A Memoir, a Movement

"In this fiercely honest, sharply observed memoir diving into the tumult of relationships, living with cancer, infertility, longing, loss, and complicated hope, Cheryl E. Klein surfaces with insights bright and beautiful as sea glass."

— SHIRA SPECTOR, author of *Red Rock Baby Candy*

"*Crybaby* is a wild ride through waves of lovehood, sickhood, motherhood, and humanhood."

— SUSAN STRAIGHT, author of *In the Country of Women*

"I'm grateful to Cheryl Klein for being real about all the messy emotions tied to the strange and powerful desire for a child. I found myself rooting wildly for Klein—and for everyone daring to take on such a common human experience from their most uncommon queer lives."

— MICHELLE TEA, author of *Knocking Myself Up: A Memoir of My (In)Fertility*

"*Crybaby* is a story of perseverance, of understanding, of showing up—for oneself and for one another. I felt my own body move with the turn of a page."

— MIAH JEFFRA, author of *The Violence Almanac*

CRYBABY

Infertility, Illness, and Other Things That Were Not the End of the World

CHERYL E. KLEIN

CRYBABY © 2022 by Cheryl E. Klein

First Edition

Brown Paper Press
6475 E. Pacific Coast Highway #329
Long Beach, CA 90803

Cover and interior design by Zoe Norvell

Library of Congress Cataloging-in-Publication Data

Names: Klein, Cheryl, author. Title: Crybaby : infertility, illness, and other things that were not the end of the world / Cheryl E. Klein. Description: First edition. | Long Beach : Brown Paper Press, 2022.
Identifiers: LCCN 2021043490 (print) | LCCN 2021043491 (ebook) | ISBN 9781941932193 (paperback) | ISBN 9781941932209 (ebook)
Subjects: LCSH: Klein, Cheryl,—Health. | Breast—Cancer—Patients—Biography. | Lesbian couples as parents. | Pregnancy.
Classification: LCC RC280.B8 K5684 2022 (print) | LCC RC280.B8 (ebook) | DDC 616.99/4490092 [B]--dc23/eng/20211108

LC record available at https://lccn.loc.gov/2021043490

LC ebook record available at https://lccn.loc.gov/2021043491

Portions of this book previously appeared, in slightly different form, in *The Manifest-Station* ("Love in the Time of Drought," 2014) and *MUTHA Magazine* ("The Tribe of Broken Plans," 2013; "Everything I Wanted to Know About Parenting but Was Too Much of a Kid to Ask," 2019).

This memoir is a representation of the author's memory, translated into narrative. As such, certain omissions and inaccuracies are inevitable. Some conversations capture the gist and spirit of what was said, but are not exact transcripts, and some names have been changed.

To my esposa and to my sister.
Thank you both for walking into it with me.

TABLE OF CONTENTS

DIAGNOSIS

I had hoped my three weeks at the MacDowell artist colony would be a happy ending to a harrowing two years.

I wrote in my cabin all day, watching deer and wild turkeys in the New Hampshire meadow outside my window. The deer were graceful and slow moving; the turkeys made me think of dinosaurs, slick and prehistoric. Every day around lunchtime, I called CC and asked whether she was ovulating. Every night, I drank with other writers and artists: the twenty-one-year-old writing about her mother's suicide, the middle-aged sociologist writing about all the suicides in Las Vegas.

Hurricane Sandy hit New England midway through my residency. I didn't need a reminder that storms could disrupt any idyll. I spent the night curled on an air mattress in the old farmhouse that served as MacDowell's communal building. Wind rattled the shutters and whipped the power lines outside as I thought about ghosts and loss and the dent that I'd discovered in my right breast shortly before my arrival.

I flew back home on a Sunday. I voted. Obama won again, and the country seemed to exhale. I resolved to lose the weight I put on at MacDowell. And on Friday, I took an Ativan for anxiety and drove to the Huntington-Hill Breast Center for the annual ultrasound that my cautious doctor had recommended because of my fibrous breast tissue. I was committed to believing that the dent was not a *thing*, but that's not the same as actual belief.

I watched the technician's face as she moved the ultrasound wand over my gelled-up breast. She had dark eyes, a badge that said "Dulce," and the poker face of a professional. I'd spent so much time in the past year trying to read technicians' micro-expressions as their machines searched my body for fertility problems. They'd scanned my uterus, ovaries, and fallopian tubes, but my chest had been spared scrutiny . . . mostly. Dulce clicked and typed and left the room, revealing nothing.

I waited for her to return and say everything was fine, because that's what happened the last time I'd found a tiny lump in my breast; it had been declared benign. And the thing that's happened before is always the easiest to imagine. Still, I was shaking. I'd had bad-news ultrasounds, too, and could translate them to this situation.

She came back into the room and told me I needed a mammogram. Today, she said. Now. That was new. The second waiting room had a gurgling fountain, recent issues of *InStyle*, and Cirque du Soleil playing on multiple TV screens. It was an ideal waiting room, except that it was still a waiting room and I was crying.

A woman with a caramel-colored weave asked if she could pray for me. She put her head close to mine, and her hair swung over both of us. I hadn't prayed since college, when it had dawned on me that if God had a plan at all, it wasn't likely to be altered by the constant buzzing of human suggestion. I associated strangers' offers of prayer with televangelists and faith healings and people who thought people like me were headed for hell. Yet the woman's physical presence—this act of kindness aimed in my direction— was something. I took a breath, cradled for a moment in the quiet curtain of her hair.

When my name was called, I murmured my thanks and stood up. *Walk into it,* I told myself, not sure what "it" was.

"Are you doing a mammogram because you see something that's an issue, or is it just, like, standard?" I asked Dulce. I hadn't even mentioned the dent because I hadn't talked to a doctor yet. I had hoped to get through the whole visit without seeing a doctor face-to-face, which would mean there was something to discuss. Magical thinking has a way of seeping through hospital walls.

"Well, the mammogram we have on file for you is two years old, so we have an incomplete picture with just the ultrasound," Dulce said.

After the mammogram, I waited in what I supposed was a special room for crying people who might spook healthy patients. When Dulce came back with a doctor in tow, I knew it wasn't an all-clear.

"We found a couple of spots where there's evidence of calcification," she explained. "That *can* be an indicator of early-stage breast cancer, but it can also be caused by an injury or hormonal changes."

"Well, I've had a lot of those lately. Hormonal changes, I mean," I sniffled. But injuries too—mostly the emotional variety, but they seemed to reside in my body like squatters.

"We want to do a biopsy to find out for sure," she said. "Is there someone you can call?"

Was there? Things with CC still felt so delicate. I'd dumped my problems on her, and it almost ruined us. How could I possibly hand this exponentially bigger problem to her? I called my sister.

"It will be okay," Cathy said. "Lots of people have biopsies, and it's nothing."

"But with Mom—"

"I know."

When I was at MacDowell, I'd called Cathy and made her run through the calculations with me. How old was our mom's cousin when she was diagnosed with breast cancer? She must have at least been post-menopausal, right? That seemed to be an important factor, a cliff you fell off as a woman. The point after which you were no longer considered sexy, couldn't have babies, and had a higher risk of cancer.

I was crying. I imagined the nurses whispering into walkie-talkies: *We got a live one on our hands!* But I wasn't putting up a fuss. Just crying. I could cry while driving on the freeway, doing the dishes, ordering at Starbucks, writing a novel. If I let crying slow me down, I'd never get anything done.

I came home and yelled and threw things and cried some more. Two days later I called in for my biopsy results. The woman on the phone said the good news was that the cancer probably hadn't spread to my lymph nodes.

I lived in America and had health insurance and my parents never hit me and my dad gave me generously loaded American Express cards most Christmases. But the things I wanted—love, health, a baby—didn't seem like such first-world things to want. Fairness was a fraught concept, but I could still wish for it.

The woman on the phone told me what to do next, and for that small guidance, I was grateful. Call this number. Get this test. With a shaking hand, I wrote down the number. I wrote down the name of the test. When I was writing, I was making a world instead of just being trampled by it.

PART I

CHAPTER 1: FERTILE

When I moved in with my first girlfriend, Bari, we sketched a floor plan of our new apartment and mapped out how we'd paint it. The front room would be eggplant, the middle room sunshine yellow overlaid with goldenrod diamonds, the bedroom pale blue and a rich coffee brown. The kitchen would have a pineapple theme.

We sat across from each other at Psychobabble, the coffee shop around the corner from Bari's old place, which for now was still her current place. I was giddy and caffeinated, imagining a life out of a Francesca Lia Block novel, even if my girlfriend was a grad student in public policy.

The apartment was on the bottom left of a Pepto-pink fourplex near the University of Southern California. The landlord gave us the key early and, at our request, ripped up the royal blue carpet in the front room. The original hardwood was lovely, but stained and gummy with glue. With a handheld belt sander, we made our way from door to dining room, inhaling dust and varnish fumes. After hours of work, we had aching backs and a floor that was slightly less stained and gummy.

What was eggplant in the can was purple on the walls. Next to the yellow dining room, whose diamonds tapered off because we got tired of stenciling, it looked like an homage to the Lakers. The brown in the bedroom looked, literally, like shit.

So much had gotten lost in the translation from dream to reality. We were much better at the future than the present. In the present, we fought about the papers Bari piled on the dining room table and whether I loved her enough. I maintained that I did; she said something was missing and it was on me to find it. In the future, though, we'd adopt two little girls from Eastern Europe and name them Yana Walker and Leland Winter. Their middle names would be our mothers' maiden names.

Our upstairs neighbor was a film student named Tania. She had a long face and long white-blond hair and wore long hippie skirts. She made a movie about a woman with amnesia and convinced a minor lesbian movie star to play the protagonist's girlfriend. She just walked up to the movie star at a film festival and asked her. She wrote movies about queer women, but she'd had a boyfriend as long as we'd known her. Once, I told Bari I wished we could be as interesting and stylish as Tania, and Bari didn't appreciate the implication that we were boring, or that stylishness held any value at all.

One afternoon I was washing dishes when there was a hard knock at the door. The man on the porch wore a black polo shirt with the word *Coroner* on it.

"How well do you know your neighbor?" he asked.

Tania had been crossing the street on her bike, and failed to see the bus rounding the corner. The other way to tell the story was that a bus driver had made a right turn and failed to see the cyclist in the crosswalk.

The coroner asked who else Tania knew. She had a boyfriend, we said. He wanted to know how long they'd been dating. We said a few years, and the coroner deemed that sufficient, so we gave him Norm's number.

While we waited for Tania's boyfriend to come over, I finished washing the dishes. A part of me stood outside myself, watching me shake soap suds from my elbows. So this was what I did when something terrible happened. My mom was going through chemo for her third round of ovarian cancer, and the treatment seemed to be working. Still, Tania's death felt like a dress rehearsal.

Seeds had already been planted: disease, worry, a connection to my mom that was simultaneously deep and threatened. One of those thematic life arcs only visible in hindsight. For now, it was just a vague unease.

Years later, when I would insist that it *was* in fact possible that I had this disease or that disease, that this or that bad fate might befall me, people would sometimes say, *Sure, it's possible, but you could just as easily get hit by a bus*, and I would think of Tania.

At her memorial service, our landlord said, "It's so sad. She and Norm wanted to buy a house and get married and have a baby." I seethed. The Tania I knew, or thought I knew, hated capitalism and wanted to adopt one kid of every race. Then again, maybe both versions of her were true.

The last conversation I had with my mom that did not take place in a hospital was on July 26, 2003. By that time, she'd gone into remission twice and relapsed twice. The cancer shrunk dramatically every time her team of oncologists unleashed a round of chemo, so no one ever gave us a timeline; no one ever told her to get her things in order. We were in my childhood bedroom, sorting through the artifacts of my youth: yearbooks and journals, cheerleading uniforms and pom-poms shedding metallic green strands like stray mermaid hair.

I'd been living with Bari for a year and we'd had a huge fight. I was vacuuming our apartment when I glanced up and apparently gave her a look that proved I didn't love her. Bari claimed she'd seen it in my eyes—some deep proof of my lack of appropriate feelings toward her. My claims to the contrary were unconvincing.

My mom and I sat on the edge of my twin bed, on the periwinkle-and-white quilt she'd patched when my pet rat nibbled a hole in it. At the end of the hallway, outside on the deck, my dad napped on a patio chair next to a week's worth of comics saved from the *Daily Breeze*. The neighbor kids threw a ball that would probably end up in our backyard.

"Every couple argues," she said. "It will be fine, honey." Her reassurance was convincing, at least initially.

"I don't know what she wants from me," I sobbed. I listed the ways that I was a good girlfriend and Bari was a bad one—or if not bad, at least unfair. My mom listened. Her khaki-green eyes were mirrors.

My mom paused and studied my tear-streaked face. "Oh honey. Your relationship really *is* just like a heterosexual one."

Sometimes I let myself imagine what might have happened if my mom and I had been able to continue our arc. I discovered I was queer when I was in my early twenties, around the same time my mom discovered that her bloating and abdominal pain were ovarian cancer. We were both hopelessly, forgivably self-absorbed, each calling out to the other from our respective universes, trying to meet in the black cosmos and rekindle our closeness.

I drove to my parents' house every weekend when she was in treatment, starting in 2000. I mailed postcards from the desk of my dot-com job during the week. She asked for hugs and I cringed at her neediness. But I always hugged her. I talked with false bravado about gay rights and *Rent* and she never missed a beat in accepting me, but she admitted, "This is going to take some getting used to."

Her epiphany, that queer relationships were made from the same human building blocks as straight ones, was genuine—a necessary step on a path to a deeper, more comfortable acceptance. Even if she didn't meet my needs in that moment.

My argumentative, oversized modus operandi—accusing her of *lacking intellectual rigor*—was a necessary but belated act of separation I hadn't quite gotten around to in my teens. I wish I could have been more forgiving.

We loved each other through the tension. But we never got a chance to see what lay on the other side.

In August 2003, she was hospitalized for a bowel obstruction. She had a feeding tube down her throat and couldn't talk those last weeks. She wrote a few notes. I can hear her voice saying, in that reassuringly minimizing way of hers, "Oh honey, I'll be fine." I don't know if she actually got a chance to say it, before the tube, or if it's a manifestation of desire and nonlinear memory.

I still hear it. *Oh honey, it'll be fine.* When I'm worried about my own health. My job. My marriage.

Things were and weren't fine. Are and aren't. I grieved in a thousand ways. The circle of mother-child-mother and life-death-life turned into a black hole. Its gravity nearly crushed me.

Two years after my mom died, Bari broke up with me. She explained she was embarking on some sort of self-improvement path and needed someone stronger and more convincingly loving by her side. I fell to my knees on the remaining Dodger-blue carpet in our apartment, surrounded by our Laker walls, heaving with sobs. Yet I knew that if I could live without my mom, I could live without Bari.

Four months later, I made myself a MySpace profile (it was a dating site for a minute, sort of) and selected whom I wanted to meet from the drop-down options: female, seeking women, twenty-five to thirty-five, ten-mile radius, open to children. CC's page played a Jenny Lewis song when I clicked on it. *What are you changing? / Who do you think you're changing? / You can't change things, we're all stuck in our ways.*

Before our first date, she told me, "I'll try really hard to be on time, but I tend to run late."

Bari, like me, had believed in perfection; more specifically, she believed that I should better myself in order to successfully extract her own dormant perfection. I should be like that girl she flirted with for a while in college, the one who moved to Ireland, who most certainly would have been The One had she stayed.

I was instantly smitten with CC and her casual awareness of her own flaws, not to mention her acceptance of them. She was on time that night in March. She had straight dark hair, strong cheekbones, a boyish gait, and girlish nervousness. We drank vodka and cranberry juice and discovered our parents had attended Santa Ana High School a few years apart. My mom and grandmother were buried in the same cemetery as her cousin from the rougher side of her family tree, the one shot by a rival gang member.

She did run late. In the months before she made me a key, I spent a lot of time on her porch with her black cat, Ferdinand, waiting for her to get home. She rented a Craftsman bungalow in Highland Park, a hilly neighborhood between downtown Los Angeles and Pasadena. To get there, you had to make an abrupt right-hand turn off the 110 freeway.

One night we played Frisbee in her backyard, between the lavender bushes and the Vespa that her roommate was forever working on. Until that night, the subject of children had been limited to our online profiles (we both checked "someday"), but I liked CC enough that I wanted to hear it out loud.

"You want kids, right?" I asked as casually as possible, which is to say: not very casually.

The lime green Frisbee sailed between us. She jumped and caught it with one hand, giving her jeans a tug with the other. She was short-waisted and long-legged, with shiny dark hair and kind eyes that sloped down at the corners. Lying in bed, looking at the tribal tattoo on her back, I felt like I could exist in that space forever. She'd gotten the tattoo on a whim, and she liked that it kind of looked like a runner.

"I do," she said. "I'm not in a rush. My ex was really revving her engine. She had it all planned out, where we'd each get pregnant with one, and she'd go first."

"So you'd want to, like, have kids biologically or . . . ?"

"I don't know. I kind of like the idea of having one biologically and adopting one."

I imagined her pregnant—big belly, bare feet, and all. It was kind of sexy.

Years later, as we started to circle in on the specifics, she clarified that she liked the idea of *me* getting pregnant. Pregnancy itself wasn't something I had thought much about—the point was kids, not how they came to us. But just because you've never thought about doing heroin doesn't mean you won't fall in love at first hit, or that it won't destroy you.

CHAPTER 2: INFERTILE

I traveled to New York for work in the slushy spring of 2010. I was thirty-three years old and spent my days chaperoning the winners of a writing contest to meetings with agents and editors. I spent my evenings hunched over my laptop at the Chelsea Pines Inn, teaching an online class. The walls were decorated with old Blackglama fur ads. Judy Garland and Angela Lansbury gazed over their cheekbones and asked *What becomes a Legend most?* The hotel cat, Charlie, curled at the foot of my bed and licked his own black and white fur.

Most of my students were writing vampire novels or chick lit. Keely was writing a story about an elderly woman who grew up in the shadow of her older sister who had died in infancy. The woman's mother always compared her living daughter's mundane life to her dead daughter's imagined perfect one.

Keely's writing was honest and funny, full of exquisite Midwestern detail. She was also the mother of two young boys and had trained as a doula. In an email, I said something like, *I don't know how you find time to write with two kids! I hope I can do the same when I'm a mom.*

Before leaving for New York, I called my health insurance company to see if they covered the cost of IUIs. (I was learning the lingo. An IUI, intrauterine insemination, involved placing sperm inside the uterus while a woman is ovulating. Sort of turkey-baster-plus.) The woman I talked to seemed to be thinking out loud. "Well, we cover some infertility costs. If you've been trying for a year."

"My partner is a woman," I said. With a small laugh, I added, "I guess you could say we've been trying for four years."

"You could find a guy and like . . . " She trailed off.

Eventually she connected me with her manager, who promised we'd be covered. I was aware—not for the first or last time—how my situation teetered between challenge and privilege. Making a baby was never going to be a matter of romance or accident for us. It would be work. But if there was one thing I was good at, if there was a thing I'd been raised for, it was work. And I had a so-called Cadillac health plan and an official email from the manager.

Don't get me wrong, it's HARD, said Keely's quick reply. *I couldn't finish my fiction workshop fall semester because I went into labor with Halston early. But you do it just because you do it.*

It's not like my life now is just brimming with free time, I emailed back. *But it's good to know people make it work.*

You will be an awesome mom, she assured me.

The next morning, I woke up and took my temperature: 97.9. I put a dot on a graph I'd photocopied from *The Ultimate Guide to Pregnancy for Lesbians.* The way your body temperature rose and fell on certain cycle days was supposed to tell you when you were most fertile, although I wasn't sure how, or even when, my cycle started.

I assumed it started the first day after my period ended, because that was when I felt newest.

The book's author recounted her own story: three home attempts, some frustration, and an IUI that resulted in a baby girl. I hoped it wouldn't take us four tries, although part of my rationale for nudging CC to get started was *It might take us a year.*

I checked my email, and then the Lambda Literary website. The Lammy Awards were due out. My editor had submitted my novel, and there weren't that many new queer books published in any given year, so I thought I had a shot. But it wasn't even on the short list.

I closed my laptop and put on running clothes. The sky was a chilly pink-blue and the streets of Chelsea were bustling with people in peacoats and dark jeans. I jogged up a set of metal stairs to the High Line, a defunct section of elevated railway remodeled as a park. Locals and tourists lay on wooden lounge chairs in jackets and scarves, practicing the rituals of summer. People walked small dogs and large ones. My panting turned to crying, as it sometimes did. If I ran long enough and hard enough, an emotion would work its way to the surface like an old splinter.

My novel was as flawed as any first book, published by a small press and printed on stiff paper. But it was my heart, and I'd hoped it would win. I ran and cried and wished my mom was there to tell me how smart I was and how stupid the selection committee was.

In May I made an appointment with a fertility specialist. Dr. Saadat's Beverly Hills office was filled with heavy furniture and photo albums of babies and their grateful parents. Dr. Saadat was teddy-bear chubby with a relaxed Farsi drawl. A little bit nasal, a little bit sardonic. Had he treated same-sex couples before? we asked. Yes, many. Was there any risk of ovarian cancer? Because I had a family history. "Only if you do more than twelve cycles," he said. I was thirty-three. No one was worried it would take twelve cycles. Being thirty-three in a fertility office was like wearing a crown and a sash.

Dr. Saadat said he'd order some basic tests. CC and I parted ways at the elevator to go to our offices on opposite ends of the city. As I was crossing the street, CC pulled up in her red Honda. She leaned out the window and yelled, "Hey, Mama, lookin' fertile!" and I laughed.

The word *endometriosis* seemed to fall from the sky. I think my friend Nicole was the one to mention it, as a possible cause of her irritable bowel issues. My mind grabbed it and began to sew a story, like a pearl around sand, like rogue endometrial tissue around an intestine. Hadn't I always had really bad menstrual cramps? Didn't my mom have endometriosis? (My dad confirmed she had, although it didn't prevent her from having two kids in her mid-thirties with no medical intervention.)

I started studying my shits in the toilet bowl for bits of blood or endometrial tissue. I didn't know what it would look like—I imagined something wavy like a jellyfish. My shits became tea leaves that would tell me whether I was worthy of carrying a child.

Later, when fact and fiction collided and erupted, I would remind myself of this: My first self-diagnosis came before any actual diagnosis. I never had endometriosis. It all began with fiction.

In early June I went to another office in Beverly Hills. They put a tube in my uterus and shot purple dye up my fallopian tubes, where sperm might one day swim. I was warned about "mild to moderate" cramping, but the test made my abdomen cramp harder than even my worst period. And my worst periods were bad. The tech who administered it said my left tube was fine, but there appeared to be a blockage of some sort in my right. A blocked fallopian tube would mean eggs from that ovary would have no path to my uterus, reducing the likelihood of pregnancy by half. Or, he added, it could just be a spasm.

I started to cry. The tech slowly backed away. He dealt in hysteria only in the most historical/mythological sense. He wanted no part of female emotion.

After the dye test, I felt like I was dragging my heart around on the ground, tethered to a frayed string. CC said, "I'm sorry, I should have gone to the test with you." Keely emailed, *Don't worry, you only need one good tube.* As the weeks went by and I continued to mope, CC started to rescind her sympathy a bit. What was the huge deal?

What *was* it? Certainly nothing I could name. And yet it was as if something I'd been trying to name my whole life—a particular kind of internal wrongness that would rain fire upon my attempts to find love—had been dyed purple and made visible.

The day before our flight to Seattle, I was still mourning my potentially imperfect fertility. As I scooped cat litter from the box in our bedroom, I speculated out loud, "What do you think the chances are that it was a muscle spasm?"

"I don't know," CC sighed. "That's impossible to know." She was in bed, reading *The New Yorker.* Our flight was early, but I knew she would fall asleep without setting an alarm and pack in the morning while I paced and nagged.

On the table at the end of our bed, I made neat piles of folded jeans and shirts and dresses, sorting them into ten days' worth of outfits. I put the new dress my sister had bought me on top. It was printed with big, impressionistic teal-and-black flowers, and it made me look like I had a waist. It was my $80 wedding dress.

"Endometriosis can block your fallopian tubes, but—"

CC put down her magazine with a smack. "I feel like this is the only thing you care about. Do you even want to get married in Vancouver? We could just take a vacation. Obviously we need one."

It was as if someone had just handed me a bomb, and I needed to handle it very, very carefully.

"Are you really . . . I mean, obviously I'm not going to *make* you marry me if you don't want to, but no, I don't want to just take a vacation."

California had legalized same-sex marriage for a minute, then rescinded it with a nasty amendment to the state constitution, but the state still recognized marriages performed in places where it was legal. Vancouver seemed like the nicest viable destination. I'd googled "gay marriage Vancouver officiants" and found an accountant named Lynn who performed civil ceremonies at her office. The plan was to spend a few days in Seattle with friends, then rent a car and drive across the border. Neither of us felt particularly romantic about it. Maybe we would have a reception someday, but for now, the point was to get the legal stuff over with and make a baby. We had lived together nearly three years. I figured we were pretty much married already.

So why did I feel like I was about to be left at the altar?

"You've been so depressed lately," CC said. "I just don't feel like that's a great time to get married."

"I'm not depressed." I climbed onto the bed and looked her in the eye. "I got some bad news. I'm sorry I haven't handled it well, but I love you and I want to fucking marry you."

CC did not like to feel forced into things. I'd learned that during the first bumpy months after we moved in together, into a duplex that wasn't her first choice. She carried that grudge coldly, alternately ignoring me and making mean barbs until eventually we went on a ski trip with friends and made up.

"Look, we don't have to decide anything now," I said. "Let's just go to Vancouver and keep talking about it."

"Okay." She switched off the light and fell asleep almost immediately. I was painfully awake. In the light from the hallway, I finished packing. My non-wedding wedding dress now looked tainted and sad, like a white gown at a thrift store. I zipped my suitcase shut.

I sat on the bathroom floor and cried some more. My natural instinct was to wake CC up and make her reassure me of her love, but I knew that wouldn't make her want to marry me more. I also knew that if I didn't get any sleep, I'd be in poor shape to play the part of Person You'd Want To Marry in the morning. I took a shot of NyQuil and knocked myself out.

We worked our way up the coast. In Washington, we visited my old friend Daisy, who'd bought a mid-century house with her older girlfriend, Laura, in a tiny town on the Hood River. They ran an antique shop along the highway, selling vintage toys and board games and novelty glassware. Daisy decorated clocks with old Scrabble tiles and game pieces. Most of their friends were retirees.

At the private beach near their house, I helped Daisy collect driftwood she planned to turn into a garden trellis. She told me about some drama they'd had involving their septic tank.

"It was a mess," she said, "but it helped us get to know our neighbors. They're all really nice, and they treat us like we're their kids."

"You guys have created something kind of amazing here," I said.

"We thought about trying to buy a place in Olympia." They both worked there, for the Washington State Department of Health. "And we like Olympia. It's cute. But this seemed like the chance to have a really different kind of life."

Daisy was an old soul. She wasn't on MySpace or Facebook. She didn't drink, because alcohol messed with her antidepressants. Her email signature said *Wisdom is the reward you get for a lifetime of listening when you'd have preferred to talk.* And she pretty much lived up to it. The things she said *did* seem wise, and over the next few years, as my own life zigged and zagged and failed to unfold as I had hoped, I would keep myself going by thinking *Maybe this is my chance to live a really different kind of life.*

I tried to listen, but I did a lot of talking. About my blocked fallopian tube, my borderline progesterone levels, and the rough patch CC and I were going through.

"I don't know if we're going to have kids," Daisy said. "Laura's already going through menopause. But I think if we did, I'd want to take in kids who were already in the world."

The wind whipped our hair and turned our noses red. The river was wide enough to pass as the ocean at first glance.

"That makes sense. It's part of the secondhand worldview thing, right? Like recycling."

She laughed. "Exactly."

I took it as a given that there was a moral hierarchy to kid-having. Fertility treatment was the most self-indulgent, and adopting an older child—especially one with some type of disability—was the most noble. I was comfortable with the fact that Daisy was morally superior to me.

Daisy pulled a small, heart-shaped stone from the sand. "Look how pretty this is. I'm thinking of building a treasure chest and filling it with sand and little odds and ends that kids could hunt for while their parents shop. Wouldn't that be cool?"

CC and I showed our passports at the Canadian border and checked into a weird little bed-and-breakfast in Gastown, a half-gentrified neighborhood where you could buy a ceramic berry carton for $25 but wouldn't want to walk alone after sunset. We visited the aquarium and smiled at beluga whales.

The pre-written vows that Lynn, the accountant, emailed us called for rings, which we hadn't planned to exchange. Before we left, I packed a little silver ring that had belonged to my mom, but CC didn't have an heirloom to give me. So she bought a dolphin mood ring at the aquarium, and on the afternoon of June 23, we met Lynn and her assistant, who would step in as our witness.

The official Canadian civil ceremony only required us to testify that neither of us was already married to someone else, but Lynn added an Apache prayer as a romantic flourish. I cried. CC didn't.

Afterward, we ordered oysters and cocktails at a restaurant called Chill Winston. We phoned our families and exhaled and ate and laughed. Neither of us said *Thank god that's over,* but I suspect we were both thinking it, maybe for different reasons. Getting married was just so *weird*, even when you tried not to make a big deal out of it.

CC's family was effusive on the phone, which was noteworthy considering that her mom had cried why-must-my-daughter-be-gay tears when CC announced her engagement to her ex-girlfriend at Christmas dinner years ago

After she clicked her phone shut, she said, "Maybe we could have a party when we get home. To celebrate." She was warming to something—an institution, an idea, me?

"Wasn't that kind of the plan? To do the low-key thing with the paperwork and then just have a casual reception kind of thing in LA?"

"No, we never talked about that."

"We definitely talked about that."

Instead of debating, we ordered a second round of drinks.

CHAPTER 3: TRYING

CC started grad school the week I started a common fertility drug called Clomid. We went to a diner so she could study (psychology, with a plan to get licensed in marriage and family therapy) and I could write, and at exactly 10:00 p.m., I took my first pill—a small, white disc that turned bitter on my tongue and would, hopefully, convince my ovaries to make more egg follicles in advance of the IUI. The plan, if it could be called that, for dealing with my possibly-faulty fallopian tube was essentially trial and error.

The only vegetarian items on the menu were salad, mashed potatoes, and milkshakes. I ordered black coffee and poured in two plastic tubs of cream. I was trying to eat extra healthy; I had a feeling that today my real life was starting.

I had been starting and restarting my *real life* almost daily since fourth grade, when I began imagining that I could abandon my unruly hair and dorky habits if I just tried hard enough. *As soon as I step over that crack in the pavement, I'll start over and never say anything embarrassing again,* I told myself. In seventh grade, I started dieting, not because I was fat but because I was tall. It didn't occur to me that this was a recipe for failure. I pinned a picture of teenage contortionists on my bulletin board and imagined that if I ate only apples and bell peppers, I, too, would be waifish, ethereal, and exceptionally talented.

The summer before tenth grade, I whittled myself from 130 pounds to 110. I learned how to take an hour to eat a granola bar, one oat at a time. My too-big breasts shrank, my period stopped, and a downy layer of hair grew on my lower back. Everyone complimented me, even teachers. I lived in a town that regularly sent volleyball players to the Olympics: Manhattan Beach liked its residents thin and athletic. I dressed up as a go-go dancer that Halloween, my first "sexy" costume ever, but in my vinyl boots and thrift store minidress I felt both sexy and sexless. I gave myself the night off from dieting, and my best friend and I melted down our Halloween chocolate and dipped marshmallows in it.

I felt sick the next day. Even though I'd planned to pig out (that was always how I referred to it in my mind: *pigging out*), I felt like I'd failed. As fall gave way to the holidays, I pigged out more and more. By spring I'd gained ten pounds.

The school guidance counselor pulled me out of English class one day and into her office, where I sat on an itchy upholstered chair and studied posters of University of California schools.

Ms. Aldrich got right to it. "A couple of your teachers have noticed some changes recently, and they're worried about you. They wondered if you might be pregnant." They had noticed my weight gain, my bigger boobs. Ms. Aldrich didn't phrase it that way, exactly; she said, "Everyone develops at a different rate, but they just wondered if maybe—"

I was wearing cutoff jean shorts and a loose tank top, the kind a girl might choose to cover a three-months belly. I burst into tears.

"I'm not even sexually active," I said, borrowing a phrase from the family life unit of biology class.

I'd never been on a date. I'd never kissed anyone, not even during a game of Truth or Dare. I was a fifteen-year-old old maid. During the day I harbored a crush on a boy from the drama program. At night I stayed awake worrying I might be a lesbian, although I wasn't sure why. I wasn't a tomboy, and I didn't fantasize about girls. I just had a creeping sense of dread that there was something terrible about me.

Everyone said Ms. Aldrich was a dyke. She coached girls' volleyball and wore her hair in a blond mullet that was lighter than her red-brown face, except for the pale outline of sunglasses around her eyes. She went to the same gym I did, and once I'd seen her playfully snap her towel against the butt of a woman on a treadmill. If Ms. Aldrich thought I was a pregnant heterosexual, I was officially, completely invisible.

She handed me a box of tissues. "It's okay, it's okay, a lot of girls just go through puberty later than others. It's all completely normal."

I'd gotten boobs in fifth grade and started my period just before sixth. She had it all wrong, except for the assumption that there was something terrible about me.

For years, I told no one but my mom about what Ms. Aldrich had said. That night I closed my eyes and mentally recited the same prayer I always did: *Family and friends. Pets and plants. Earthquakes and other natural and unnatural disasters. Please let me be normal. Please let me be normal.*

It evolved into a kind of rosary. My family wasn't religious, but I had inherited some sort of recessive Jewish-Catholic gene, prone to guilt and ritual. What would organized religion do without obsessive compulsive disorder? And what would OCD do without a flair for religiosity?

On the thirteenth day of my cycle, at exactly 10:00 p.m., I pinched a half-inch of skin to the left of my belly button, like the nurse at Dr. Saadat's office had demonstrated. I held the refrigerated syringe in my left hand and pushed the needle in, slowly compressing the plunger. The spot of blood grew ladybug-sized, and I pressed on it with an alcohol wipe. I might have moped too much about my infertility; I might be prone to anxiety; I might not even make a very good mother, but I was not afraid of needles.

The previous day's ultrasound had confirmed three good follicles in my left ovary, five in the right. Eight grainy jelly beans on a screen. Eight chances for a baby. A plastic tube would deposit Donor #5850's sperm directly into my uterus, no long swim required. And that night's "trigger shot" of the pregnancy hormone hCG would ensure I ovulated right on time. I did a kind of magical math in my head and concluded that while the average woman had a one-in-five chance of getting pregnant each cycle, I had at least a two-in-three chance. Subtract a couple of points for frozen sperm, which tend to die once thawed. Add points for eating whole grains and exercising regularly, which must have something to do with this, right? Add points for acupuncture, which I could get at Dr. Saadat's office for an extra $125. The acupuncturist, a nice, not-too-woo guy named Ryan, said it would help me relax and stimulate blood flow. How could I *not* get pregnant?

Exactly thirty-four hours later, CC and I took separate cars to Dr. Saadat's office again, sitting side by side on the 110 freeway as traffic bottlenecked toward downtown. The morning felt historic. My coworker Jamie, who was currently on maternity leave, had described the decision to become a parent as "jumping off a cliff." Being pregnant, she said, connected her with the animals. The non-clinical language of pregnancy did have an animalistic ring to it: brood, nest, welp, suckle. I wanted to taste all of it.

I thought of my mom, gone seven years, and felt connected to her too, and cried. Now I would finally understand something amorphous but important—nothing short of the secret of life.

CC met me in front of Dr. Saadat's building carrying the dry-ice canister—it looked like a small beer keg—that contained #5850's sperm. The sperm bank was near her office, so she'd been tasked with picking it up. I quizzed her relentlessly about whether she had let it sit in her car for more than a few minutes, risking an early thaw. She hadn't.

What we knew about #5850: He was Mexican, like CC, and a professor of anthropology (we called him "The Professor"; choice number two was "The Graphic Designer"). In his baby picture, he had bright, sincere eyes and a dimple.

"Do you want to keep the vial?" asked the nurse, once we confirmed that the number matched the one on the packing slip.

CC and I looked at each other. Was that something people did?

"I'm good," I said. "You?"

"No, we're good," CC told the nurse.

While the sperm thawed, I had my first acupuncture appointment. White towels and long slender needles. New Age music and my thumping heart.

And then Dr. Saadat got his speculum and syringe and tubing. When I'd first learned that fertility doctors do an ultrasound on the first day of patients' periods, I cringed. My body was closed for business at least two days a month, as far as I was concerned. But already I was becoming immune to any need for privacy. Every question about my body seemed to end with an ultrasound wand up my vagina. If it got us a baby, it was worth it. (This would become a mantra: *If it gets us a baby, it's worth it,* as the universe upped the ante on what "it" was.) CC held my hand and made little jokes.

I lay on my back with my hips tilted upward for ten minutes afterward, while CC played a mellow mix on her iPod. Despite drugs, old fertility tricks were still invoked. The general thinking seemed to be, *It can't hurt.*

It can't hurt to do acupuncture. It can't hurt to avoid alcohol during the two weeks before pregnancy can be detected. It can't hurt to wear the rose quartz ring my sister gave me for good luck. It can't hurt to give up sugar. It can't hurt to do yoga, but not inversions. It can't hurt to stop jogging.

These precautions can't hurt as far as the baby is concerned. The tightrope walk might hurt the mother, but anxiety, too, is considered bad for fertility, so better not to worry about all that worrying.

At lunch that day I ate a black bean burrito (whole wheat tortilla) and thought, *I might be pregnant.* It was like having a birthday as a little kid, waiting to feel five instead of four. Later I would learn that the fertilized egg doesn't take root in the uterus wall until day six, so only the most extreme anti-abortion activists would consider a woman pregnant by lunchtime. But at that point I was still fuzzy on the details.

I googled early signs of pregnancy:

Tender breasts

Mild cramping

Spotting

Heartburn

Nausea

Discharge

Every website cautioned that *every pregnancy is different* and pointed out that most early pregnancy signs mimicked premenstrual symptoms. Eight days into the two-week wait, I noticed cramps that weren't like my usual PMS cramps, which were dull and ugly, like a clenched fist. These were small and sharp. If cramps could be cute, these were. The only explanation I could think of—the only reason my body might be doing something it hadn't before—was pregnancy.

At home I whispered to one of our cats, Temecula, who sat on the arm of our old velveteen chair: "T-Mec, I think I'm pregnant."

She studied me with round blue eyes. She was a good listener. A calico in pastel—gray, white, and peach—and the smartest cat I'd ever had. Picking her up was like picking up a water balloon; she was cuddly and seemingly boneless, too chubby to be a huntress, but quick with her paws. She would keep the secret I was too superstitious to tell anyone else.

The secret filled me up. It propelled me. It kept me from concentrating. I emailed Keely, who commiserated: *The two-week wait is the worst! I usually start testing around day ten. Sometimes you can get a faint line. And if you don't, don't worry—it doesn't mean you're not pregnant! Oh, and don't waste your money on those expensive pregnancy tests. The dollar store ones work just fine.*

I wasted my money on an expensive pregnancy test, the only brand our sperm bank recommended. Two more days till I could try.

Our book club was meeting that night to talk about *Tattoos on the Heart,* Father Gregory Boyle's memoir about working with gang members in East LA and starting Homeboy Industries to help them leave that life. I liked the book. It was funny and simple without being simplistic. A lot of stories seemed to start with Father Greg trying to wrap up a long day, only to have a homie burst into his office with some problem. It heartened me, somehow, that even a priest who devoted his life to helping the toughest people craved peace and quiet. He wrote about *radical acceptance* and pointing angry young men toward a metaphorical light switch that they would flip themselves, illuminating their own lives. He wasn't out to save anyone.

The idea that I didn't have to prove anything to anyone did, in fact, seem radical to me. I heard somewhere that people tend to view God the way they view their fathers. Mine was kind and fair, but his fairness was threaded with a subtext that if I fucked up, I might un-earn his love. I had never put it to the test, not even as a teenager. So while in theory I believed God was a little more like my mom—someone who found me endlessly interesting and lovable—in practice, I was always trying to fill up my existential bank account so I wouldn't go into debt if I ever needed to call in a favor.

I picked up tacos from Homegirl Café, one of the businesses Father Greg had started with help from the community. Everything I did that day was tinted rosy by my secret. I waited a long time for the tacos, studying the waitresses with their hard, dark makeup. I floated to my car, not bothering to check the order, which was comically wrong, as if waiting to become one of Father Greg's stories.

I tried not to pee on my shaking hand. I balanced the stick on the bathroom sink, making sure the pee part didn't touch anything. Keely warned me the second stripe would be pale, not at all like the picture on the package.

I squinted. My heart raced. There was only one stripe.

I cried, but it was a perfunctory sort of crying. It was only Day Ten of the two-week wait. I wasn't out of the game until my period started. That night I sat in on a writing workshop that my organization, Poets & Writers, was sponsoring. It was someone's birthday, and a box of cupcakes with pink frosting and sprinkles was making the rounds. I abstained.

"Oh, come on!" one of the writers urged.

I harbored a vague feeling that sugar stood between me and pregnancy. Sacrificing this cupcake was like placing a small dead animal on an altar. I claimed my stomach had been off earlier in the day. *Early morning sickness,* I thought, holding onto what remained a secret, even to my own body.

Tuesday morning there was a pink brushstroke of blood on my underwear. The internet told me it could be "implantation bleeding," a little burst of blood released by an embryo making itself at home in the uterine lining. What a terrible invention on nature's part—to make all the signs of starting one's period (cramping, headaches, even blood) the same as signs of pregnancy. But by now I had regular cramps, not the funny little crab pinches.

I emailed Keely, who wrote back immediately. *Uuuugggggghh, that's awful, I'm so sorry. That's the worst thing I can imagine.*

No, no, I replied. *The worst thing would be getting pregnant and miscarrying.*

In my fertility-related Googling, I'd come across a blog post by a woman who identified herself as CNBC: Childless Not By Choice. She had gone through every fertility treatment in the book and tried to adopt. After eleven years, she gave up and moved to Denmark, where she was trying to build a life for herself with her husband, but she spent a lot of time alone in her car, crying.

Please don't let it take eleven years, I begged no one in particular. Even scarier was the prospect of giving up. My limbs were heavy, my eyes were puffy, and the last thing I wanted to do was lead a roundtable discussion about the literary community in Riverside. But that's what I did. For me, the path of least resistance was to do what I always did: show up and get to work.

CHAPTER 4: STILL TRYING

My mom claimed nothing good happened in November. Both her parents had died that month. And like everyone in her generation, she remembered where she was on November 22, 1963, when she saw grainy footage of President Kennedy's open car rolling through Dealey Plaza. He smiled and waved, and then his head tilted forward and whipped back, and Jackie was climbing over the back of the car, trying to stop time.

I decided I would approach the November IUI pessimistically, thereby tricking fate. I used the same strategy when taking tests in school, announcing "I'm going to fail!" no matter how much I'd studied. I usually got an A or a B. This time I didn't treat the IUI as special. I lay on Dr. Saadat's vinyl bench and held CC's hand and cried. Then I went to work.

Even things that are awful become more palatable just by becoming familiar. Now when I googled pregnancy symptoms, the links showed up in been-here-read-that purple. Links led to other links, and I found more obscure symptoms. One woman said she knew she was pregnant when her pee started to smell different. Every time I visited the bathroom, I sniffed the air above the toilet. Did my pee have a slightly . . . *nutty* smell?

Emails flew between Keely's inbox and mine. She noted my slightly low progesterone and short luteal phase (the time between ovulation and menstruation) and wondered if, in fact, I *had* been pregnant the first cycle and had an early miscarriage. In a panic, I called Dr. Saadat's office. Should I be taking progesterone supplements?

"We could prescribe you progesterone suppositories, if you want," his nurse said. Her tone was that of a waitress who didn't have a lot of faith in my choice of entrees, but ultimately didn't care what the fuck I ordered.

That, and the word *suppository,* put me off. "I guess I'll see where this goes and think about progesterone for next time."

I hoped there wouldn't *be* a next time, but then I got my period again. If the stakes had felt high from the start—$500 for a vial of sperm, a cap on how hard I could tempt ovarian cancer with Clomid—they became higher with two failed IUIs behind me. True, lots of people took a few months to get pregnant. But straight people had unlimited free sperm. And somehow my marginal fertility seemed more marginal than other women's marginal fertility. It was wronger, uglier, deeper; and the only way to stamp it out of existence was to be perfect, better, first.

We switched donors for our third IUI, replacing The Professor with The Salvadorian, who had already sired several children. So what if he wasn't Mexican? I was feeling less particular and more desperate.

This time my attitudinal strategy was humor. As I lay with my feet in the stirrups, Dr. Saadat remarked that my uterus was tilted, but he knew his way down this winding road, as he'd been there before, and we all had a good laugh.

During my third two-week wait, I made sure to develop a contingency plan, thereby decreasing my chances of actually needing it. Dr. Saadat explained that, statistically, women who didn't get pregnant after three IUIs were unlikely to get pregnant after five or six.

Just a few months before, I'd categorized in vitro fertilization (IVF) the same as plastic surgery and maid service: things that mark you as a certain kind of well-heeled, hateable woman, even if my official stance was *to each her own.* Now I found myself sitting across from Dr. Saadat as he explained the process, which involved prescribing hormones to maximize egg production, retrieving eggs from a woman's ovaries, fertilizing them to make an embryo, and then placing them directly into a woman's uterus. He showed us charts of his success rate for women in my age bracket (something like sixty-five percent). He leaned back in his tufted office chair. It all seemed very matter-of-fact.

I met with Michelle, a good friend of my coworker Jamie's, who *was* well-heeled—with a nanny and a personal trainer and a lovely Spanish-style house in Mid-City—but not at all hateable. She'd gotten pregnant with her son on her second IUI, and pregnant with her daughter on her first round of IVF. We drank tea at her dining room table, which looked as though it had been cut from an old-growth forest. She was friendly and honest.

"The thing about IVF is, if it works, it's totally worth it. I'm lucky—it worked. I don't know how I'd feel if it didn't."

"What about mood swings and stuff?" I asked. "I get pretty insane just from PMS, and I think Clomid might be making me kind of emotional, too."

It was the first time I'd given voice to that possibility. Was I feeling desperate and ravenously competitive and always on the verge of tears because of Clomid? Or because I'd built my life around being Good At Things and my mom had died and all my friends were having babies? Could I blame twenty-five percent of my despair on Clomid? Fifty percent? I didn't want to be Clomid's puppet, but there was also something liberating and solvable about it. Clomid would end, one way or another.

"I thought I was alright on all the IVF drugs, but when I talk to my husband and parents, they're like, *Um, no.*" Michelle laughed. "They're not the same drugs, though. So some people have a good experience with Clomid and a bad experience with Bravelle, and vice versa. You just never know."

"I know. I want to know, though. I'm kind of a control freak." I took a long sip of tea. "What about the money? It's so expensive."

"We were lucky that we could kind of afford it. I mean, we had the money, but also, now that money is not set aside for Alexander's college tuition, you know?"

"I have pretty good insurance, and my dad has offered to help out." I always felt the need to confess—that I wasn't rich, and also that I was.

"And that's a family decision," Michelle said. I liked the phrase, as if I weren't a spoiled rich kid, but part of a team.

A few days later, CC and I went to church and listened to Ed Bacon—a kind, funny, activist Episcopalian with a small celebrity following—talk about callings. If you did something solely because it was the right thing to do, but you hated it, maybe you were in the wrong line of work, he said. If you loved music but worked as a civil rights attorney, you might be a good person, but you weren't heeding your call. On the other hand, if you channeled your love of music into writing jingles for a yogurt company—when you had no particular passion for yogurt—you probably weren't maximizing your calling either.

I considered this as I sat next to CC beneath All Saints' peaked Gothic Revival arches. Since I was a kid, I'd contemplated adopting. Our close family friends had adopted two kids and fostered several more. CC's mom was adopted by friends in the United States after her mother died in Mexico. What if adoption was my calling? I had never liked the expression *Everything happens for a reason.* It was one thing to find a silver lining in a bad situation, but quite another to declare injustice collateral damage in a grand, unseeable plan. But *callings* I could get behind. They were one part career aptitude test, one part magic. They required careful listening to the sound of one's own heart. I had accepted that I didn't have it in me to join the Peace Corps or Doctors Without Borders. But maybe adopting a human who needed a home was my sweet spot, the thing that was for me and also for another person.

I told CC as much on the way to the car. She said what she always said, which was that she was open to it, and also to IVF. I envied how much less fraught the world was for her. I hoped it was all a moot point anyway.

I had the pinchy cramps again, and a low-grade headache. I sat through meetings and readings, counting the minutes until I could take a pregnancy test. The night before testing day, CC admitted she had hidden my box of pee sticks.

"It was making you so crazy last time. I didn't want us to go through that again. Why can't we just wait until we visit the doctor?"

"Come on. If you can't trust me with a pregnancy test, how can you trust me with a kid? It's my body."

"Okay, fine, I'll see if I can find the box."

She could not. I believed her, because almost every morning she searched for her keys or wallet or some piece of paper she'd misplaced.

I drove to the twenty-four-hour CVS in Pasadena at 10:45. The streets were wide open, the night cool and clear. I felt strange and giddy.

I was too jumpy to sleep. After tossing and turning in bed next to CC, I took a pillow and blanket into our office and made a little nest for myself on the carpet. I watched some stupid TV, tossed and turned some more, and then it was morning, or close enough.

I peed in a cup this time, and dunked the stick in it. I wanted no room for error.

I was not pregnant. It seemed both unfathomable and inevitable.

I called in sick to work. I stayed in bed and watched TV shows about awful people, and rich, ridiculous people.

That night, I went to a friend's apartment for a potluck and group critique of his novel manuscript, which I'd really loved. Nothing in me felt capable, but at least he was a gay man, hence unlikely to be pregnant. Our friend Amy was there, and I murmured my bad news to her. She was sympathetic. She and her partner, Kim, had gone back and forth about whether to have kids. They had gotten as far as browsing sperm donors. Amy was up-front about her angst, if vague. I got the impression there was relationship stuff they wanted to work through first. *Fuck all those straight women with their easy pregnancies*, Amy and I agreed.

CC and I decided to take the rest of December off and try IVF after the holidays. Wasting even a few weeks seemed like madness to me, but I wanted to demonstrate how chill I was, how good at compromise. She worked for the public programs office of an art college and always got two weeks off at Christmas. Poets & Writers slowed to a crawl. She moped when our friends went out of town. While I filled the days with writing and cleaning projects, she used them to wonder whether she really had any friends at all. And if I didn't make myself available to see movies and hike and go out to eat, it got worse.

As 2010 waned, neither of us was in good shape. We went to the Los Angeles County Museum of Art one afternoon shortly before Christmas and stared at each other across a plate of Ethiopian food afterward. Little blobs of stewed lentils and carrots sat untouched on spongy bread.

"You're so depressed lately," she said, her voice full of desperation.

"I don't know what's wrong with me," I said, meaning, *Tell me nothing is.*

Another day, we went to a bar in Atwater Village with Justine, Sam, Piper, and Piper's newish girlfriend, Lindy. Justine and Sam were our best couple-friends. Justine and CC had met years ago at a social group at the city's Gay and Lesbian Center, where, as CC described it, everyone was either newly out, newly single, newly sober, or new in town. CC and Justine were both the latter and clung to each other like life preservers in a sea of awkwardness. Justine could be overly direct, but she balanced it with a big grin and Southern manners. She had a pixie cut and clothes that always seemed perfectly tailored. I admired her ability to spend months finding the perfect jacket, whereas I bought things because they were pretty and on sale, and told myself I would somehow make my boobs smaller to fit. Justine bent the world to her, and I tried to bend myself to the world.

Sam was a civil rights lawyer, as warm and hyper as Justine was cool and slow. He was the first trans person with whom I'd spent any significant amount of time. I kept thinking about the parallels between being trans and being infertile, both our stories shaped by uncooperative bodies that didn't perform as society demanded.

Justine and Sam had been feeding a feral cat population in the backyard of their Hollywood house for a few months. They'd also been trapping, spaying, and neutering them one by one, like the responsible citizens they were. But one of the female cats escaped capture and had given birth to three kittens currently living in the couple's bathtub.

At the bar, Sam scrolled through pictures on his phone: two black kittens and a long-haired kitten with Siamese-style markings. One of the black kittens was big and fluffy, the other was short-haired and tiny.

"They are soooooooo cute," Lindy gushed.

Piper said, "Lindy would adopt every cat in our neighborhood if she could."

Sam said, "We learned that kittens from the same litter can have different fathers. Mama cats can get pregnant twice. We think the little guy here just didn't have as much time to cook as the other two. He has some breathing problems, but he's eating, so that's good."

"We want to adopt the two healthy ones," Lindy announced. Apparently they'd already discussed it. They were calling them Bruce and Marlowe. The runt was Squeaky.

I looked at my friends in the low blue light of Sam's phone. It *figured* that Piper and Lindy wanted the big alpha kittens. To live in their new house at the top of the hill. As good lesbians, the next step was to get cats. Could a baby be far off?

Then Piper told us she was taking classes to become a foster parent.

It was all I could do not to throw my beer in her face. Didn't she know we were trying to get pregnant? Didn't she know it was our turn first?

"I've been learning so much," she said. "The foster care process is actually really fast, and really interesting."

"I'm going to the bathroom," I said.

Already it was becoming a pattern: me fighting tears, or not fighting them, stumbling through public places in search of a corner to cry in and angrily text my sister. I made my way to the entrance of the bar and out to the cold air.

Since when is Piper a foster parent? I texted. *She's never said anything about this before! Now she's going to be yet another person who becomes a parent before I do.*

It occurred to me that my reaction was oversized, that someone might argue, *So what? How does it hurt you if Piper adopts a child?* But it was as if a spirit had been roused from the deep to take over my body and my texting fingers. How *dare* she waltz into my life and be better and faster at everything I cared about?

And oh, fuck you, Piper, for not seeing the irony of taking only the big, healthy kittens. Don't you know the foster care system is full of kids who haven't been given a chance to thrive? Kids who, by some measure, were more like Squeaky?

Christmas came and went as it had every year since my mom died: a family performing happiness—which wasn't quite real—out of love, which was. I told Dr. Saadat and the nice woman in his billing department that I wanted to do IVF. Around that same time, I noticed something akin to a stretch mark on my left breast. I pressed my fingers into it and looked at it from different angles. It wasn't a lump, but I'd read somewhere that misshapen flesh could signal breast cancer, too.

I'd had an ultrasound in the fall, the last in a series of follow-ups stemming from a ball bearing–sized lump in my right breast two years before. Each time the results came back saying, essentially, *It's probably benign, but we can't be one hundred percent sure, so don't sue us.* That was good enough for me. The chances that I had breast cancer at age thirty-three were low. The chances that I had some extra stealth brand of breast cancer seemed miniscule.

I told myself all those things again, but three months of fertility treatment had made me extra vigilant about my body. I wanted it to be the best possible vessel to inject powerful hormones into. So I made another appointment with the Huntington-Hill Breast Center. Just in case.

I made dinner for my dad and sister the weekend before my appointment. My dad was full of questions about the IVF process. I was already burned-out and I hadn't even started. My dad's approach to any discussion was to ask questions until he really and truly understood. It was a rare and exhausting virtue.

"Dad, I'm glad you're helping me out with this, but I kind of don't have the energy to talk about it right now." I emptied a bag of spinach into a bowl and rummaged through his fridge for other non-wilted vegetables. My dad lived on frozen dinners and low-fat ice cream.

"I've read a few studies online, and everything I've found confirms what you said—the risk for ovarian cancer is only elevated if you do quite a few cycles."

"Well, good. Thanks for doing the research. Do you have any other vegetables?"

"There are mushrooms, and there should be some tomatoes there, too."

"These tomatoes? They look kind of wrinkly."

"They're fine. Okay, maybe not that one. But the rest are fine. I just bought them."

"Just bought them in 2004?" my sister said. The spice rack still held cardamom and nutmeg bought by my mom.

"Let's remember, too," my dad continued, "that Mom's doctors said it's unlikely that she even had a hereditary form of ovarian cancer, since the onset was post-menopausal. And we know now that it could have been exacerbated by hormone replacement therapy. Which is, of course, why you don't want to do more than—"

"Dad, I *know*. I'm being cautious. Why do you always have to warn me about the opposite side of everything?" He was always willing to risk my annoyance if it meant I might be spared the tragedy of not considering a possible pro or con. Usually a con.

"I trust you to make good decisions. I just want to make sure you've considered what we can agree is a negligible cancer risk—"

"Dad!" I snapped. "I said I don't want to talk about cancer right now!" The sad spinach salad went blurry as I started sobbing. I wanted a piece of paper saying I was healthy, that my body was normal and hospitable territory for a baby, and until I got it, I was as fragile as the glass balls on our Charlie Brown Christmas tree.

Two days later, I went to my breast ultrasound appointment. Certain rituals were starting to feel familiar. Wonder about your body. Feel sick to your stomach. Drive to the doctor. Hold your breath. Wait for an image on an ultrasound screen or a number on a printout, the textual readout of a vial of blood. Hand all your power to the medical staff, as if they're curanderos with access to gods who can be appeased with grateful smiles and chicken feet. The only difference was that the stakes were so much higher now—not merely permission to try for a baby, but permission to live.

I got the paper. A technician explained that hormonal changes can cause fat deposits in breast tissue to shift, which was probably the story behind my apparent stretch mark. I always left the Breast Center feeling hugely relieved and a little bit sad for all the people who didn't get to walk away feeling lighter, and this time was no exception.

My appointment had been early, and I didn't have to work until 11:00 a.m., so I had time to go to the gym. The air had a freshly washed feeling, crisp and bright. I turned the radio on and sped east toward the sun and the mountains, passing rows of pink apartment buildings. That Florence and the Machine song, "Dog Days Are Over," was playing on the radio.

I heard "dark days." I heard that they were over. I heard something about horses. I thought about the apocalypse. A song can be an anthem, a warning, a soundtrack for a mood that shifts. In all my favorite musicals, the reprise puts a little twist on the original lyrics. In *Into the Woods,* the witch initially sings *Children will listen* as a command. Later it's a warning to other parents: *Careful the tale you tell / That is the spell / Children will listen.* I was always telling myself a story and looking for signs of its trueness. The dark days are over, I told myself.

CHAPTER 5: EXPECTANT

I went on the pill for a few weeks because, I learned, birth control creates a fertility surge as soon as you go off it. As if women's bodies had pent-up, baby-making libidos just waiting to be let loose. I was supposed to start IVF meds as soon as the first red blood of my period arrived. But after a couple of pinkish-brown days, nothing more came.

"Come in for an ultrasound," Dr. Saadat said when I called him on my lunch break. "If we missed this cycle, we'll try next month."

Another month, another clamshell of birth control pills—these were nothing to him and torture to me. In the courtyard of the Spanish-style church where I often ate lunch, there were some shrubs, two uncomfortable benches, and a small bundle of fire-wood. I was already crying, but it wasn't bringing me the usual relief. An unfamiliar emotion was refusing to be stuffed beneath sadness and frustration, and it was that feeling that made me pound my fist into the firewood over and over until my knuckles bled.

The ultrasound confirmed I hadn't missed my window. Priscilla, a young nurse with a Hello Kitty tattoo on her neck, talked fast and acted annoyed when I asked her to repeat instructions for taking the medication. I wrote everything in a small red notebook with a ridiculous purple flower on the cover.

"It's all going to be on the printout," she said.

"I know, but I remember things better when I write them down." I didn't trust printouts to include everything, or to think the way I did. When I got home, I would type up my notes to drive those grooves even deeper into my brain, and to prove I could turn a terrifying process into bullet points.

The medications and needles filled an entire shopping bag, the square-bottomed kind you might get with a new pair of shoes. There were powders in glass jars to be mixed with liquid in different glass jars. It looked like a magic potion, and it was. The names of my prescriptions sounded like goddesses: Lupron, Menopur, Bravelle. The latter was the subject of a battle with my insurance company that lasted as long as a full-term pregnancy.

Or maybe Lupron, Menopur, and Bravelle were three weird sisters, and I was their apprentice witch, mixing my potions at the kitchen table each night.

I timed and measured and mixed and shot every night for days. My ritual was proof that I Worked Hard and Was Good. It also felt like Fucking With Nature, like I had Some Kind Of Disease. It wasn't so different from praying to the Virgin Mary on my knees or burying a chicken in the ground beneath a full moon, except for the science part. But science can become a kind of religion, too; not the series of inquiries and steps it's supposed to be, but a belief system that becomes a knee-jerk answer.

My ovaries bloomed with ripe follicles. Dr. Saadat gave me a trigger shot and scheduled egg retrieval for the next day, in the smaller office on the floor above the one where I'd gone for exams. A full bladder would position my uterus at a better angle, they said, so I drank a liter of water at the Starbucks down the street. CC ordered oatmeal and said the most encouraging things she could think of, but she didn't say, *I know this will work and you will definitely get pregnant with a healthy baby,* so she was useless to me.

I lay back in a sort of dentist's chair with stirrups, and when I woke up, Dr. Saadat said they'd retrieved seventeen eggs. I beamed. Ten or twelve would have been a success. The anesthesia caused me to throw up in a plastic bag on the way home, but I was back on top, an overachiever again.

While Dr. Saadat's staff spent the weekend fertilizing my eggs, we went to a wedding in Santa Monica. Our friends said quick vows in a flurry of rose petals on the boardwalk. The February wind whipped the bride's dress and mine, and animated the petals. I was bloated and constipated. Everyone walked up the hill to a Jamaican chicken restaurant with outdoor tables. Toast after adoring toast referenced babies, as if the thirty-four-year-old bride's biological clock were the real guest of honor. I felt the distance between us, which happened at weddings sometimes, the person you knew becoming an archetypal character in a very heterocentric play. But it wasn't just that. It was also that she, like Piper, was skipping to the front of the line.

I wondered if I was getting pregnant this very minute, The Salvadoran's sperm meeting my egg. If I felt not-completely-in-my-body that day, it was because part of me (my eggs) literally wasn't.

"The transfer" happened in the upstairs office with the fish tank and the black leather couch, but otherwise it was just like the IUIs. A syringe. Some tubing. Some awkwardness. Three embryos. Signatures promising we wouldn't sue.

Then I went home, got into bed, and waited. No one seemed to know for sure whether three days of bed rest helped the embryos implant. Maybe—in the tradition of midwives asking dads to boil water while women gave birth—it was a task designed to make people feel useful. I'd cleaned the house and cooked food ahead of time. I had a stack of books and the first season of *Gossip Girl* on DVD. I planned to do a lot of writing.

During this wait, my boobs were sore, but maybe that was just the drugs. This time, though, at an Oscar party where we watched a pregnant Natalie Portman accept her Best Actress award for *Black Swan*, I felt a wave of heartburn. I remembered a friend saying that heartburn was her first symptom, one she rarely had in her non-pregnant life. I thought, *Maybe.*

This time I didn't bother with home pregnancy tests. I thought I'd read that IVF drugs created false positives. Besides, this time Dr. Saadat's office was offering to do a blood test nine days out. My case had been escalated for reasons that weren't entirely clear, as well as for some that were.

Dora, the phlebotomist, promised she would call with results as soon as my blood had been analyzed. At 3:00 p.m., I called her, my hands shaking. Still no word, she said. I hung up, deflated and anxious. The office usually closed around 4:30; by 4:15 I still hadn't heard from her. I debated whether to call again. Normally I didn't like being a pest, but when the stakes were high, I was a *relentless* pest—like the time I desperately wanted an internship at *Detour* magazine, and the time I wanted to make sure I got press tickets to *Rent.* I had called the magazine office and the musical's publicist, respectively, every day for months.

At 4:22, my cell phone rang.

I stepped swiftly into the hall. I didn't want anyone to see me cry, if it came to crying.

"We say hCG level below seven is not pregnant, and anything above fourteen is," Dora said. I knew this, of course.

HCG was one of many medical acronyms thrown about in fertility forums (along with cutesy ones I hated, like DH for "dear husband"). It stood for human chorionic gonadotropin, also known as the pregnancy hormone, also used as a shady weight loss supplement, because what wasn't?

"What was mine?" I tried to sound businesslike.

"Yours was nine."

"Oh. What does that . . . mean, exactly?"

"It means we should test again in two days. We're looking for it to double or more."

"So I'm not *not* pregnant."

"You are pregnant, but we don't know if it will be viable yet."

"Okay. Thanks."

I flipped my phone shut and sat in the hallway, leaning on a narrow strip of wall between the door to my office and the stairwell. I was pregnant. Sort of.

I hadn't made plans that night. It was the first of many that would remain intentionally blank in my calendar, reserved for celebrating or crying. But instead I felt foggy, like I was moving slowly through a pool of lukewarm water.

CC and I went to Villa Sombrero down the street. We sat in a booth and shared a giant combo plate. I did not order a margarita.

"In class we sat in a circle and had to talk about a time we felt powerless," she said.

"What did you say?"

She shrugged. "I wasn't really feeling it. I ended up talking about my first year of teaching and how much I hated it, but I don't know if that would be my true answer, if I had more time to think about it."

"What did other people say?"

"One woman talked about when she was attacked by her neighbor's dog when she was a little kid. It just kind of came out of nowhere and mowed her down, and she had to get a ton of stitches. And then Adrienne—she's one of those people who, the more you know her, the more stories come out. She's been a model and she's dating this guy in Queens of the Stone Age. Anyway, she had an awful childhood. She told a story about her dad taking her on some kind of drug mission and just brutally beating her in his truck for no real reason. Because of some typical kid thing she was doing."

I told myself to be more like Adrienne. If bad things happened to me, I wanted to emerge from them strong and glamorous, my scars a veil of mystery. Right now I was wearing sweatpants and sitting cross-legged on a red vinyl bench, eating beans.

Finally CC said, "How about you? What was a time when you felt powerless?"

If the Inuit people have a hundred words for snow, shouldn't every culture have at least a dozen for crying? For the tears that surprise you, gushing like a burst dam; for the ones you have to coax out because you know you'll feel better after a good cry; for crying with your eyes and crying with your mouth and crying with your whole body. The tears that found me now were a slow but steady build, like a faucet filling a bucket.

"Now," I said.

On Friday morning I tested again. On Friday at work, again, I did nothing but look at my phone. Again I debated the right time to call Dora. I didn't want to bug her, but I didn't want her to leave for the day without calling me. I was starting to learn her schedule, like the stalker I was.

"Cheryl Klein . . . " She had a Filipino accent, full of hard *d*'s in place of *th*'s, and a friendly voice. I vastly preferred her to Priscilla, whose every sentence seemed to have a subtext of *It's weird that you'd care about* that, *that thing that is definitely not* my *job.* "Your hCG is nineteen."

"Oh! That's good, right?"

"Yes, we want it to double, and it doubled and just a little more. We will test again next week."

"Thanks so much. Okay, I'll see you on Tuesday. Have a wonderful weekend, Dora."

I truly, deeply wanted Dora to have a wonderful weekend. She *deserved* it. She was so kind and gentle. I wanted *everyone* to have a wonderful weekend. We all deserved it! We were all wonderful! If this were a movie, I would run outside in the snow barefoot, shouting Christmas greetings to everyone. Instead I called CC and emailed Keely.

I wanted to describe the experience of pregnancy, but even at the time, it was like trying to see a shadowy figure who was always disappearing around corners. I kept trying to catch a real glimpse, to look pregnancy in the face. It was, perhaps, like losing your virginity—one of those life experiences with a before and after, but the after is so different than you imagined—so mundane, so much like the before—that you wonder if you did something wrong.

That first weekend of knowing, CC and Justine and I went to an art show at the Brewery, where I avoided the wine and ate just one cube of cheese, because the acupuncturist at Dr. Saadat's office had told me there was no good reason to eat dairy except for Greek yogurt. I studied each painting dutifully, but they might as well have been neon signs blinking *Cheryl is pregnant.* It was the only fact that mattered. It didn't feel like a fact.

I was so scared and elated; I knew it wasn't a sure thing until the second trimester, and even then there were horror stories, and I knew that meant I should enjoy this moment of undeniable good news. But how do you enjoy the present when the thing you are celebrating feels like an idea, i.e., the complete opposite of being present? It was a mental exercise I wasn't quite up to. All I managed to do was teeter around in my tall shoes, trying to imagine my stomach big and my center of balance shifting.

I worked and I googled and I compiled my symptoms into a growing Word document. According to the internet, if my baby was healthy, I should feel like shit. I had those strange pinching cramps, and sometimes I got a little woozy. Sometimes my head ached. I didn't feel nauseous, but Keely encouraged me to count my blessings and eat what I could while I could, because I might puke like crazy later. She'd had hyperemesis gravidarum so badly she had to wear a backpack containing a Zofran drip.

I found a website for neurotic, barely pregnant women like me, where you could enter your hCG level and gestation and see what percent of pregnancies with the same levels had survived past the three-month mark. It was hope, crowd-sourced and dressed up as science. I couldn't stop visiting the site, a Wiki of Destiny.

I tried to be vague with my closest coworker, Jamie, and my friend Nicole. Information is currency, or so it was to me. As Jamie told it, she'd gone off the pill, and when she didn't get pregnant immediately, the next month she'd "*really* tried." In the world of a fertile straight woman, "really trying" meant figuring out roughly what time of month she'd be ovulating, and having a bunch of sex that week.

I suspected the universe was punishing me for all the good luck I'd had with my writing, whereas Jamie remained frustrated by the slow pace of her poetry and publishing. My therapist summed up my feelings tidily and not inaccurately: "You got the book, Jamie got the baby. That's how you look at it." An echo of all those years ago when my sister had wrested my mom's love, and I'd done my best to reel my mom back with academic excellence—or, truly, with stories. My mom had been my biggest supporter, delighting in the narrative scenarios I wove even before I could read, right up through early drafts of my graduate thesis. But I supposed I couldn't have both: mother love and book love.

Now I tried to punish Jamie by sneaking into the hallway and stairwell for all my medical conversations. I told Nicole, "The results are inconclusive." I didn't feel a sense of competition with Nicole, I just knew you weren't supposed to tell anyone until the magical twelve-week mark.

One Friday afternoon at work, I went to the bathroom and saw a smear of red in my underwear. Again, my ghost-self stood to the side and narrated, trying to wed the horrifically unimaginable (which I had, nevertheless, imagined constantly) to what was happening in front of me. *This is what it feels like to miscarry.*

I called Dr. Saadat's office. They told me to come in, and not to give up so quickly. Spotting was common.

I didn't and still don't know how to live in the liminal space between elation and devastation. I could only pin my hopes one place at a time. So I wove down Olympic Boulevard in my bloody underwear thinking it was all over, calling CC and going to voicemail over and over, crying but hoping. Hope was like a secret I was trying to keep from myself.

Dr. Saadat did an ultrasound. He showed me a little flutter in the blur. "Do you see that? That's a heartbeat."

"Oh. So the baby is . . . okay?"

He continued to study the screen. "Look, there's another heartbeat."

Twins? "But I thought it couldn't be twins because my hCG wasn't high enough," I said.

"With fraternal twins, you grow two placentas, but, with identical, you just have one, so it doesn't make hCG higher. The chances of identical twins are one in a thousand."

I thought about how a friend and I always pretended to be identical twins named Hazel and Haple when we were kids. About how the writer Darin Strauss had written a novel called *Chang and Eng* about the original "Siamese twins" years before his wife became pregnant with identical twin girls. I didn't technically believe in fate, but maybe, once events were set in motion, there was a way to sniff out your own most likely future. Maybe life was threaded with motifs, and twins were one of mine.

"I'll make you an appointment with a high-risk specialist," he said. "A friend of mine who has an extra powerful ultrasound machine. But don't worry too much about the bleeding. It's especially common with twins; no one really knows why. Just stay off your feet until it's stopped for twenty-four hours."

I finally got a hold of CC as I rounded the bend from the 10 to the 110 freeways, Friday afternoon cars in front of me like hundreds of iridescent beetles.

"I know it'll be a lot to manage," I said apologetically.

"I love twins!" she said. "Remember the Hopkins kids?" Three boys she'd babysat as a teenager, two of them blond-headed twins.

"You're not worried?"

"Nah, we'll manage it. Twins!"

Her giddiness gave me permission to feel excited too, and relieved, finally. Maybe everyone else had gotten pregnant more easily than I had, but I was going to show them by being *extra* pregnant. I was on my way to being an *extra* mom.

I crawled in bed when I got home, and that evening, CC joined me. We watched *Brothers,* in which Natalie Portman hooks up with her MIA military husband's troublemaking brother and cares for her two young daughters. The girls tumbled in the snow, charming and real, and because we'd heard IVF babies were more often girls, we imagined them as our future, despite the lack of snow in Southern California.

CHAPTER 6: BEDRIDDEN

Bed rest arrived out of the blue this time. The house wasn't clean and meals weren't prepared. I didn't know what I would do if I was still bleeding on Monday. On Wednesday, I was supposed to emcee a reading of women poets. I had to be able to walk around by then, to care about poetry by then.

Our bedroom was the biggest room in our house, two tile steps up from the living room to accommodate the hill on which our duplex was built. From our bed, I could see the tiny living room—too small for a real couch, so we'd purchased a gray suede loveseat on Craigslist for fifty dollars. Outside the bedroom window, I could see telephone wires and the neighbors' fence. CC brought me cereal with too much soy milk.

"Justine and I are going to see *The Girl with the Dragon Tattoo*," she said.

"Oh . . . you're not gonna, like, hang out with your bedridden baby?"

"Do you want me to?" It was clear from her face that she didn't want to stay.

"I guess there's not really anything you need to be doing here. And I don't want you to be bored." I'd learned the art of guilt-tripping from my mom.

"I mean, I could stay," CC said. "It's just I told Justine—I didn't think it would be a big deal, since we had all of last night together."

CC lived in fear of not having fun; she panicked when a weekend rolled around and her calendar wasn't full. She wasn't a party girl, but she was reassured by a steady flow of brunches and movies and housewarming parties. I was overwhelmed if I didn't have time to write and clean, and until now, our biggest conflicts had unfolded along this extrovert/introvert divide. But this particular movie date seemed extra loaded, as another divide emerged. An unspoken plan in which CC would carry all the light and joy, and I would hold the worry, the planning, the drudgery. She would wonder why I was such a spoil-sport, and I would make her feel bad for being shallow.

"You should go," I said.

"Now you're mad at me," she said.

"I'm not *mad*, I just feel like this is a thing we're in together, you know? You've been incredibly supportive, and I'm so grateful for everything, seriously, but I guess I also feel like I could use a little solidarity. You should go to the movie, but maybe just think about carving out a little time at home in the future. We'll still have fun."

If I seemed to be arguing for two conflicting things (go, don't go), it was because I was terrified that if she capitulated to my homebody needs, she would want to back out of this parenting project or, even worse, this Cheryl project. The two were no longer separate. The kids were inside me. They had already taken over, as kids are known to do.

She went to the movie. I convinced my sister to drive up from Hawthorne and hang out with me. We watched movies CC wouldn't like—chick flicks with a lot of costume changes. Temecula poured herself between us on the bed.

"How's T-Mec doing?" Cathy asked.

"She's hanging in there. She's lost some of her chub, which might not be a bad thing under normal circumstances, but I don't think it's good in this case."

That was the other piece of bad news from the summer of 2010. Our vet had initially diagnosed a cluster of pink bumps on Temecula's chest as a reaction to fleas. But he decided to biopsy one just in case, and the results came back malignant. He called me at Kinko's, where I was photocopying my novel to send off to a contest. The papers shook in my hand, and fat tears fell on the gray plastic machines.

Six months later, Temecula already had outlived the two-to-four months the vet had expected her to live without treatment. She'd slimmed down and her front leg was stiff, but she ate and purred and nuzzled as much as ever. I was happy, but also shaken. Doctors were supposed to know these things.

I took my drugs and waited for my appointment with the prenatal specialist. I wasn't sure exactly what this doctor and his fancy ultrasound machine would be looking for until I went to my next scheduled appointment with Dr. Saadat. CC attended this time. I wanted her to hear the heartbeats.

She squeezed my hand as we watched the fuzzy screen. The heartbeats weren't a thump-thump—more of a crackly whoosh, like a white noise machine. One twin's heart rate was much higher than the other's. They were at opposite ends of the normal range. Dr. Saadat wasn't worried. My own heart beat fast.

"When you see Dr. Dubicki, he'll be looking for a membrane in the amniotic sac," Dr. Saadat explained. "I can't see it here, but his machine is stronger."

I'd already read everything Wikipedia had to say about twins. Half-identical twins grew from one egg and two sperm. Chimeras carried cells from their twin or mother. "In one case, DNA tests determined that a woman, mystifyingly, was not the mother of two of her three children; she was found to be a chimera, and the two children were conceived from eggs derived from cells of their mother's twin," the entry offered. It was a Grimm's fairy tale, full of witchcraft and orphans and mothers who deserved to be punished.

"So what you're looking for," I said, "is a wall between them to make sure they're not conjoined?"

"Yes, but conjoined twins are very rare."

He checked some boxes on his clipboard and told me he'd see me in two weeks. When he left the room, I crumpled.

When my friend Cara and I pretended to be identical twins as kids, we set up house in my backyard, in the playhouse my dad had built by hand with salvaged linoleum, a loft, and running water. Haple and Hazel were sometimes children, but other times, these personas morphed into adults with a gaggle of children of their own.

"Let's pretend our kids think it's totally regular to have two moms," Cara said. "They're like, 'What's a dad?'"

In my more private narratives, the ones I forced upon my sister, I was sometimes a twin who'd been surgically separated from my erstwhile conjoined sibling. Once, we had shared an arm; now we both wore a prosthesis. This enabled me to indulge both my twin fantasy and my desire to be disabled.

An older cousin of mine was born deaf, most likely part of a generation whose mothers contracted rubella during pregnancy.

I was fascinated by the bionic accessories that went along with disability: hearing aids and hook arms, wheelchairs and guide dogs. I liked the idea of being special—not in the pejorative sense, but in the way of a princess in a tower, with something external to explain whatever limitations I might have. But my disabled protagonists were inevitably as beautiful and accomplished as they were frail.

It was the eighties, only a dozen years after the Rolling Quads, a group of wheelchair-using Berkeley students, had loudly rejected the stereotype of the disabled as vegetables to be warehoused in institutions. The Americans with Disabilities Act was still half a decade away.

Surely I was a weirdo. Surely I had done something terrible. Surely mothering actual conjoined twins in the cold light of reality would be my punishment.

"I did this," I told CC in the doctor's office. "I used to play 'Siamese twins' when I was a kid because I was a weird child, and now I made our babies conjoined."

It was an absurd, impossible idea, of course. Thoughts don't create reality. But *The Secret,* a self-help book that encouraged people to manifest their destinies using the "law of attraction," sold twenty million copies. And the idea of a random universe was depressing.

"Oh, you did not," CC said, with just the right amount of dismissal. "We're going to see the specialist, and he's going to show us that they're just hugging, not conjoined."

Upon further Googling, I realized we did not want our babies to be hugging. We wanted a thin wall between them; if it wasn't there, they would be "monoamniotic" twins. If a fertilized egg split early in the game, you'd get identical twins. Doublemint, *Sweet Valley*

High twins. They might even get their own placentas, eliminating potential problems relating to uneven nutrient delivery. At the other end of the spectrum, if embryo cleavage didn't happen until two weeks in, you got conjoined twins. It seemed like a lonely life in which you also never got to be alone.

My babies were probably somewhere in the middle—hopefully in Doublemint territory but possibly in the realm of monoamniotic. When babies swam in the same sac, they risked getting tangled in each other's umbilical cords. The survival rate for such twins, according to Wikipedia, used to be about fifty percent; aggressive fetal monitoring and a drug to lower amniotic fluid—making for a smaller, tighter swimming pool—had bumped that number up to eighty-one percent.

Mothers of monoamniotic twins went on in-hospital bed rest at the point of viability and had C-sections between thirty-two and thirty-four weeks. Could I do that? Could I leave my job and go on disability and make CC feed the cats and clean the house and cook her own dinner for months? It sounded like a terrible sentence, and also a terrible indulgence. I would, naturally, have to start working on a memoir from my hospital bed. The thought filled me with dread. I didn't want to be one of those people who wrote about *herself.* But I was a writer, one who might soon have a lot of time on my hands, and if something happened to me that only happened once in every 35,000 pregnancies, a memoir seemed mandatory.

In the weeks that followed, I performed the motions of daily life. I went to work and made writing dates with my novelist friends. But instead of working on my novel about a traveling circus troupe, I looked up statistics about monoamniotic twins. At some point CC and I went to San Francisco; I have a memory of shooting up hormones in my friend's bathroom, but I can't tell you when.

My timeline was broken into gestational weeks and rigidly timed dosages, yet it was also a blur.

At night I placed my hands in a heart shape over the place that cramped when I had my period. I didn't want one of the cats to jump on me and jar a fetus. But it wasn't just cats I was trying to keep away. It was the whole world, including whatever defects, whatever evil, lay curled inside my own body.

The morning of April 7, I put on old jeans and a T-shirt I'd gotten free from CC's sister, Elena. I had an unfortunate ability to remember what I was wearing on almost every really bad day of my life, starting with the beige corduroy pants I wore to my grandmother's funeral when I was four years old; and if I got bad news from the specialist, I wanted to be able to toss my clothes in the trash. Preparing myself for bad news was part of my ritual for ensuring good news. It was a pessimist's version of *The Secret*.

Another early morning in traffic, another glass-and-brick building in Beverly Hills. CC and I told the receptionist we were expecting twins, and she said, "Oh, you should apply for a handicapped parking placard. A lot of people don't know, but when you have twins, you're eligible."

It felt a bit hubristic, but I nodded and took the stack of forms she handed me.

The woman across from us puzzled through her own forms out loud. "How am I supposed to know my insurance number? What does that mean? Where would I find that?" She appeared to be in her early thirties. Had she ever been to the doctor before? How many times had I written my insurance information in just the past three months?

A nurse in Bugs Bunny scrubs ushered us into the exam room, where the dildo cam made its appearance. This time on the ultrasound screen, instead of grainy clouds, we saw billowing sepia jellyfish. I explained to the nurse what we were looking for, and she said, "Oh, yes, there it is, right there."

That beautiful, gauzy membrane.

"They're not hugging, just waving," CC exclaimed. "Hi guys!"

"I'm going to go get the doctor. He'll be right in," the nurse said.

In our moments alone, we joked about her Bugs Bunny scrubs and our waving babies. Relief was my favorite drug.

Dr. Dubicki was a round-bodied man with a stubbly beard; he had a contemporary Santa-ness about him. "Let's take a look," he said. He planted his large fingers on my labia and reinserted the dildo cam. I winced and realized for the first time that Dr. Saadat had never, ever touched any of my external genitalia. Was Dr. Saadat extra skilled, or was Dr. Dubicki a little molesty? The question would stay with me. I told myself that, if things had turned out differently, I wouldn't have cared how he touched me. Isn't that what they tell women who've been raped, though? *You just had a night of bad sex and regretted it later.*

Dr. Dubicki agreed that, yes, the membrane was quite clearly there, "but the reason I'm being subdued is because I'm not finding a heartbeat."

"Not for either of them?" I didn't know what to do or how to feel, so I became a vessel. I ripped myself open and let the information pour in.

"It looks like a neural tube defect. See how the head on this one is way too large?"

"But I've been taking so much folic acid."

"We don't always know why these things happen."

He was telling me my babies weren't conjoined twins, but that they were, still, misshapen freaks. I pictured their little shrimp bodies blown up newborn-sized. Cradling and loving them and not being strong enough to parent them. He was telling me that nature had called it. There were disabilities that humans could live with, and disabilities you never heard about because they killed their inhabitants before they even got a chance.

What I remember is being ushered out the back door in tears. CC and I sat in my parked car and cried together. Dr. Dubicki had told me to call Dr. Saadat and schedule a procedure that would end the pregnancy. My babies had died, and I had received my marching orders: a punishment, a to-do list. But we gave ourselves that time. A minute by the side of the road. We hugged like mono-amniotic twins, long and hard. So often over the past few months we'd existed in different universes, but right now we occupied the same, terribly sad one.

I'd been so focused on the number of amniotic sacs in my uterus that I'd forgotten to campaign for healthy neural tubes. I'd tried to pin my worry to a board like a moth. If I examined it in detail, I believed I could conquer it. Meanwhile a flock of more venomous insects had descended.

That afternoon, I called Dr. Saadat's office to schedule an abortion. ("Stop calling it that," CC pleaded. But it seemed like the right word, because it was the harshest.) His staff explained that, due to confusing reasoning around the floor on which the procedure took place, my insurance wouldn't cover it. I called Planned Parenthood.

"How far along are you?"

"Nine weeks."

"That's too late to take medicine that would induce an abortion, so we'd need to do a D&C." D&C referred to dilation and curettage, a literal description of the act of opening a body and spooning out the fetus.

She was saying I was too pregnant for the first procedure. It was hard to believe I was one of them, the fortunate pregnant, the

chosen maternal, and any little bit of external evidence was vali-
dating, regardless of the context. I imagine that this is how a trans
woman might feel after being sentenced to a women's prison. *Who,
me? Thank you.*

"I went through fertility treatment to get pregnant," I explained.
She needed to know these were wanted babies. "But today they told
me there were no heartbeats."

"Oh, I see," said the woman on the phone. "I'm afraid that's not
a service we provide. You'll have to call your regular doctor."

My attempt to bargain-hunt for my own abortion had failed.
Because they were dead, they could not be aborted. Because they
were wanted, they had been rejected. Because I had wanted, I had
been rejected.

I made an appointment with Dr. Saadat, for the upstairs room,
for the procedure that wasn't in any of the photo albums in the
waiting room. Then CC and I got veggie burgers and fries and
taro milkshakes at The Oinkster, because where had those months
of healthy eating gotten me? We watched *Eat, Pray, Love,* a movie
about unexpected turns and happy endings after sad middles. There
were some beautiful, golden shots of pizza. I fell asleep after *Eat,*
woke up for a few minutes of *Pray,* and missed *Love* entirely.

CHAPTER 7: SICK?

I thought The Bad Thing had happened and now I would begin to feel better and better until I felt okay. I was at work, sitting in my new desk chair, when I got the strange feeling that I was wet between my skirt and the chair. Discreetly—I hoped—I explored the space with my fingers.

In the bathroom, I saw that my underwear and skirt were covered with blood. Was I hemorrhaging? Was this what hemorrhaging felt like? Would I faint soon? Or die?

I went into the stairwell to call Dr. Saadat. I shivered amid the tile and echoes. I told him I was bleeding.

"How much? How many pads?" He always sounded relaxed.

"Um, I don't know. I just went to the bathroom and it kind of gushed."

"This happens sometimes after a miscarriage. The D&C might not have gotten all the tissue. If you fill more than one pad in an hour, you can go to the emergency room."

The bleeding slowed to a trickle a little while later. No emergency after all.

Lately, I'd been waking up in the middle of the night with numb fingers. Usually the last two, ring and pinky. They would tingle and ache. I shook the feeling back into them and lay awake wondering what was wrong with me.

A woman whose blog I followed had been diagnosed with multiple sclerosis—the relapsing/remitting or "good" kind. It didn't sound very good, but yes, it was better than the degenerative kind. I wondered if *I* had MS and would soon lose feeling in all my limbs. The internet told me that the tingling could also be a sign of estrogen leaving my body after pregnancy, or a pinched ulnar nerve—sort of like carpal tunnel, but different.

My regular doctor, a Russian woman who wore short skirts and got to the point, tended to order tests just in case. I sat in her small waiting room, hands shaking (this, too, could be a sign of MS). Dr. Jasper was probably going to make me get an MRI. Would it show lesions on my brain? I hated living in the maybe space; I was always trying to google my way out of it. Answers as antidotes. Every time I got online, my intention was to reassure myself that I *didn't* have some particular awful disease. But every page led to more pages and more questions. It was impossible to prove a negative. At least without an MRI.

Dr. Jasper did not order an MRI. She said it was carpal tunnel.

"You mean like an ulnar nerve thing?" I asked.

"Yes. Same thing. You can get a brace for sleeping."

For months after that, I slept with soft, black elbow braces from CVS on my arms, like an injured tennis player. I stuffed socks in the creases so I wouldn't bend my arms past a forty-five-degree angle.

Another symptom of MS—or maybe it was lupus, or both—

was blurred vision. I was terribly nearsighted, and had astigmatism too, but "blurred vision" seemed to be a separate and special symptom. How do you know if you have it? I found myself looking into the middle distance, trying to catch myself in the act of seeing. This was how the floaters began etching themselves on the inside of my vision. I'd noticed them before, over the years, and my eye doctor had said they were just proteins or something. Basically dust in the unswept corners of an eyeball. Nothing to worry about.

But there was one in my left eye that was so big, like a long strand of black spaghetti. And in my right eye, two tiny circles and a squiggle. Whenever I looked at the sky, I saw tangled black nests. Looking at the sky started to suck, but I couldn't stop doing it.

At work, I looked at the scuffed white wall behind my computer monitor. It seemed like a nice blank space on which to test my vision. When I looked closely, it seemed to move. Not moving, exactly—nothing so psychedelic—but it wasn't a pure, flat surface. Shadows were layered upon shadows, and they seemed to take turns stepping toward me.

One night CC and I went to see Florence and the Machine at the Greek Theatre. We parked in the dirt lot at the bottom of Griffith Park near sunset. The streetlights were just coming on, extending long, yellow-orange fingers toward the ground.

"What do those lights look like to you?" I asked CC. I couldn't remember what streetlights were supposed to look like. What did they look like to normal people who weren't dying of MS or lupus? Did they always have fuzzy tendrils like that? Or were they supposed to be sharp? Or invisible?

How were you supposed to see light? How had I forgotten everything as it was before I lost the babies?

"What do you mean?" CC asked. She'd made us tuna sandwiches and pretzels.

"I mean, like, do you see long blurry lines coming out of them?"

"Yeah."

Later this kind of conversation—this nervous and constant checking in—would begin to annoy and exhaust her. I would prove my insatiability. CC would max out on reassurance. It appeared that, like my health insurance for infertility, CC had a lifetime limit.

"I've been thinking maybe I should take antidepressants," I said. I knew CC had taken them for a while in her twenties, when she was working as a teacher and hating it, then unemployed and hating it. CC lived on the verge of melancholy, but she could stave it off with exercise and parties.

"You should do it," CC said.

It felt good to have a plan. We found our seats, and I stopped worrying about my blurred vision. Florence and the Machine was okay. She sounded like she did on the radio. The dog days were not over. I started worrying about my shaking hands again.

The more I watched my hands, the more they shook. There were also the bumps on the back of my tongue—had they always been there? And the fact that sometimes my middle toes felt kind of numb, in certain shoes or while running. And the bumps in my neck. I decided these were knots in my muscles—maybe from all this stress!—and tried to rub them out. Obsessively, for one entire drive home. The next day my head and neck hurt, but for a little while I thought the bumps were gone.

The next time I saw my chiropractor—whom I'd started to see because of the tingling, because it was less scary than a neurologist—I asked about the neck bumps. My chiropractor, who gave me lots of stretches to do and encouraged people to check out his YouTube channel, showed me a plastic skeleton. "See those yellowish things that extend off your vertebrae?" They were some kind of connective tissue. I can't remember now. Just that they weren't tumors and everyone had them.

CHAPTER 8: SAD

We hadn't seen Amy in a while, but one morning she texted and asked if it would be cool if she went to church with us; she was going through some stuff and needed spiritual comfort. Of course, we said, and we sat together in the chapel at All Saints Pasadena, feeling our smallness in relation to God and all those pointed stone arches. I didn't know what was up with Amy, but her face was shiny with tears, so I figured she and Kim weren't a happy, expectant couple, and that was all I needed to know. I held her thin hand.

After church, people mingled on the grass and signed up with All Saints' various activist cohorts: the LGBTQ group, the peace-in-the-Middle East group, the group that gave secondhand eyeglasses to developing nations. All Saints served a relatively well-off congregation, and most of the rector's sermons focused on social justice. But he always linked his calls to action to personal struggle and biblical stories. He described our community as a lake; generosity flowed into and from it. As such, All Saints felt like a reprieve from the narrative of privilege in my head. The world wasn't divided into haves and have-nots. We were one big lake, and the force from which we drew was the same as the force to which we gave. It was a place that would remind me to write to my congressperson, *and* a place where I could hold Amy's hand and cry.

"Kim and I broke up," she said. "I will always love her, and if it was just the two of us, I could handle her temper. But I want kids, and I can't raise them with someone who shoves me and pounds her fists into walls."

Later that month, CC's friend Justine got pregnant (second try, fresh sperm from a known donor), and she and Sam stopped being a safe space. Justine was a fierce, angry pregnant person who did not give up her evening beer and would not let anyone carry her lawn chair for her when we walked to an outdoor movie screening at Hollywood Forever Cemetery.

At the Easter craft party of a mutual friend, Justine sat at the dining room table, which was strewn with pastel paper and glitter glue, stencils of chicks and bunnies, birth and rebirth everywhere. Sam stood behind her, rubbing her shoulders.

Afterward, I told CC, "Seeing the two of them—I realized *that's* what I'm envious of. Not the baby. Or not just the baby. But how close they are right now."

At that moment, the idea that CC would voluntarily start rubbing my shoulders seemed unfathomable.

"I don't believe you," CC said. "You're totally envious of Justine's pregnancy. You're envious of everyone's pregnancy."

It was an accusation, unquestionably, and accurate. Looking back at pictures from that party, I see how bloated my face was. The pregnancy hormones hadn't even left my body. If my task was to conquer all obstacles using reason and intellect—and I believed, always, that this was my task—my body was waging a separate war, trying to sabotage me not with MS or lupus but with its own grieving process. And it refused to be hurried.

"Please," CC said, not for the first time, "will you go to a miscarriage support group? You deserve to be around people who know what you're going through."

"I told you, it's not that I'm *against* it," I said. "It's just that it will be full of straight women, and half of them will be pregnant again within months. That's not my experience."

It sounded like as much of a nightmare as my Facebook feed. And even though I was a vocal fan of therapy, being told to get help felt like getting a bad grade on my grief report card.

"Then can we see someone together? Can we go to couples therapy? I'll find someone for us." This was not a first request, either. And the fact that she was half of the couple in question made it harder to refuse.

She found Julie, a large, friendly woman who had adopted her younger son after experiencing secondary infertility. She freely shared personal stories. She ran a little late for our morning appointments. When I mentioned the miscarriage, she asked when it had happened. I said "Five weeks ago" and she gave a small, sympathetic gasp.

"Oh, so this is *very* fresh."

I erupted into grateful tears and said, "I didn't think I was going to cry so soon."

"Did you not expect to cry?"

"Oh, I definitely expected to cry, but I thought I'd make it until the second appointment."

She laughed. I liked her. She knew exactly how seriously to take me.

On April 9, I was getting ready to go see *Hanna,* a movie about a fifteen-year-old raised in the Finnish wilderness to be an assassin, when CC opened a group email from her friend Jeff, the husband of her old roommate Rachel. Jeff explained that, shortly after their family had left Los Angeles for Colorado, Rachel had started having stomach problems. She didn't feel full, but she couldn't eat much. They'd done some tests, rooting for Crohn's disease, but knowing that stomach cancer was possible. A biopsy confirmed stomach cancer, stage IV.

My mom had been diagnosed at stage IV, too, although no one ever said so, at least not to me. We knew where it had spread—from her ovaries to her peritoneal wall—but we didn't have the grim perspective of linear staging. Maybe the doctors told my mom and dad, and they failed to pass the information along, wiggling through the loophole of omission in their general policy of honesty. I don't know. But as they say, there is no stage V.

There are more than two kinds of twins. There is more than one way to have cancer, and more than one way to have stage IV cancer. My mom had lived for three years after her diagnosis. It wasn't long enough, but in that time, I'd come out and met Bari and lost weight. My sister had graduated from college and started her teaching career. She and my dad had bought a big new RV and traveled through the Southwest and dipped into Mexico. My mom learned, finally, to ask for what she needed without apologizing. A lot can happen in three years.

Jeff's email explained that they would try one type of chemo, the kind that worked best in the most cases, and if that didn't work, they'd try another. Each subsequent chemo option was linked to a more dismal prognosis.

I rubbed CC's shoulders as she read out loud, and felt the peculiar mix of emotions that descends when someone else's hard time proves worse than your own. Relief. Gratitude. Humility. Rachel was thirty-seven. She was a runner who grew her own vegetables. She had two little girls. There was no reason why it should be her and not me.

This truth—this deep knowing that *It could happen to anyone*—should be the root of empathy. At its best, it inspires us to give money to homeless people and support after-school tutoring programs and cut grouchy baristas some slack. But my brain always likes to take empathy one step further. It echoes, *Yeah, why not you? In fact, maybe you* do *have stage IV cancer. Probably not stomach cancer, because what are the chances you'd have exactly what Rachel has at the exact same time, but how about breast cancer? That's a good one.*

So the thing that brought me relief on April 9 made me poke and prod my breasts on April 10 and throughout the months that followed. Not just my breasts, but my neck and that bump on my lower back I'd once gotten X-rayed. It made me study the size of my pupils (why not a brain tumor?) and the bruises on my arms (why not leukemia?) and the bumps in the back of my throat (why should mouth cancer be limited to smokers?). Rachel didn't deserve to die. My babies didn't deserve to die. Why did I deserve to live?

The first line of chemo didn't work. They tried a second one. Rachel and Jeff posted updates on a blog platform called CaringBridge, which sounded to me like Rainbow Bridge, the thing people said their pets crossed when they died. Rachel posted a picture of herself in a layered, brown wig that looked like a wig. She was so skinny; her teeth were too big. She posted about the relief of having fluid pumped from her stomach and finally being able to poop. She maintained her humor and grace, at least on the blog. But my own blog was always funny and graceful too, and CC and I both knew the truth about me.

Rachel didn't get three years. She got four months. Jeff wrote about her final days, in which she was in and out of lucidity, the cancer having found her brain. Because my mom had, technically, died of a complication from cancer—pneumonia resulting from a bowel obstruction resulting from cancer—I didn't have much experience with cancer just marching ahead like a victorious army. Could it really grow that fast? Could a person be blogging and hanging out with her kids—sick, but recognizably herself—one day and hallucinating the next? But cancer grew exponentially. That was its thing.

They had a funeral in Colorado and a memorial in Los Angeles at an old carriage house surrounded by rolling hills and low stone walls. It was late summer, and the San Gabriel Valley held heat like a grudge, but the day had started to give over to a cool evening. I filled a paper plate with chips and carrot sticks and chatted with Holly, the wife of CC's college friend Joel. For a while we'd been in a book club together, but I hadn't seen them in a year or more. CC, Rachel, Jeff, Joel, and Holly had all been evangelical Christians together, and then they'd all thought better of it and become other kinds of Christians.

"How have you been?" I asked Holly.

"I've been having a hard time. I'm just kind of trying to take care of myself—taking a break from social media and stuff."

"I hear you. Is it just, like, all the people living perfect lives stressing you out . . . ?"

"Well, Rachel's death hit me really hard. She was such a mentor to me."

I had just asked a person at a memorial service why she was sad, and then been surprised when the answer was: because someone died. I'd hoped, for a minute, that Holly's answer would be more like mine—tangled and self-absorbed.

The service started, and people shared stories of Rachel's work and mentorship, her kindness and creativity. I thought about how she had miscarried before getting pregnant with Jane, and how, perhaps, the one consolation of not getting to see them grow up would be getting to see the baby who didn't get to grow up. I sort of believed in an afterlife. I doubted it looked like anything humans had imagined thus far, but I believed because I wanted there to be something rather than nothing, and wanting created its own energy. So what if God was a human invention? That didn't mean God wasn't real. Maybe God was the exact manifestation of all those animal wishes vibing off each other.

I pictured my babies as two balls of light, one in each of my mom's hands.

I sobbed so hard it was embarrassing. People who knew me knew that I didn't know Rachel all that well. I hadn't earned this level of grief, and grief seemed to me like yet another thing that had to be earned, rationalized, and accounted for. After the service, CC talked to old friends while I sat on a stone railing and stared at the place where the lamp-lit grass gave way to residential darkness. I cried and cried, grateful for this public container, even if I had stolen it.

Years later, Holly became one of my best friends. She alluded to her difficult time so casually that it became clear she thought she'd told me something she hadn't, and finally, in pieces, it all came out. A plunging depression that led to a ten-day stay in a psychiatric hospital and a diagnosis of bipolar I. I think about that August night sometimes, how we were two raccoon-eyed people staring at each other across a refreshment table. Being as honest as two acquaintances could be, and still not communicating the half of it. Lonely ships, lonely ocean.

CHAPTER 9: **MAKING A PLAN**

I don't consider myself an optimist, but I am an Aries and an American, which is to say I'm stubborn and willful, and I buy into the myth of self-creation even as I rail against it. I fumbled around for catalysts to happiness. I wanted to read the classics as well as experimental fiction from small presses; I wanted to be the most flexible person in my yoga class; I wanted to campaign for social justice and cook things with kale and answer all my emails in a timely manner. I wanted to *write* new classics and experimental fiction. I wanted to win awards and use my platform to question society's systems of reward and punishment. The myth of self-creation—of the possibility of rebirth around any corner—sustained me.

If I was going to grieve, fine, but I was also going to be productive. At some point, back when it was all hypothetical, CC and I had talked about her trying to get pregnant if I wasn't able, but she hadn't said much about it lately. It was her body, her choice—and I was nervous that if she made the choice to try to grow a baby in her body, I would hover like a mosquito, whining at her to track her cycle and hormones and medications. Or she'd slack off and there would be no baby. Or she'd get pregnant easily and I would resent her like I resented every other pregnant woman. Adoption felt like neutral ground, something I could pour myself into without the baggage of pregnancy.

CC and I attended the Independent Adoption Center's Weekend Intensive—the first serious step to becoming adoptive parents. When I got the physical required for our home study a month later, there was still a swirl of miscarriage blood in my pee sample. Lots of women at the Weekend Intensive had miscarried. Some of them cried when they introduced themselves. The guest speakers included parents who'd adopted two little girls, and a woman who'd placed her baby for adoption.

Placed was the word we learned. They hadn't abandoned their children. They'd made a plan.

Maybe I could save myself by making a plan.

The seminar was led by Lane, a middle-aged, gay, white guy who wore his cell phone clipped to his belt. He and his husband had adopted two Black-and-Latinx boys, now approaching middle school, from two different birth families. Lane was loud and New York-ish. When CC asked a question about the required training for transracial adoption, he waved her off: "You'll be fine. You already know this stuff."

Because she was Mexican? I watched her bristle. I watched him not really look at her.

As homework, we all had to read *Children of Open Adoption* by the agency's founder, plus two other books of our choosing from a table of options. I selected *Secret Thoughts of an Adoptive Mother,* because I already had some secret thoughts, and CC and I both chose *The Kid* by Dan Savage, because we'd already read it. That's how we got here. Between the seminars and the required reading, the agency seemed to be driving home two messages: Open adoption was the best kind of adoption, and birthmothers were not crack addicts who'd abandoned their children. They were women in crisis who'd made a brave choice for the sake of their children.

I did not disagree. But I did begin to resent what I saw as a corollary assumption—that adoptive parents had to always present themselves as mature, capable, chill, and able to hold the birth mom's grief. I *wanted* to be all of those things, but I was still a mess.

I started the home-study paperwork, a combination of legal documents that were a slog and personal essays that I blew through with ease. The agency wanted to make sure we were not criminals, and that we were financially, medically, and emotionally sound. I wasn't sure we were any of those things, but soon we would have papers saying we were. I tried to make the process painless for CC. I'd already put her through so much. And even though I knew she wanted kids, something about her role in all this felt fragile, as if she might reach her breaking point at any turn.

But I grouched and raged against the paperwork, which didn't make things particularly easy on CC at all. At the same time, I dove in whole-heartedly—not just because it was something to do, not just because I wanted a kid, but because on some level it made perfect sense to me that I would need to prove myself worthy of motherhood.

Manhattan Beach was Reagan-loving and socially libertarian, and as a teenager, I defaulted to demonizing affirmative action as an enemy of meritocracy

Then I went to UCLA. For the first time, most of the people around me weren't white. Asian Americans didn't benefit from affirmative action, but the ones I went to school with were nevertheless for it. They pushed against the model minority myth and wrote essays about their interned grandparents. There hadn't been a single out gay person at Mira Costa, but at UCLA, I saw women cross the lawn holding hands.

On weekends, I came home and argued politics with my dad. Over the next twenty years, the patterns of our conversations didn't change much.

> CHRIS: [Dangles bait.] Those damn deadbeats are a drain on our system.
> CHERYL: That's a myth. You don't understand how hard other people's lives are.
> CHRIS: Prove it.
> CHERYL: [Cites anecdotes and generalities, occasional statistics.]
> CHRIS: Well, if that's true, that's very sad. But don't be hoodwinked. Nonprofits have a vested interest in staying in business.
> CHERYL: Everyone does. No one is objective. You're not objective. Why put your trust in business and religion and assume the worst of poor people and nonprofits and government?
> CHRIS: No one is perfectly objective, but I strive for objectivity, and you're the most objective person I know.
> CHERYL: I'm not objective. I'm a critical thinker, there's a difference.

If you argue with a stubborn but kindhearted and open-minded man weekly for twenty years, he will inch to the left like a house settling on its foundation. The other thing that has changed is my awareness of what we're really arguing about. As much as I want to believe in my own compassion, my dad is right—we are self-interested creatures. At their essence, our arguments came down to this:

CHRIS: Some people do not deserve love.
CHERYL: Everyone deserves love!
CHRIS: Not people who mess up. But don't worry, you haven't messed up. You have earned love.
CHERYL: But what if I do mess up? What if I become a deadbeat?
CHRIS: But you're not a deadbeat.

His actions—his keys in the lock every weekday at 4:30 p.m., his infinite patience with my math homework and political rants—painted a picture of unconditional love. Deep in my bones, he knew this and I knew this. But his worldview was a rigorous meritocracy: outcomes as proof of worthiness. If you're poor, you must not have worked hard. If you get lung cancer, you must have smoked. My mom's diagnosis and death softened the edges a bit; he confessed sympathy for "victims of circumstance." But that's everyone, I argued—no one "chooses" to join a gang, no one "chooses" to be an addict—and then we spiraled into our familiar patterns. Meanwhile, I walked a tightrope. I argued on behalf of the deadbeats and welfare queens, while trying not to put his love to the test and risk finding out if it was as conditional as I believed.

I went on Zoloft for depression, chased with the occasional Ativan for anxiety. Neither stopped my obsessive thoughts the way I'd hoped, but that feeling of sinking—of looking up at a merry world from the bottom of a well—occupied short stretches instead of long ones. I had lost my appetite and was skinnier than I'd been in years. I discovered eBay and stalked small, attainable prizes: Anthropologie tops, Lucky Brand jeans, ankle boots with elfin toes.

I went to Palm Springs with my sister and blogged about combing through vintage shops and outlet malls. In the hotel/spa she'd found via Groupon, we practiced yoga headstands and took mineral baths. Once, a friend had mentioned that sitting in a hot tub could trigger her MS. Why or how I didn't know, but the fact stayed with me. Every time I encountered a Jacuzzi, I waited for confirmation of my doom. Would my skin tingle or go numb? I didn't know what to expect, just that I expected something, and expectation itself can make your nerves fire.

I jumped in and out of the hot mineral bath to prove I could. Months later, my sister told me that she'd noticed my pupils were different sizes that weekend. She knew my fragile mental state, but she was a bit of a hypochondriac herself. Did her sister have a brain tumor? Was Cheryl having a stroke? On drugs? She sneaked off to call my dad, who is a worrier too, but an anti-alarmist. He told her it was probably nothing; just keep an eye on it. Whatever that meant. Keep an eye on her sister's weird eyes.

When I observed the same symptom on my own, months later at the gym, I made an appointment with my optometrist, which seemed like a compromise—medical attention that wasn't a trip to the emergency room or an immediate referral to a neurologist. I had that feeling again: *Finally, the other shoe is dropping. My external reality merges with my internal reality.*

But I had been happy and healthy for enough of my life that it seemed possible I could be again. Hope was faith that there was something on the other side of a seemingly insurmountable mountain—that it was, in fact, surmountable. This, and a reluctant belief in the principle of Occam's razor (the theory that the simplest explanation is usually correct), prompted me to tell my optometrist that I had soaked my contact lenses in eye drops that said *Not for use with contact lenses.* He doubted I was having a stroke. Believe what the bottle says, he said with a chuckle, and come back when you're ready for new frames.

In the fall, CC and I went to Montana, which she'd wanted to visit ever since reading *A River Runs Through It*. I read the story collection on our flight to Missoula. The phrase "big sky country" had never made sense to me; wasn't the sky the same size everywhere? But then it did: a magnificent blue alternative to the suspicious and undulating walls of my office. It spread out as far as the flat brown prairie. We spotted a black bear cub our first night in town, in the parking lot of our Motel 6.

We bought itchy wool gloves at the army surplus store and drove our rental car to Glacier National Park. The main road was called Going-to-the-Sun, and it was closed, so we went the long back way, through the Blackfeet Indian Reservation. It was the flattest, brownest part of our trip, the landscape confirming a genocide mapped out in land treaties. It was beautiful in the way of an old woman whose life is written in wrinkles and scars, not the cover-girl beauty of the park itself, with its abundance of megafauna, its glassy blue lakes, snow you could touch in the summer. But even in the park, the glaciers were melting as a result of climate change. Everyone becomes wrinkled and scarred eventually, or they die young.

We hiked eleven miles up a mountain to the touchable glacier. We got even closer to a bear. This time I smelled it—dank and pungent—before I saw it nosing through a thicket of berries. We kept bear spray—like pepper spray but stronger—at our sides and made loud noises and stayed close to other hikers. I was scared, but also physically exhausted and moving forward, which made for a different kind of fear than the doom thoughts that spun donuts in my head while I was stuck in traffic. For the first time, I could sort of understand why people jumped off of bridges tethered by a bungee cord. I'd thought of that stuff as a self-created, first-world problem, but maybe it was more of an ancient-world solution—a way of stuffing the uncontainable back into a box our lizard brains could understand and triumph over. I could not categorically prove I didn't have MS or ascertain whether I would be a mother, but when we emerged jelly-legged and dirty at the bottom of the mountain, I could say with confidence that we had not been eaten by a bear that day.

In the expanse of Montana, we were happy. I usually felt like a C-minus student in happiness, and all the after-school tutoring in the world wasn't bringing my grade up. But in Montana, happy seemed simple enough, measurable in steps hiked and Moose Drool beers consumed.

CHAPTER 10: **SEESAWING**

Lane approved our "Dear Birthmother" letter after numerous edits. It was a literal glossy brochure (and website) written like a dating profile for a process that was almost exactly like dating, except with very high stakes, and only one party could do the asking-out. Hopeful adoptive parents were debutantes, dressed in our best ball gowns, flaunting our dowries, and waiting for a good man. I was never very good at dating. But I could write a damn good profile. I could tone-shift and dog-whistle. We painted a not-completely-accurate-but-also-not-untrue portrait of a culturally voracious urban couple grounded in family and spirituality. It was who we had been at our best, for a moment, three years back.

And then we "went live," meaning the agency would start sending our paper letters to expectant mothers who were potential matches (them: open to same-sex parents, Californians, etc.; us: open to a child of any race, mild alcohol and drug use, etc.). Anyone at all could contact us through our online profile. I checked our dedicated Gmail account every day. It was always empty, which was to be expected at this point. The average wait for a match, according to the Independent Adoption Center, was six to eighteen months. The longest anyone had ever waited, the counselors said, was three years, and that was because the couple was very picky and took a couple of breaks. People often asked me, phrasing it as politely as they could, whether it would likely take us longer because we were gay. Birth moms who were open to queers raising their babies had to be in short supply, right?

Our agency and I liked to point out that, statistically, same-sex couples actually matched slightly sooner than straight couples. This tended to be because same-sex couples had more open profiles. Once those factors were accounted for, the wait time was almost exactly the same. Although birth moms also didn't skew as young as outsiders assumed—the average age was twenty-four—they were youngish, and youngish people were usually not homophobes in my experience. Dar Williams wrote a song called "The Mercy of the Fallen," in which she claims that people who've fucked up in life are the least judgmental. And even though we were being trained to see accidental pregnancy as a crisis instead of a tragedy, I felt most generous when I imagined birth moms as people like me, people whose plans had gone all to hell. As such, I hoped they would see falling in love with someone of the same sex as just one more unexpected turn that a life might take, not a thing weighted as inherently good or bad.

I told myself we would wait eighteen months but secretly hoped we'd be a unicorn, one of the outliers who matched almost instantly. Checking our email and answering calls from unknown numbers gave me little adrenaline rushes. *Something amazing might happen today*, a little voice whispered. Those boom-and-bust neurological pathways grooved deeper. Dopamine flooded the empty rooms of my brain.

Days and days passed with nothing amazing happening. Christmas reared its garish head, and CC's mood slumped per usual. We were seesawing. Montana had been a moment of equilibrium, and now she was on her way down while I was pumping upward, trying to make up for lost time. During our days off between Christmas and New Year's, I laid out newspapers on our back patio and spray-painted an old brown file cabinet a light apple green. It was the kind of project I never got around to, and finally doing so proved . . . something. About intentionality. About the future.

Temecula had outlived the vet's estimate by more than a year, which said something about her strength, and/or what doctors don't know. The bump they biopsied had never quite healed and eventually started to fester. Her armpit grew lumpy with tumors, her front leg grew stiff and swollen. Still, she made her way up the carpeted cat tree on three legs, and continued to snuggle, purr, and eat. She was her squishy, sweet, intelligent self. She continued to listen with her shaky blue eyes. We gave her buprenorphine when we suspected she was in pain.

I wanted to make sure I wasn't "putting her out of her misery" when the misery was in fact mine. I wanted to make sure I wasn't mistaking a compromised life for an unbearable one. But as 2011 waned, her appetite went, and we decided it was time. I decided she wouldn't want to spend her last moments in a car and on the vet's cold steel table, so I made an appointment with a home euthanasia doctor for a Saturday.

The Friday night before, I woke up to a strange sound, like coughing. Gingerly, I lifted her off the cat tree and woke CC: "I think this is it." I crouched on the stone floor of our bedroom with T-Mec in my lap. With a cough and a shudder, she died in my arms.

I held her and CC held me, both of us sobbing. It felt like

Temecula had given us something—her life, but also her death. We let our other cats, OC and Ferdinand, in the room so they would know what had happened. They sniffed her body curiously and then moved on. I carried her body to the vet's office in a towel. CC drove. I sat in the parking lot with her curled on my lap, feeling her specific weight and shape for the last time.

CHAPTER 11: **CHOSEN**

I was sitting in bed with my laptop when an unknown number appeared on my cell. My heart leapt, the way it always did right before I found myself talking to a recorded message telling me I'd won a cruise. This time, though, a live woman spoke my name.

"This is Crystal," she said, as if we'd already met. "I saw your listing and just really liked everything you said. My fiancé and I are pregnant, and we thought you all looked like you'd be great moms."

Crystal's words tumbled out freely, in the way of people too quick to trust. She was on the pill, she said, but she was just *that* fertile. She and Jesse, her fiancé—who seemingly was not the biological father of this child, but it was hard to keep up—were ten months sober from meth. They'd moved to Orange County to get away from Nebraska. She wanted to know my opinion of medical marijuana. She smoked it for her bipolar disorder, and cigarettes, but didn't do any of the hard stuff anymore.

I tried to remember our training: Save the hard questions for the IAC counselors. Ask her why open adoption appealed to her. Don't talk about yourself too much. Basic first-date best practices.

"I'm so glad you called," I said, my voice too high and bright. "It's really brave—I mean, it's a big choice, and uh, so, what made you consider open adoption?"

"This is my fourth baby. Two of my kids got adopted by a family in Fresno. But the youngest is only eighteen months, so they couldn't handle a newborn already. My oldest, Aliya, lives with my parents. We Skype all the time. Do you like Skype? We could talk right now."

I was dressed in boxer shorts and an ancient T-shirt. I was not ready to Skype. But birth moms who'd already placed children for adoption were the holy grail. A woman expecting her first child might easily see adoption as preferable to all the challenges of parenthood—especially if she was single, poor, in an abusive relationship, or facing any variety of crises—but she might not factor in the love, the tiny hand wrapped around her finger, the rush of oxytocin. A woman already raising children knew about the love, but also the unceasing demands of parenthood; if she made an adoption plan, she'd be more likely to stick with it. Then again, she might also think, *Well, I've made room in my life for two. Why not one more?* But a woman who had actually placed previously—

"CC is going to be home soon. I could check in with her and we could set up a time when, uh, we could all Skype. The four of us."

"You're gonna love Jesse, and he's gonna love you," Crystal assured me.

I had no idea what she was basing this on. "Do you have any questions for me? About me and CC?"

"What do you all do for fun?"

"We keep pretty busy. We like doing, like, cultural things— seeing movies and going to plays and museums." There was no way to answer *What do you do for fun?* without sounding snobby, generic, or weird. "We spend a lot of time with friends, and our families are local. CC's pretty into running. We're just, like, always doing something."

"Oh my god, we're the *same* way," Crystal said. "I just can't sit still. See, I knew we'd hit it off."

"So, um, I guess the next step—well, the next step would be talking on Skype—but also, would you be interested in calling the organization we're working with?"

Don't say "agency." Agency is clinical, and evokes ugly chapters in the history of adoption. Maternity homes where young mothers were hidden away and coerced into surrendering their babies.

"Oh, sure, no problem," Crystal said. "We already have a lawyer. She wants to set things up pretty fast because the lady we're staying with out here knows we're doing this adoption thing and can get our rent money to her after we find parents for the baby."

Crystal said she was five months along. Could we pay four or five months of Southern California rent on top of our own Southern California rent?

"Okay, yeah, I don't know exactly how that would work—our agency, our uh organization, and your attorney, but obviously we could talk and figure it out."

We said our goodbyes and promised to talk soon. I paced the length of our house, from the tiny living room to the oversized bedroom. Where was CC? Every time she went out lately, I felt ill at ease. I couldn't quite place it. She'd always been bad with time, returning home later than planned. But now my need to call or text to check in with her felt stronger than ever, and more poorly received. I was the old ball and chain, keeping her from the freedom she claimed not to be pursuing.

As long as I'd known CC, she'd harbored a series of friend

crushes on slightly bitchy, distant, cool girls. The latest was her classmate Adrienne, a former model who still got paid by Marc Jacobs to attend parties in their clothes. Once Adrienne got in a surfing accident that caused her to lose her voice for a year, during which time she dated a lot of older, wealthy men who weren't really interested in a woman who talked. She was friendly to CC, but flaky, the perfect combo. CC fixated and analyzed, and I played wingman while reminding myself it was me she returned to every night. I consoled myself that she was a bad liar and not the cheating type. I reminded myself that narratives about never desiring another human being once you were in a committed relationship were heteronormative and stupid. I was frustrated and a little jealous, but I didn't mind having a little kick in the ass to remind me I had to win CC's heart time and again. One of the first things Julie said to us when we started couples therapy was that marriage is a decision you make every day.

Lately, though, CC's heart felt harder to win. It wasn't just that I had to listen to her and maybe put on a little eyeliner; it was like I was starting a lap behind and always trying to catch up, tripping over my own feet in the process.

When she got home, it was well past dark. She went straight for the refrigerator and pulled out a container of leftover pasta.

"I got a phone call from a birth mom," I said. I tried to shake the feeling that I was confessing to something. As if this were *my* cheating-but-not-cheating thing. "I mean, an expectant mom." This was part of the language of adoption—no woman was a birth mom until the baby was born and handed over. She was a pregnant woman in the process of making a decision. It made sense, but it was yet another reminder that thinking of *myself* as a mom was presumptuous and not allowed.

"Really? What did she say?"

I recounted the conversation, doing my best impression of a level-headed Hopeful Adoptive Parent. Like Expectant Mother and Birthmother, it was a semi-official term, HAP for short. It sounded like it should mean chump, or mark, or dolt. At the very least, I felt hapless, a dinghy bouncing around on choppy waters, waiting for something to happen.

CC always saw my act for what it was. She was attuned to the world's micro-emotions, mine especially. Plus I'd already shown my hand to everyone who would listen. They knew about my infertility, my pregnancy, my devastation. I couldn't imagine holding all of that inside, but walking through my life as a weeping wound wasn't so great either.

"Bipolar disorder is for real," she said. "And it's hereditary."

"I know. And the expenses. I think we checked the 'up to $3,000' box. But my dad would probably help. If we decided this was a good option."

She forked the last of the pasta and left the container on the table. I washed it and put it on the drying rack, then followed her into the living room, where she was already slouched in the arm-chair, flipping through a *New Yorker*.

"So I guess the only thing we need to decide now is whether to Skype with them . . . ?"

She shrugged. "Sure."

Her "sures" had always been a pet peeve of mine, whether in person or as replies to the emails I sent her during the workday. There was something infuriatingly noncommittal about them, but how could I argue with "sure"?

Everything was so delicate. I didn't want to ask another question that might make her rethink her first "sure." I was so unsure.

"Are there, like, specific days or times that would work for you? Would tomorrow be too soon?"

"No, tomorrow is fine. I want to go to yoga in the morning, but any other time."

That night, I went to my sister's birthday party without CC, who had plans with grad school friends. Those friendships were the delicate bubble she was protecting. Adrienne first and foremost, but also Jessica, the daughter of a housekeeper and wife of a guy who earned enough in his corporate job at a toothpaste manufacturer to allow her to be a fulltime student. Jessica was serious and always slightly stressed out. She'd had a miscarriage of her own. They wanted kids but didn't talk about it much. Summer was a single mom and sometimes actress, whose baby-daddy was a somewhat well-known Native American actor. Her Antioch friends had what I thought of as Westside lives. They had worked in The Industry. They were massage therapists and recovering addicts. They did not captivate me.

My sister was self-conscious about turning thirty-two single. She was a high school teacher who was still friends with all her high school friends. We all went to dinner at Macaroni Grill and ate Italian food cooked with lots of butter. Cathy was always the designated driver.

At the end of the night, Cathy handed out eighties-themed gift bags decorated with pictures of cassette tapes. We put on star-shaped plastic glasses and took selfies. With matching glasses, big teeth, unapologetic noses, and curly hair, Cathy and I could have been twins.

I told Crystal we'd Skype at 3:00 p.m. on Sunday. She said they'd be around all day, so whenever. At 2:54, CC still wasn't home from yoga, which had ended at 2:00. She'd stayed out late Saturday night and had slept through the 9:00 a.m. class. The studio was only a few blocks away. How could it take her an hour to get home?

I texted Crystal to let her know CC had gotten tied up, and prayed that she wouldn't think we were irresponsible or not taking this seriously.

No worries we r here, Crystal replied.

At 3:02, CC walked in the door with two CVS bags, which she flung on the couch. "Hey, sorry, should we Skype—what are their names again?"

"Crystal and Jesse."

The picture was choppy and they shifted a lot, full bodies coming in and out of the frame. Crystal was heavyset and didn't look particularly pregnant. Light brown bun, dark eyes, sweatpants, Big Gulp in hand. Jesse was skinny, with bad teeth and a twang. He held a Big Gulp, too.

"I'm so hungry now, I'm eating all the time," Crystal said, laughing.

"How do you guys like California so far?" CC asked. All her bristles were gone. She was in party mode now, chatting and riffing and happy to make new friends.

"Oh, we love it," Crystal said. "I'm so glad to be far away from my ex. He was coming around way too often, making threats and such. It was a bad situation. He tried to kick Jesse's ass two days before we left."

"He did kick my ass," Jesse offered, with an undefended laugh.

"You got in a couple good punches, baby," Crystal said. "I miss my daughter, though. She stays with my parents, and we Skype with them too. But I still miss 'em."

"And your other daughter and your son, the ones you placed—" I tiptoed toward the question I wanted to ask, and Crystal answered it for me.

"I talk to them, too. Mostly I talk to their parents, 'cause they're real little. But we're really open. Do y'all mind if we go out on the balcony? I need a cigarette."

The screen blurred and bounced. When Crystal and Jesse settled into the frame, I saw a backdrop of tan stucco and suburban street. A few cars, a row of palm trees. Despite Crystal's candidness and my reminders to myself that generations of healthy babies had been born to smokers, it was still weird to see Crystal flick her lighter and take a long drag.

I wanted to ask if they were in a twelve-step program, if Jesse or her ex was the biological father of this baby—the chronology she presented was confusing—and if they would still like us if we couldn't pay their rent. I didn't.

CC and I debriefed in bites over the next few days. The gist of her thesis was: bipolar disorder plus $10,000. The gist of mine was: baby. Our trainings introduced hypothetical birth moms and asked HAPs to assess risks—of the adoption not going through, and to the hypothetical babies themselves. The implication was that multiple opportunities would come along. I tried to believe this wouldn't be our only one, but I wasn't wired that way.

Keely understood me. She was a go-for-broke type, too, always entering quilting and weight-loss competitions. When I told her I was backing off the Crystal situation as a gesture of respect to CC, Keely wrote: *You deserve the chance to make your case. Did I ever tell you how Brandon and I got married? He hated the idea of marriage so much, he wouldn't even say the word, but he had health insurance and I needed health insurance. So I laid out why this was a logical choice for our relationship. When we got married, he said we got "M'ed."*

So I laid out why Crystal was a logical choice for our birth mom: She'd placed before. She was a sweet person. Bipolar disorder was manageable with therapy and medication, and we'd know to be on the lookout. The baby would be a mix of Latino and white like us; Crystal was Puerto Rican, and Jesse was white (although we still weren't sure if he was the father).

CC turned on Keely. "She manipulated her husband into marrying her? That's the kind of person you're taking advice from?"

And so I defended Keely alongside Crystal and Jesse. To me, Keely's tactics were not only normal, but they were the *only* tactics. My dad had taught me that the way to get what you wanted was to make a logical case. If you had enough bullet points, the other person had to acquiesce. Ideally, they would realize that this was what they wanted too. How could they not, when it was so logical? You had created a tidy little cage of evidence.

CHAPTER 12: SEPARATE

We said no to Crystal and Jesse. We cited money as the main issue, and said nothing about bipolar or the growing tension between me and CC, which moved through our house heavy as a ghost.

Tuesday nights, I went to IAC support group meetings at a hospital in the Valley. CC saw patients at her clinic internship and was uninterested in turning adoption into some sort of lifestyle. Gay and straight couples and a few singles gathered around pushed-together tables and ate dry cookies. Ostensibly we were there to learn about particular aspects of open adoption, but mostly we coached each other on how to deal with The Wait. People said things like, "I always thought I'd have kids younger, but on the plus side, I'll be able to retire in five years, and I can spend all that time with my son or daughter." And, "People talk about the adoption roller coaster, but actually matching with a birth mom feels like riding a roller coaster while holding a puppy and juggling knives." And, "My sister is pregnant right now, and I want to be happy for her, but—"

Sometimes we were joined by parents who'd recently adopted. A new mom, who stood in the back of the room swaying with her baby in a sling, replied to the pregnant-sister comment by saying, "Or don't. You can be nice to her, but you don't have to be *happy* for her. You don't owe anyone happiness. She'll be fine without your happiness."

I wanted to hug that mom for saying it, for throwing me this lifeline. Yes! I could hate pregnant women and new moms and birth moms all I wanted! As long as I didn't actually run them over with my car in parking lots, I didn't have to knife myself with shame just for *thinking* about running them over with my car.

We sifted through our fears one by one. If a baby landed in our arms, we wanted to know, what forces could snatch it away? How long did a birth mom have to change her mind once the baby was born? In what ways might we fuck it up ourselves? The social worker told a story about an adoptive dad who'd gotten a DUI before his placement was finalized. The baby went back to her birth family until the agency found a new adoptive couple.

CC was not a big drinker in general, but she drank the way she did many things—with friends, haphazardly, and without checking whether I'd mind driving home before she ordered a third drink. Suddenly I had a new fear, as looming and theoretically possible as MS. Her obsession with her therapist friends. Her unpredictable outings. Her increasingly aggressive disinterest in my insatiable needs, and in talking about the future.

I started doing the relational equivalent of researching diseases. Now, instead of running my fingers over the bumps on my neck or making mental checklists of MS symptoms, I told CC, "Have fun. Take a taxi if you need to." I put $80 in cash in her glove compartment.

We saw Julie, our couples therapist, Wednesday mornings before work. Sometimes I managed to squeeze in some writing time at McDonald's next door. I'd show up on time and caffeinated and wait outside Julie's second-floor office for Julie and CC, who both ran late. One day I went to the bathroom in the middle of a session, darting down the hall with her Legoland keychain.

When I returned, Julie said, "CC has something she wants to say. I told her she could tell you or I could tell you."

CC said, "I kissed someone."

Part of what makes bad news bad is the moment of impact. You have to figure out what to do with your face and body—to behave as if the world is not ending while your world ends.

Then again, this was not the end of the world, was it? I'd read a lot of Dan Savage's sex advice columns, and I repeated his words in my head and at our session. Cheating wasn't good for any relationship. Dishonesty wasn't healthy. But wasn't it oddly puritanical to act as if cheating was worse than any other indiscretion?

"Who . . . was it?" I asked.

"Someone from Antioch. No one you know. We all got drinks after class one night, and we kissed at the bar. I told her I wanted to go home with her, but we both knew that was a bad idea." She paused. "I'm sorry."

"I'm glad you told me," I said.

It was a strange moment that had been carved out for me, both by CC's actions and by every story of cheating spouses that came before. She'd behaved badly, and that gave me a certain amount of power, a not-terrible hand to play. But it also gave me a window into how she saw me: a sad, baby-obsessed homebody, a person she perhaps loved, but who existed separately from the world of things she wanted: the heat of liquor, the gravitational pull of sex, the promise of the unknown.

One night I made tilapia with pico de gallo for dinner, and it was only a little bit cold by the time CC got home from work.

CC seemed quiet and exhausted. Finally she said, "There's something I need to say." A piece of advice I'd once received from Keely: *Don't bother worrying about problems you haven't encountered yet, because your actual problems will be different ones. You don't have to go searching for them. They'll find you.*

CC said, "I want to separate."

I might as well have been tilapia, white and flabby and common, skewered on a fork. *So this is how it ends,* I thought. I didn't move or say anything. The chemicals of panic surged through my veins, some ancient response to some ancient threat. The bear's claws hook the fish.

"I've been so awful, for months," CC said. "I kissed someone else, and you forgave me. Immediately. Then I had this terrible revelation. You would never leave me."

I was loyal because I wanted to be with her and no one else. But two things can be true at once. I loved her and wanted to be with her, and I knew how to manipulate my innocence. Grief-stricken, semi-cheated-on spouse. Damn right I was going to make her be the bad guy in this. I was going to make her *do* something, be someone. That was probably a good step for both of us, *and* it was a knife to my fish heart, a sad, slithery bit of organ meat.

"All the color drained out of your face," she said.

"How could it not? Did you think I would be like, 'Okay, cool, see you later?'"

"I don't know. You don't seem like you like being with me. All you talk about is wanting a baby. You're not interested in me, and you don't even listen to me. Your pain is so loud I can't fucking hear myself think. I need time to hear myself think."

In my head, I began assembling proof that I loved her.

Exhibit A: kiss forgiveness. Exhibit B: couples therapy. Exhibit C: my mom's ring on the chain around her neck. But listing ways I was Not So Bad was going to be about as effective as listing my needs and drawing fine-lined portraits of my grief, as I'd been doing for months.

"I'm sorry," I said, knowing that wasn't going to work either. "What do you want to do now?"

"I want to separate," she said.

"Do you want me to move out? Do you want to move out?"

"I don't know," she snapped. "I just need space. I am so miserable, and I know you are, too."

"I am not miserable. Or, I'm not miserable in our relationship. Don't tell me how I feel." I dug my fingernails into my forearms. I didn't want to cry, but I needed to perform an act of alchemy. I needed to turn love and fish-heartedness into physical pain. I imagined CC looking at the gouges in my skin and wanting to take it all back.

She did not take it back.

I wriggled the aquarium ring off my left finger and handed it to her.

"Really?" she said.

"This is what you're saying," I said. "This is what you're asking for. Don't just throw words like 'separation' around."

When I'd stopped shaking, I realized that she had not said "divorce." Maybe just because that sounded like something from the realm of adults and heterosexuals, because it still only half seemed like we were married. I contemplated life as a person who had broken up after less than two years of marriage. Making this about my personal failures would be a replication of everything CC was bucking against right now, but it was there in the background, like the hum of the refrigerator.

I clung to this bit of hope: Maybe she really did want a pause and not an ending.

Simultaneously, I wanted to throw this bit of hope in the trash. The only thing I could imagine more tortuous than waiting for the results of a pregnancy test was waiting for CC to decide whether she loved me enough to forgive my selfishness. I could not stand in either place—hope or grief—without eyeing the other.

That night, I unrolled my sleeping bag in our spare room and poured an inch of whiskey into a glass. I lay there watching *RuPaul's Drag Race* on my laptop, falling instantly in love with a queen named Latrice Royale. She was older than the other queens by a decade or two, with a few missing teeth and a Compton backstory. She wore a thick cat-eye, a purple beehive, and sequined evening gowns. Rather than masking something, her performance brought out all the pain and beauty behind the makeup and sparkles. When people threw around the word *fierce,* Latrice Royale is what they meant. I let her giant, feathery eyelashes cover me like a blanket.

We hatched a plan: We would spend two months apart, May and June, splitting custody of the house and cats down the middle. We would keep going to couples therapy on Wednesday mornings and meet once a week for a sad, awkward "date."

She took the first shift at home, while I spent nights at Nicole's and then at Piper's. Nicole hosted her annual Motherless Mother's Day tea at her sister's house, and I was even more alone than the previous year. No child, no mother, no spouse. I stepped away from Nicole's sister's spread of teacups and raspberry tarts and tiny glass jars of crème fraîche to take a call from a high school friend who was weathering a breakup as well. We railed about our selfish still-significant others.

I joined CC for a yoga class in the Valley, and we ate Thai food afterward. I told her she looked hot doing downward dog, and she told me that made her feel weird, and I raked my nails along my arms some more.

My weight dropped below 130 for the first time in years. I went for long runs with Piper and declined her offer to house-sit for a friend who had a husband and a new baby and a recently published book. I called my sister daily and asked her to repeat my hopes back to me as if they were facts: CC wasn't behaving like a person trying to leave. We would probably work this out. Didn't every couple have rough patches?

I polled my friends in long-term relationships. Colin said he and his wife had it easy for the first eight years, and then their mortgage and jobs and dog and existential *stuff* made things . . . heavy. Kat said she'd been toying with the idea of leaving John, and then he had a heart attack. This provided her with laser focus; now they were solidly together, and vegan. Lizzy said that once, during an argument, Mars had said: *Don't you ever stop talking?* She wanted to settle into her life with him and their two daughters by making big travel plans. He wanted to mow the lawn and watch TV. Bronwyn said that if she and Melissa had decided to have kids, they would have had frustratingly different parenting styles. Terry said I should let CC go and learn to live in gratitude, and I hated her.

In couples therapy, I listened. I imagined myself as all ears after months of being a bottomless, sobbing mouth. I drew CC a mini comic book breaking things down as I saw them. Even in the midst of crisis—especially in the midst of crisis—I didn't know how to stop storytelling. I opened with a panel of my sentient uterus and ovaries, flashed back to my dad soapboxing about hard work as salvation in the 1980s, and depicted CC's bubbling interrogations of her own childhood as they collided with my meltdowns. I shaded the backgrounds pink and yellow and blue.

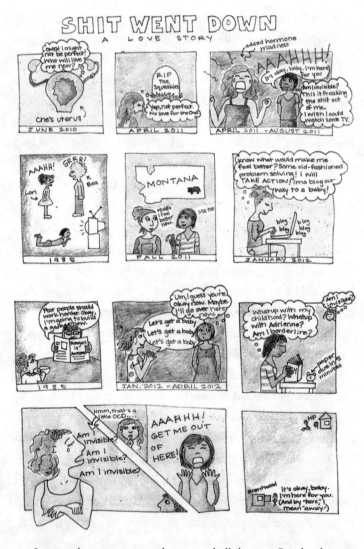

I spent the next two weeks at my dad's house. On the drive to Manhattan Beach, I decided to inhabit Terry's idea. What if it was over? Let's call it over.

When Bari broke up with me, I'd been more certain of her certainty. She had called from her parents' house in Syracuse to say she wanted to talk to me about something when she returned. I said,

"Are you breaking up with me?" because I had an unfortunate habit of joking my way to reassurance. She remained silent. She'd gotten me to do the dirty work myself. In the days that followed, I wrote her long pleading emails insisting that I loved her. But I never really expected her to change her mind. It wasn't her style, and I was a little bit excited about having an apartment without giant cardboard boxes stacked in the corner of our bedroom "just in case" we ever moved.

I rode the 110 and attempted to simply mourn CC. I tried to get excited about a tidy apartment to myself. I arrived at my dad's house sobbing. My dad was on the deck he'd built himself, in the exact place he'd spent weekend afternoons since the eighties: reclined in a folding chaise lounge, eating microwaved leftovers with a week's worth of *Daily Breeze* comics sections collected next to him.

Counseling my sister and me through our traumas had been my mom's job, though it frequently ended in her pleading, "I just wish I knew what to *say.*" But like a blind person whose hearing attunes to the slightest ruffle of feathers, my dad had learned to do what was necessary for the survival of our family.

"People have hard times in marriages," he said reasonably. "She told you she needed time to think, and she's doing that. There's no reason to believe this is forever. You're giving her space and listening to her, and that's the best thing you can do. You'll work it out."

When I was at the bottom of a hole, my dad's rhetoric was the only thing that could get me out. We each knew our role and snapped to attention. My job was to state the worst case scenario. His job was to list *logical, factual* reasons why said scenario wouldn't come to pass. He was the voice of a god I knew better than to believe in.

"Terry said I should give up and let her go," I said.

"That seems premature," my dad said.

"Right? I think so, too."

I made pasta with a sauce patched together from ingredients in my dad's bare cupboards. My dad proclaimed it delicious. He was my best audience. He liked how I used "herbs and flavors." In our small steamed-up kitchen, I felt competent and loved. And because my dad was the Voice of Truth, it must be true.

Later that night, we watched procedurals on network TV, followed by the local and national news. A reporter stood in front of a swirling weather map and talked about Tropical Storm Cheryl, which was rapidly heading for hurricane status.

In the communication workshop we'd done at church, we learned that in most couples, one half tended to be a "hail storm," while the other was a "turtle." We knew who was who. I took a risk and texted CC and got a *hahahaha* back. She had replied! She had not retreated into her shell. I curled up in my childhood bed that night to watch old episodes of *Law & Order: SVU* on my laptop and eat low-fat ice cream. I slept.

In the mornings, before driving to Westwood for work, I jogged to the Hermosa Beach pier. Down a wood-chip trail, alongside fit white people and their dogs. Past the sleeping sites of evening douchery—Sharkeez and Hennessey's Tavern—now closed and smelling of old beer. Past the tsunami warning zone sign, which, as far as I could tell, just told people to run. I tried not to think of earthquakes and tsunamis, and failed. I ran to the very end of the pier, until all I could see was ocean, flat and dark for the time being. The sun did its best in the thin, gray morning. I've never been good at this—at seeking out and rooting myself in nature, which never negates all the problems that would be waiting for me as soon as I turned toward land—but it was big and I was small but part of the big thing, and that was something.

CHAPTER 13: **CLOSER**

CC went to Justine's, and I returned to our house. The first night, I cleaned furiously and drew Xs on our wall calendar over all the separation days that had already passed. I felt a burst of energy. Not quite optimism, but something that required hope as its pilot light. After cleaning, I wasn't sure what to do with myself. I went to CVS and bought myself a gothy shade of nail polish. I wasn't used to this aimlessness; I was too antsy to rest and too distraught to be creative or productive.

Saturday morning, CC asked me to meet her for brunch at the York. My heart fired off little hope rockets while my stomach churned, another tempest in the larger storm of Hurricane Cheryl. This wasn't planned. Was it good news or bad?

Over eggs and bacon and biscuits, she said, "I'm so lost. I don't know what I want. I called up that girl, the one from Antioch. I tried to go see her, and she said it wasn't a good idea. She was right. I don't know what I'm doing."

Was I supposed to console her about being rejected by the person she'd cheated with? The thing is, I didn't mind doing it. I was either a desperate pushover, or I was rejecting heterosexist narratives about desire and loyalty, or I was a grownup coming to terms with the complexity of real life.

"Do you want to be with her?"

The biscuit toppled from the top of her egg sandwich. She stabbed it with a toothpick. "No. Not really. I just want to have a good time and not feel invisible. But I don't know how to do that. This is the most lost I've ever felt."

"Well, you know what I think would be *great* for you. But I'm going to stop telling you what that is. That's the part I'm trying to learn."

"When I was a kid, I spent so much time in my head. I was so into movies and books. Not just in that normal creative-kid way. Like, beyond that. It was an escape from reality."

She looked miserable, but she wasn't freezing me out the way she had the night of yoga and Thai food. Had that really been just a few weeks ago?

She walked me home—to our home—and we stood on the steps outside the gate. They were too narrow to stand on together, so we stood escalator-style, me a foot above. The June gloom of the morning had parted, and the overgrown yucca plant outside our living room window was leaning toward the street like an eager alien.

"You know," I said, unsure of my intentions, "I'll be okay. I'll be fucking devastated, but I'll survive without you. If I can live without my mom, I can live without you, too. I'm strong."

"I know you will," CC said. "I know you are."

I hated being at home. I looked at the calendar and thought *Five more hours before I can cross off another day. Forty-two more minutes before it will only be four hours.* I hated work, where Jamie sat across from me, turtle to my hailstorm, quiet and kind and professional.

I had to go to Fresno to host a literary roundtable meeting, a meet-and-greet of local writers and teachers and publishers with a loose agenda. On the drive up, I stopped and called Bari. It had been a while since we'd talked, and I was looking for a punching bag.

"I'm sure you're thinking, 'Of course she'd get dumped again.' But what's going on with CC and me is really different from what you and I went through."

"I'm not thinking that," Bari said.

I asked her, more or less, if she thought CC would take me back—a terrible and impossible question to ask an ex. I made a flimsy, obvious trap. A pile of leaves over a cartoon hole.

"Well," she said. "You know that was a thing for us, too, where you said you cared about me, but I didn't always feel it."

I exploded at her, drawing her into my deep hole, where my sob-yelling reverberated off dirt walls.

"Don't you see the difference? I *actually* hurt CC. She stuck with me and wanted to have a family with me and didn't just set up a bunch of hoops for me to jump through to prove my worthiness. And I shit all over that. I was completely self-absorbed, and now I have to live with the consequences. I wasn't a perfect girlfriend to you, but I always paid attention to you and did nice things for you. You were the one who set the terms of the test and then decided I'd fail it. CC never set out to test me."

I all but yelled, *You're half the woman CC is.* As different as they were, as different as their motivations were, they'd essentially arrived at the same conclusion: I was a person who didn't know how to love people. I didn't understand how I could be "selfish" when I didn't even like myself, but maybe it was true—time spent hating myself was time away from the people I loved.

I white-knuckled the roundtable meeting, feigning investment in poetry workshops for underserved youth. On the drive home, I stopped in Keane, a tiny town outside Bakersfield, where my reporter friend and her ER doctor husband had recently bought a house. I helped her make dinner, and the three of us crowded around her laptop screen to watch *Downton Abbey*. I couldn't keep the characters straight. I retired to the guest room—people my age were starting to have guest rooms—to unpack.

My phone buzzed and my heart leapt. CC?

Not CC. Justine.

"I just wanted to see how you were doing," she said.

"Not good. I know you can't, like, tell me everything CC has said, but how is she doing? Have you guys been . . . talking about things?"

"Yeah. She's been thinking about what she wants. I've been asking her what her values are. What marriage means to her."

"What did she say?"

"I don't think she knows yet."

CC emailed and said she wanted to talk some more. I thought that was probably good, and then I thought it was probably bad. I wanted to hope, and I hated hope. Back on the road, I called Nicole to puzzle over possibilities. She said what I needed her to say, over and over. And then, when I got home, I saw a text from Nicole: *I need to take a little break from talking about CC. It's stirring up a lot of anxiety for me. I love you.*

I flopped down in our living room chair, my suitcase at my feet. Well, fuck. Here was written proof that I was officially Too Much for everyone who attempted to love me. Why couldn't Nicole be one of those people who secretly enjoyed other people's drama by virtue of being separate from it? Or, better yet, be one of those people, and then successfully disguise herself as being one hundred percent invested in the fate of my marriage?

I called my sister, complaining that Nicole had abandoned me, too.

"I keep thinking about how this whole experience reinforces my worst fears," I said. "That if I'm too needy and not helpful, no one will want me."

"You're not too needy for me," she said. "I'm never going to stop taking your calls."

"Thank you," I said. I curled in the stained green armchair in our living room. "If she takes me back, it will be such a good lesson for that subconscious part of me. I've told you what my therapist said, right? About how, when you were born, I got the message that the best way for me to win Mom and Dad's affection was to be really capable and independent? So, like, I always believe that as soon as I'm needy, like baby you, no one will want me. So if CC wants to reconcile, it will show my subconscious that I can be needy and loved, and that broken things can be repaired."

"Sorry I did that to you as a baby," Cathy said sincerely.

"Well, obviously it wasn't your fault. It wasn't Mom and Dad's fault, either. I know they loved me, but my kid logic extrapolated from the cues they sent me about being a big kid."

"Yeah. I guess I see that."

"But if CC doesn't want to get back together, I don't know what I'll do. I guess I'll have the biggest self-help project ever. But it seems like we'll get back together, right? Like things are moving in that direction?"

"You still see her more often than I've seen a lot of guys *while I'm dating them*," she said.

"We're lesbians that way," I said.

Near sunset that night, I stepped outside to lock the front gate.

We rarely bothered, and the padlock was beginning to rust, but I felt edgier when I was alone in the house. A small black cat stood on the bottom step of the staircase that led to our neighbors' house. I'd seen him around, initially as a kitten; now he was a teenager. CC and I called him Mini Ferdinand. Like Ferd, he had a tuft of white fur at the top of his chest like a small ascot. I reached out my hand and Mini Ferdinand sniffed it. We thought maybe he belonged to the family in the house behind us. They had caged birds in their cluttered backyard, which faced ours, and a narrow dog run that housed a rotating cast of cooped-up dogs.

Slowly, I petted Mini Ferdinand's silky black fur. He wasn't as shiny as Ferd, and I wondered if he was getting enough to eat. He arched his back beneath my hand and emitted a small purr. I texted CC *Mini Ferdinand let me pet him!*

She replied: *!*

The next day, she texted again: *Do you want to get a drink and talk?* Of course I did. We met at the Verdugo, a wine-and-beer bar tucked away in a residential neighborhood. I ordered a dark beer and she ordered one the color of summer, and we sat at a picnic table on the back patio. Around us, people played Jenga and laughed and waited for greasy sandwiches at the grilled cheese truck parked next to the bar.

After a minute, she said, "So it seems like we're doing this, doesn't it?" She didn't have to clarify what "this" was. *This* was our life together.

My heart leapt, and I could feel myself trying to reach out and catch it.

"I'm asking you," I said.

"I want to stick with our plan. I don't want to move back until July. Maybe longer."

"Okay, I can live with that." During the long days in Manhattan Beach, I'd worked out on the elliptical at the gym, moving my body without going anywhere, trying to re-imagine the next handful of years. I'd refused to imagine life without CC, but I could picture us as cool older moms—thirty-seven, thirty-eight, thirty-nine, wizened and crow's-footed, giving zero fucks about the things that didn't matter. It had been like that, in a way, with coming out, too. I just had to work myself up to a place where something terrifying seemed desirable. I just had to write a convincing novel in my head.

"No rush," I said.

We talked about small things. Work, Justine and Sam, Mini Ferdinand. The conversation twisted back to our big thing. It was like hiking in a big urban park; you could convince yourself you were in the woods for a while, but all trails eventually led to the freeway, and when you thought about it, the vast rushing sound of it had never gone away.

"I asked you to get help and you ignored me," CC said.

"I know. I'm sorry. And this doesn't make it okay, but it's like—" my voice caught and I fought it, because here I went again, being dramatic, making it about me. "It's really, really hard to follow a map or, like, create a new one when you're just trying to keep the car from running into a ditch."

"Yeah," she conceded.

When our glasses were empty she said, "You know Laura from the clinic? Do you want to go to her wedding with me next weekend? It's on Saturday. It's on some ranch out in Temecula."

Saturday was our anniversary. Why not spend it at someone else's wedding with my semi-estranged spouse? I laughed. "Yeah. Why not?"

I knew better than to get her a real anniversary gift, or to make a big deal about it. She was a bird eating out of my hand. I tried to stay perfectly still. But I was still me. After Bari had broken up with me, I'd bought a T-shirt at a craft fair depicting a dish running away with a spoon, and a sad, lonely fork in the foreground. I explained to CC that I was the forlorn fork and the spoon was Bari's idealized girlfriend. CC had said, "But now you have a new colander."

Now I bought an actual mini colander in the home section of Macy's. I made a little face for it with paper and colored pencil, and did the same for an old fork from the set I'd grown up with. I gave the fork very big ears.

"It's not a *present* present," I said, handing her the gift bag as we set out for Temecula. "See, those are my big listening ears, and that's your talky colander mouth."

She smiled with her regular human mouth, one I'd always liked. Wide and cranberry-dark, with a bottom lip that stuck out a little.

Temecula was ninety miles east and south, past dry rolling hills and the Pechanga Reservation and the Pechanga Resort and Casino. I thought of the radio commercials for Pechanga, a pop diva scream-singing *Take me away / a secret place / a better day.* Geography did its magic, and the heavy blanket of our Los Angeles lives peeled back. We got lost, of course, and had to ask for directions at a place that looked like a saloon in a Western.

Eventually we arrived at a dirt parking lot and a pen full of horses. A bartender poured mojitos into mason jars and we mingled with Laura's friends, none of whom we knew. We could be anyone. We could be the most solid couple in the world. We could have just hooked up three days ago.

We hiked to the top of a small hill where there was a tree and a hammock we could both fit in. Her body was warm and right-sized next to mine. The sun was low and red-orange. I thought about kissing her and decided against it. I remembered when we first got together, how lusty-grateful I'd been to lie in bed staring at the tattoo on her back. The scales had tipped a bit—more gratitude, quieter lust. But the world stretched and paused again.

We hiked back down the hill in time for the sunset ceremony. We sweated in rented chairs, but it was short and sweet, and Laura and her new husband's dogs wore bow-tie collars. Every place setting at dinner included a small three-legged pig made of red clay. A tiny scroll of paper tied to each said they were Chilean symbols of abundance and happiness. Even smaller pigs, no bigger than the tip of my thumb, were twined to cloth napkins. Between us, we had a family of four. Two big, two small. I knew that if I chose to believe good omens, I had to believe bad ones too. I had to entertain the possibility that the knobs in my neck were tumors. And yet.

It was after one in the morning when we got back to Highland Park. For the first time in months, we slept in the same bed.

PART II

CHAPTER 14: HONEYMOONING

Was our honeymoon the tense trip we took in 2010 to Washington and Canada on our way to get married? Or are honeymoons, when there is no wedding and no limo and no sunset to drive into, only defined retroactively? As in, *the honeymoon's over.*

We got the summer. Our first day back in the house together, we fought on the way to a Dodgers game. I said something I shouldn't have; CC panicked that nothing had changed. Then we settled down and settled in. Mini Ferdinand returned, and one night he walked in our bedroom door, the one that opened to the outside, and helped himself to Ferdinand and OC's food. CC and I looked at each other in quiet conspiracy. You weren't supposed to feed strays.

"It kind of seems like you're moving in," she said to the small black cat.

"We're going to need to call you something other than Mini Ferd," I said.

We tried out a couple of names, and then CC came up with Cousin Oliver, for the bespectacled kid who joined the *Brady Bunch* household when the rest of them were outgrowing their cuteness. Like the Bradys, we needed an injection of cuteness; like an aging TV show, we were a little desperate. Ollie ate and grew and had a stealth determination about him that I admired. His matte coat turned glossy.

I still had obsessive thoughts about my health. There was an indentation on the top of my right boob that troubled me, and any mention of multiple sclerosis—just its existence in the world— made my toes tingle. But I tried to keep the volume low, for my sake and CC's.

I knew better than to bring up adoption, but one night we were thumbing through used books and records at a store in Hollywood when CC relayed a story about her sister trying to get pregnant back when she was married to her ex. Now she was engaged again, and ready to try again. CC and Elena had, not a rivalry exactly—it was more like Elena did things bigger and louder, and CC tried to carve out a space for herself in the world, off to the side. No wonder she'd been drawn to me. No wonder she hated me.

I looked at the table-to-ceiling rows of books in front of me and took a deep breath. "I know we're not talking about kids yet, and I'm in no rush. But I don't want you to feel like you can't try to get pregnant—like it would hurt me somehow. It's your body, and you have every right to try. If you want to try, I promise not to be a jerk about it."

Her face was surprised and soft. "Thanks. I mean—maybe I do. Thanks."

We booked tickets to Atlanta to visit Amy. We always did better out of town, and with friends. A honeymoon.

Not long after splitting with Kim, Amy had met Carrie on a work trip to Atlanta. A few months later, she moved out there to live with Carrie and Carrie's son, Cooper. Before she left, she said, "It's weird to be leaving the Childless Woman Club, but I hope you'll keep my picture on the wall and think of me during your meetings." She meant it kindly, but I fumed for months.

I was still wary, but CC had mentioned that Amy was struggling with step-motherhood, with Carrie's ex, with the transition to a whole new life. Schadenfreude got me on that plane.

They lived in a three-bedroom house that Carrie owned, in a thicket of green that conjured up stories of moonshine (which we bought at the liquor store in mason jars). In the morning, CC peed on a stick to see if she was ovulating, and she was. It was just a test run, to make sure that she would be able to get pregnant when we were ready to bring in the sperm, but it was another tally mark in the optimism column. At night we drank fireball whiskey on the enclosed porch while Cooper slept. A few drinks in, Amy and Carrie got into a low-grade argument about the scientific validity of the aptitude testing service for which Amy had recently started working. I tipsily attempted to channel our couples' therapist, and observed that Amy had fully immersed herself in Carrie's life; her job was one thing that was hers alone. Of course she was a little defensive about it.

I was drunk and full of hubris and relief that their life wasn't so perfect after all. Cooper was a cutie, but also very much a four-year-old hurling his way through the world. When he elbowed a toy off a shelf in a store we visited, Amy and Carrie paid for it and *still let him play with it even though he broke it.* I judged, smugly and gratefully.

Back home, I packed for my three-week writing residency at the MacDowell artists' colony. I'd gotten the acceptance letter while

CC and I were separated and had been so angry at the weird lack of balance in the universe that I'd pounded my fist into the seat of my office chair. Now I worried that CC would change her mind about me while I was gone. I worried that I would lose my mind in all that quiet. I made lists of how I would spend my time (reading, jogging in the woods, writing), and how I wouldn't spend my time (giving myself breast exams, Googling diseases).

I flew into Boston and rode through small towns and wet woods with MacDowell's driver, a grant-writer-turned-medical-writer who told me a long story about the time when, in the middle of a move, his pickup truck containing all his possessions was stolen. It had been a fork in the road of his life, or maybe not a fork because that implies a choice, but a sudden curve, when he'd almost fallen over the cliff. He survived, shaken and cynical. I could relate.

Some of the cabins at MacDowell were close to a hundred years old, but mine had been built in the late nineties. It had heated floors, two perfect reading nooks, a bathtub overlooking a meadow where deer and wild turkeys gathered. An older jazz musician joked every day about the bathtub. "Are you using it? Not every cabin has a tub like that, you know," he said. I forced myself to take one bath, my pale boobs floating in front of me, begging me to examine them for lumps. There was that funny dent, almost like a stretch mark but not quite, on the right side. But I *had* gained some weight recently, and the tech at my last breast ultrasound said that fat shifts around with menstrual cycles and weight fluctuations. My next breast ultrasound was November 9. I'd contemplated bumping it up, to get it out of the way before MacDowell, but my therapist encouraged me to try to manage my anxiety instead of perpetually choking down life's vegetables before allowing myself dessert. I didn't use the tub again.

During the day, I read and wrote and wrote. Over the years working on the Westside, I'd written three and a half novels in the time I spent waiting out traffic at Starbucks. Three and a half novels in one- and two-hour stints. I didn't think I could or even wanted to be one of those mad recluse writers who wrote for eight hours at a stretch. But it turned out I could be, in the paradise of Mac-Dowell, where I had no job, no spouse, nothing to cook or clean. No TV, no internet except in the main hall, no pets, no traffic, no car, no friends, no family. I was surprised how quickly my brain filled with words, how the problems of my novel would arrange themselves like puzzle pieces on my lunchtime walks through the woods. I knew I was tasting the good life, and I was scared by how much I liked it.

At night, we gathered for dinner in Colony Hall, an old farmhouse with a high-ceilinged central room, a big fireplace, and a pool table. There were always vegetarian options. There was always wine and dessert.

I tried to make friends, because I knew it would stave off my crazy. It was an odd feeling, carrying all my recent tragedy with me; not talking about it, but feeling a certain confidence among other people who had Lived. The recent college grad whose mother committed suicide. The WASPy horse girl who wrote about all her psych meds and ended up in the emergency room one night after alcohol mixed poorly with them. The guy with the 9/11 memoir who sort of flirted with me. As I waited for the van to take me back to the airport on my last day, he was the one to whom I told My Story—about miscarrying and sinking into a place I'd never known existed. I felt like I had to tell someone, to stitch my life there to the one I was flying home to, to make MacDowell more real and to carry a little of it with me.

CHAPTER 15: **SICK**

I wasn't actually diagnosed until November 12. On the ninth, they held me down, smeared more goo on my right breast, and extracted a needle full of cells from the ominous mass on the mammogram. Between the ninth and the twelfth, I zombied through the world. Nicole and I watched a campy horror movie called *Jennifer's Body*. I told myself more biopsies than not came back benign. I stared at CC while she ate a hamburger at Fusion Burgers. And then I went home to call the number they'd given me to get my results.

Yes, said the voice on the other end of the line—it was malignant. No, it did not look like it had spread to my lymph nodes. She told me what to do next: Make an appointment for an MRI, call Dr. Jasper, and call this other number to make an appointment with an oncologist.

My hands were still shaking, and I was still floating outside my body, but I was also beginning to understand that I was being plugged into a system. It was complex and no fun, but someone—

many people, many dollars from pink-ribbon relays—had taken the care to make it navigable. Go here. Do this. Miscarriage had no such map. Miscarriage was met with shrugs and averted eyes.

By that point, my dad and sister were waiting in the living room while I made calls and took notes in the kitchen. I could go here. I could do this.

But after I'd followed all the instructions I'd written on the back of the gas bill, the sense of free-falling returned. I sent my family home. They reassured me we would get through this, too, as a family. We'd gotten through my mom's death, we'd gotten through my miscarriage. I felt a surge of love for them, which was its own kind of pain. I was grateful to share the weight of this. I didn't want to hand them the weight of this.

And the darker thought: Had we really gotten through anything? Did events that failed to kill you make you stronger, or did it just pile up, compressing like sediment until they combined with something that finally did kill you? The time had come to raise my hand and say, "This is not fair. This is more than my share of shittiness. This is above my fucking pay grade."

I called a college friend who had attempted suicide once, before I knew her, and flirted with it as recently as a year ago. She was a voice actor with a cult following and a boyfriend who never acknowledged her publicly. But she received me that day, the only vessel deep enough for the expanse of my darkness. She gave me the gift of being unafraid of me.

I threw some things at the wall. Nothing that did permanent damage. I called my therapist, who made me promise that as understandable as my feelings of overwhelm were, I wasn't actually suicidal. At the depths of my miscarriage insanity, I'd reasoned that I must not be suicidal because I worried about death all the time.

It felt more like I'd already died but somehow missed the train to the afterlife. Being stuck among the living felt wrong and torturous. This was more of that, and something slightly different.

I had done everything right. Or, well, "right." I'd established a career before trying to get pregnant, but I didn't wait so long that my eggs were shriveled. I'd sought fertility treatment, but not enough to put myself at risk of ovarian cancer. When I sank into a depression, I barely missed work.

And now I still had no baby, and I had cancer.

So how the fuck was I supposed to live my life? Jane Smiley has written that the premise of every novel is: *Things are not what they seem.* It takes a while for the protagonist to realize this, and the realization and what comes after is their story. The world of cause and effect, working and earning, was not what it had seemed. I had already known this on some level. If I'd truly believed in meritocracy, I would have been a Republican. My whole family had been shocked when my mom was diagnosed: *But she eats a bowl of peas and carrots with nothing on it for lunch every day,* we said. *She goes for long walks. She's never had more than a sip of alcohol in her life.*

It was only then that my dad stopped obsessively talking about and saving for retirement. They bought a fancy motorhome and toured the Southwest. Their Christmas gifts got more and more generous.

But there are layers of knowing, and each one adds to the total weight. They can crush you. Another layer of knowing engulfed me: Life had nothing to do with fairness. It unfolded in a completely separate universe from fairness. How was I supposed to move through a world that still believed in it? How was I supposed to shower and get dressed and face people who still placed faith in vitamins and resumes? How could I move among them as anything but a ghost?

Some people learn the fundamental unfairness at a younger age than I did. I heard an interview with a reformed con man who endured a horrifically abusive childhood. He knew early on that trust can be torn apart and manipulated, and so he swindled people. Once he beat up a woman in an elevator just for looking like his mother. She'd been the kind of mother who prompted such a reaction. He committed a series of identity thefts and massive cyber-fraud. Even after he went to jail and tried to get "back" on a track he'd never known existed, after he fell in love with a woman who knew his history, he ran up bills on other people's credit cards. I know it sounds overly Freudian, but of *course* he was looking for an identity.

CHAPTER 16: RICOCHETING

The month of my diagnosis, four sets of friends had babies. Justine had a C-section the same day I had a biopsy. I wanted to thrust my bruised, cancerous boob in all their smug faces.

Suddenly I had as many doctor's appointments as I did during fertility treatment. The mammogram had shown no cancer in my lymph nodes; the higher-resolution MRI would confirm it, hopefully. The techs on duty at the Huntington-Hill Imaging Center told me that MRIs *usually* didn't reveal anything new, but I was already unusual. People didn't usually get pregnant with identical twins. They weren't usually gay or left-handed. Women didn't usually get hernias, and I'd had surgery for one.

CC came with me to the Imaging Center. Our couples therapist had encouraged her to get more involved with the logistics of Hard Things; apparently I'd done her no favors by driving to all those Beverly Hills fertility appointments on my own. The Imaging Center was next to the Breast Center. A sculpture made of glass and stone and flowing water stood behind the reception desk. When the nurse approached me in the waiting room, she said something about the office being closed and not having my paperwork. What office? What paperwork?

"I don't know what you're talking about," I said. "They told me they'd already obtained referrals from my regular doctor."

CC stepped right up. "You're trying to call Dr. Jasper's office to get her to fax over paperwork that they should have already sent. But it's closed for lunch. They always take really long lunches, so call Dr. Jasper's emergency line."

"I did. She said the office will open soon."

"Okay, so keep calling."

They must have gotten what they needed, because I was ushered into a maze of spa-like dressing rooms. Put this robe on like a jacket. Put this other robe over it. Now these teal socks with orange tread on the bottom. Now lie face down on a thing like a massage table but with holes for your boobs, and no massage.

A few nights later, in the safe after-doctors'-hours of our kitchen, I stir-fried vegetables and shrimp pot stickers and invited Nicole over. She showed up with purple flowers and a sucks-you-have-cancer card, and folded her long limbs into one of the Ikea chairs.

She wanted to make sure CC was being appropriately support-ive. It felt like CC and I had lived at least two full marriages since I'd called Nicole on my way home from Fresno, but I know time functions differently when you're looking at someone's narrative from the outside. It's why widowers who remarry quickly receive dirty looks: people look at the number of days they've grieved rather than the hours.

"CC gave me flowers, too," I said. "And she is kicking ass when necessary, like with doctor bureaucracy stuff. And we're still going to move ahead with trying to get her pregnant. I know that probably sounds crazy, but it's really important to me. To not feel like I'm being punished, like 'Oh, you have cancer, so now you also don't get a baby.'"

"No, that makes sense," Nicole said, appeased.

"She's going to do an ultrasound next week, and an IUI after. That's the glorified turkey baster thing. I don't know how fast they're going to shuttle me into surgery, but I hope I can schedule it around the IUI."

"Are you nuts?" Nicole said. "You don't get to choose a surgery date. They tell you."

"But this is the one thing I'm looking forward to—I feel like the universe owes us a fucking baby. Also, CC already took Clomid this month, and I don't want it to go to waste."

Nicole said, "See, this is how I know I don't want kids. You'll do everything to have them, and I wouldn't put up with any of this. I would be like, cancer trumps all of it."

I knew cancer was the most important thing. I hated it for being the most important thing. After months of feeling dead, I had to decide whose side I was on: that of death, or my own life. But what could be more anti-death than the literal creation of life?

Later, I talked to CC about it. She said, "I can handle the IUI alone if I need to. If you would be okay going to surgery with just your dad and sister."

I would learn soon enough that, in the vast spectrum of medical emergencies, pre-symptomatic cancer was fairly non-urgent; my surgery wouldn't be for another month. But right then, I loved CC for being as impractical and unromantic as I was, as nontraditional about what required our presence as a couple. Maybe we were both still in the denial phase of this annoying new grief process. But we were there together.

This time, I had a road map. I made an appointment with my psychiatrist, who studied the fine print to see which antidepressants were contraindicated with chemo drugs. I talked to my Uncle Robin and Aunt Connee, to my therapist, and to Dr. Jasper, who said, in her brisk Russian accent, "This isn't the cancer that will kill you. There are a lot of spots on your MRI, so they'll probably recommend a mastectomy, but they'll do a very nice reconstruction."

Adrenaline and momentum and dreams of the spaghetti-strap tank tops I would wear braless with my new gamine boobs kept me going. And then a brochure arrived in the mail. Its title was something like "So, You've Got Breast Cancer!" The guide helped me figure out that my "early stage" was probably stage IIB, which didn't sound early at all. Anything up to IIIA was considered "early stage," but I would have preferred a little more leeway. The language of the booklet was careful never to say things like "bad" or "death." Some cancers were just more prone to a "favorable outcome" while others were more "difficult." It was factual and informative and, despite its pinkness and Papyrus font and one "smell the roses" quote on the back, it didn't bullshit you, the cancer lady, too much.

This wasn't just a free boob job. I decided I probably had an aggressive form of cancer. I decided chemo probably lay in my near future, and didn't chemo and radiation increase your risk for some other cancer? How bad off did you have to be if your doctors were willing to put you at risk for other cancers?

I'm trying to describe the arc of this experience. I think there was an arc. I wanted to live in a happy story, not a tragic one, but even a tragic one seemed preferable to no story at all. Still, there are stories within stories. Ripples within waves. I was bad at living in the unknown, at not knowing what story I belonged in, and so I squatted in a hundred versions—but really two versions—switching my surroundings by the day, by the hour. I started thinking about, and inevitably Googling, the BRCA gene mutation, and grew despondent. BRCA1 and BRCA2 are cancer-suppressing genes whose inherited mutations put people at higher risk for certain types of cancer. I made myself throw up in the hallway bathroom at work, the same one where the last of the Squeakies had gushed out of me. But these moods weren't any more sustainable than my good ones, and eventually I'd ricochet back to spaghetti-straps optimism. Or, if not full-scale optimism, at least a wholesome determination.

I'm trying to tell you, as honestly as language allows, how it was. But know that every death thought was interrupted by a tiny hopeful spark of "But maybe . . . " and that on easy, average days—of which there were many—I had a little goblin pulling at me, saying "But maybe . . . " We were plotting our future and I was plotting my death. The life impulse and the death impulse are both relentless, and daily.

Dr. Hills was a tall woman in her late fifties. She wore a loose-fitting skirt suit and had long, wavy blond hair and a warm smile. I could imagine someone pitching her as the subject of a documentary reality show, the tasteful kind. She told us she only did breast surgeries. ("No gallbladders or hernias for me," she said.)

She drew a picture of a breast from the side and the front, with nipples like raisins and milk ducts like the spokes of a wagon wheel. I kept thinking, *Let's get to the part where we talk about* my *breasts and what we're going to do about them.*

She worked up to it. She was a pro, explaining each option (lumpectomy, single mastectomy), then gently explaining why it wasn't the best option. CC was impressed. Finally, she told me my left breast was healthy, but there was so much dense tissue and fuzzy ducts that finding cancer there would be a needle-in-a-haystack venture.

"That's what I was thinking about doing anyway," I said, "as long as my insurance will pay for it."

"They will," she said. "Younger women are usually pretty amenable to a bilateral."

"We came of age in the plastic surgery era," I said. For a second I felt young, like I was there because I was an overachiever, not because my body was flirting with death. When it came to death, my friends' bodies were still in the girls-on-one-side-of-the-cafeteria, boys-on-the-other stage. My body was like, *Hey death, let me show you my tits. Want 'em?*

The surgery part was easy, she said. But then she talked about radiation and chemo. She said that radiation made reconstruction with implants trickier. The plastic surgeon would have to use my own tissue instead, and the results would be lovely, but they'd need to hack into my stomach or thighs for material.

Dr. Hills talked about the BRCA gene test, which would require mailing my blood to Utah. Whether they wanted to admit it or not, Mormons were, apparently, concerned about inbreeding. I was one quarter Ashkenazi Jew, an inbred people. You marry your own out of loyalty, and because everyone else thinks you're a pariah, and it bites you in the ass. *Yes,* your body decides, *you are a pariah.*

A BRCA gene mutation would give me an eighty-five percent lifetime risk for breast cancer and a forty-to-sixty percent risk for ovarian cancer. Pancreatic cancer, which had killed my mom's paternal aunt in her forties, and melanoma were sprinkled on top, like free-gift-with-purchase cancers. It was (probable) bad news on top of bad news, but at the same time, it was just adding specifics to what I already knew: I had a family history of cancer. People had known about family histories of disease long before medicine tried to do anything about it. And yet these specifics—the numbers and the architecture and the infrastructure—felt like an injury all on their own.

Dr. Hills said I should talk to a medical oncologist about chemo, and about doing a "risk-assessment" for other cancers. I started to melt a little bit.

I imagined getting my ovaries sucked out via laparoscope in a couple of years. I thought, *If I have to go through menopause before I have a kid in my arms, so help me god I will . . .* I couldn't fill in the blank.

Dr. Hills was the type of bright, slightly bossy older woman that CC—raised by a passive and uncertain mom—adored. She'd hung on Dr. Hills' words, and I could tell that some new reality was sinking in for her. In the car, CC said, "When you told Dr. Hills your story of getting this diagnosed, how it started like three years ago with a lump that the doctor said was probably nothing, and then you moved into making ultrasounds a yearly thing—I really saw what an advocate you are for yourself. You knew what was up."

"But I also thought I had MS and lupus. I was wrong about a million things. I hope I was wrong about a million things."

I was not a hero in this story. I didn't want to be a hero, I wanted to be a mom and maybe a widely published writer. Still, it wasn't often that CC considered the upside of my anxiety, and I paused to absorb it.

"Yeah, but when the doctors dismissed MS and lupus, you believed them. And the things they told you were worth looking into, you pursued doggedly."

I wanted to show CC that, unlike when I miscarried and left us both wandering the wilderness, this time I was seeking all the support I could get. I went to the cancer support group at All Saints in the same little room where we'd once taken Covenant I classes. A thin, chatty woman introduced herself as Susan and asked what a Leapfrog laptop was. She was holding two red tags from the Foster Care Project Christmas Tree.

"I don't have grandchildren, so I don't know what these toys are," she said. There was a slight note of longing in her voice.

"I think it's like a toy laptop," I said. "Leapfrog makes electronics for kids."

She introduced her friend Claire, a small woman with a cane. I studied Claire's flat chest beneath her fleece vest and wondered: *Breast cancer?*

They'd met at the gym where they both swam, back when they both swam.

The group leader, Zelda Kennedy, arrived. I'd never seen her out of her priest robe, but tonight she was wearing jeans and a black sweater and a felt hat, even though she didn't have cancer. I'd gotten blessings from her at church before, and her hugs and prayers always felt deep and true. She was a large-ish, older Black woman, and sometimes I worried that the peace I felt in her presence was my own racist projection of a "Magical Negro" stereotype. But she was undeniably gifted.

She asked people to check in; I was new, so I could go first.

"How does this work? Just my name and cancer and stuff?"

Cheryl, breast cancer, newly diagnosed, treatable, I said. But the bigger story, the backstory, I said: fertility problems, miscarriage, relationship problems.

"I'm just going to go ahead and cry," I said, and I did.

Susan and Claire: early seventies, pancreatic cancer, hospice. Daniel: prostate cancer. Daniel talked a lot about a leak in his apartment. Was that what we were here to talk about? What about the part where I got to feel God's love firsthand?

Loretta: early fifties, breast cancer seven years ago that was now in her bones. Maybe treatable. She'd adopted two kids from Kazakhstan a year before she was diagnosed. I liked her instantly. I was worried I was looking at my future. I *hoped* I was looking at my future—she'd gotten to be a mother for six whole years!

I couldn't remember crying this hard in a long time. Maybe not even when CC left. My fears tumbled out of me. I hogged the stage, stole it away from Daniel's plumbing problems and from Claire, who talked quietly about how she didn't like complaining and didn't like pity from others.

I liked complaining, I said, and I complained.

I could feel my sinuses puffing up as I talked and cried and shook. Susan rubbed my shoulder, and I felt like she was my mom. I kept trying to get the most out of the shredded Kleenexes in my hands, and she kept taking them from me and handing me new ones.

"You're the age I was when I thought I'd never have children," Susan said. Her daughter was thirty-four now. "And you have this whole other thing to deal with."

She and Loretta were both quick to say my story wasn't theirs, to imply that I perhaps had it harder because I got cancer before I got a kid, and I appreciated both their deference and their example: They weren't people who'd gotten married at twenty-nine and popped out a kid at thirty-one.

I told them I wasn't someone who had trouble letting it all out—clearly—but that I'd been trying to contain my emotions a little bit to be strong for my partner and my family, that it felt right. But so did this. I told them how I worried about burdening CC with more trauma when they did the biopsy.

"You can call me," Zelda said. "That's what I'm here for. You can always call your priest. I'll give you my number."

"Your job must be hard," I said. "All these snotty, crying people like me."

She laughed like, *Don't get me started,* but said, "I can do this because I've experienced it all. The only thing I haven't been through is losing a child—a child who was born and lived. But I've had miscarriages. I've been through almost everything else."

She brought out prayer shawls knitted by other All Saints members. She joked about how the crochet club called themselves "hookers." We could choose one that spoke to us, she said. None was pink, thank goodness, but too many were purple, which seemed like the color of some other cancer, or some kind of awkward lesbian event. I took a plain mint green one with uneven stitches and skinny fringe.

"It's kind of a baby blanket, but I love it," I said.

"It's not a baby blanket," Zelda said gently but firmly. "It's a prayer shawl."

But I meant it as a compliment. I wrapped myself in it and felt like someone who was mothered, if not quite like someone who could be a mother. Zelda hugged and blessed each of us.

"I guess I'm wondering where God is in all of this," I said. "I mean, I have some thoughts about where God *isn't,* and maybe some theories about where God is, but I want to ask that. To hear what you guys have to say, I guess."

I think Zelda thought I was questioning God's existence, which wasn't exactly true. It was more that I was looking for it. It was more that I knew everything in the world was uncertain, and so I was looking for the one thing—the thing of and not of the world—that was certain.

"I don't believe everything happen for a reason," Zelda said. "But I do believe in God. I believe in a divinity. I see God in you, Susan, and you, Claire, and you, Loretta, and you, Daniel, and you, Cheryl."

For a minute, I wasn't sure she'd say she saw God in me. I mean, of course she was going to say that, but I think my uncertainty was why I was there. Was why my nostrils were red from all the snot-wiping.

We held hands and prayed, and Loretta gave me her number, and Zelda took my information for the cancer group mailing list and gave me her card. For maybe the tenth time that night, I felt grateful for all of them and nauseated to be one of them.

I got in my car and sobbed just a little bit more. I tried to rub the spots from my glasses, but some of them had dried already. I felt like I had witnessed my future and my death and accepted it. And it all felt a little premature and not quite healthy. The perfect thing, it seemed, was to love life and accept death at the same time, all the time. I had no idea how to do that.

CHAPTER 17: **SOBER AND DRUNK**

The Friday before Thanksgiving, I visited Dr. Sam Chung, a medical oncologist at City of Hope. CC had to work, so my dad came with me. He understood science and knew how to rattle off facts and statistics to deescalate a situation and reassure me in ways CC could not. His presence also cracked open memories of being at the hospital with my mom. His complete disregard for the number of questions a doctor might be willing to endure. The smell of his hair pomade. His deep voice, always calm but sometimes tinged with phlegmy emotion. He was grayer now than he'd been in 2003, and he seemed physically smaller, too. We triggered each other and leaned on each other and tried to pretend we weren't leaning on each other while vocally affirming, *This is what families do, they lean on each other.* We leaned away, trying to protect ourselves and each other. It was all too intimate, like a dream where you find yourself underwear-clad in an auditorium.

Dr. Chung was exactly my age, and I imagined it must be weird for him to see cancer in a peer. He was casual and matter-of-fact in a way that instantly endeared me. The City of Hope website said he'd gone to UC Riverside as an undergrad, and I could easily imagine him as someone I'd known in college. A framed picture of two little black-haired boys in matching plaid shirts hung above the exam table.

My dad stepped out so Dr. Chung could examine my boobs. He said, "Yeah, there's no way you would have found that on your own. Don't waste any time blaming yourself."

The fact that he guessed I might be prone to self-blame, and the swiftness with which he dismissed its validity, convinced me he was the doctor for me.

When my dad returned, Dr. Chung went over the results of my biopsy. A closer read was always possible. "You have cancer" was the headline, and now we were reading the article, following the jump to exhaustion.

"Many cancer cells have receptors on them," he said, explaining what I'd already read. "The kind of receptors determine the kind of treatment we do. Ninety-eight percent of the cells in your tumor have estrogen receptors, and seventy-five percent have progesterone receptors. That means that we can do hormone therapy after your initial treatment. You're also negative for HER2 receptors."

"Oh," I exclaimed. "That's good news."

"It is," he agreed.

I'd been expecting the more aggressive, somewhat harder to treat triple-negative cancer just because all of this *felt* so aggressive. Just because I believed my luck was bad. Estrogen- and progesterone-positive cancer was good news for medical reasons, but also because it hinted that 1) my spiraling bad luck might not be as catastrophic as I'd thought, and 2) I wasn't psychic after all. I didn't want that burden.

He also talked about tumor grade, which had to do with how differentiated the cells had become while they were busy photocopying themselves inside my body. Just how off-the-rails had this office party gone? Just how many naked asses had been pressed to the glass of the Xerox machine? My tumor grade was two on a scale of one to three, so, a medium number of naked asses.

He talked about the chemo drugs I'd be taking and how they might shut down my ovaries temporarily or permanently. He asked if I wanted to freeze my eggs, and I said, no, I'm good, I still have some frozen embryos, waving it away like the suggestion of dinner out after a big lunch. He asked whether I'd taken antidepressants, and I told him about the miscarriage. He said, "Oh, well *this* is perfect timing, isn't it?"

He got it. He got it.

I did what I'd done after every fertility appointment. I wrote down what Dr. Chung said. I repeated it back to him. It wasn't entirely unlike couples therapy: unpleasant, an act of surrender, clarifying, lifesaving.

As we waited for the elevator, my dad said, "You were so focused and organized. Much more than I was. You got everything he said and asked exactly the right questions."

This was high praise from my dad, second only to the times he'd told me I was objective and responsible. He had expected me to be more like my mom—because I was female, because I was emotional—and I'd shown myself to be like him. I read that anxious people tend to be good in a crisis because 1) they spend their whole lives preparing and 2) they are focused on *actions* in the *present*, for once, instead of on imagining terrible things that might happen in the future.

We drove up the street to a little café and ice cream parlor called Buster's, home of many writing dates, and ordered sandwiches.

"Knowing now that the cancer is estrogen-positive, I can't not think about what might have happened if I'd stayed pregnant," I said. "If I'd had all that estrogen pumping through my body for another seven months. I guess I should be grateful. I mean, I *am* grateful, but it's still hard to think about my babies dying for me."

My dad repeated something from the grief group he'd attended for years after my mom died. "Just because you enjoy or appreciate something that a person's death made possible doesn't mean you wanted it to happen. It's okay to enjoy or appreciate that thing."

"I know."

It was all so sobering—the universes unfurling alongside us, a spectrum of utopia to apocalypse, and the infinite in-betweens.

On the way home, I called Cathy and gave her a bossy-big-sister lecture about getting therapy. I knew how hard my diagnosis and treatment would be on her and my dad, and I didn't want to worry about them more than I already did. When my mom was sick, she fretted that our family would drift apart in her absence. Fussing over her family's emotional health was how she put her affairs in order. And even though death was an *unlikely* outcome based on my prognosis, I was essentially doing the same.

I told Cathy she was more emotionally savvy than my dad. She could take it; she could understand it.

Except she couldn't.

"I told you I'm *thinking* about therapy," she said. "I'm not saying I won't go. But I see how torn up you are after therapy, and I'm not sure I want to be any unhappier than I already am."

"That's couples therapy," I said. "It's totally different. Individual therapy is really gentle and affirming."

"But I've been talking to Karly and Delia and Jenny," she said.

"It's not the same," I snapped. "Delia and Karly are alcoholics.

Jenny has two little kids and is pregnant with a third. They don't seem like people who can be there for you like a therapist could. And I want you to understand our family dynamics better."

"I know you see our family differently than I do, but I like how I see our family. I don't want to change that."

It was like when we were little, and my mom was complaining about something my dad did, and I heartily agreed and my sister piped up, "I *like* Dad." It became this family joke, because of course my mom and I liked my dad, too.

But I was enjoying being angry, because I needed to be angry at someone or something, and why not the people who broke my heart the most?

"So the message you're sending me is that *I'm* the fucked-up one who needs therapy. Not only do I get to have cancer, but I have to do all the emotional legwork. I'm the freak. I have to take all the risks, and you and Dad will stick with what you know. Even though we're in a totally different situation, and you'd *think* that might be the *exact time* to take a risk and try something different."

She was crying now. "I'm not saying you're a freak. I don't want you to feel like you're all alone. I just don't think I'd get much out of therapy if I went only because you wanted me to go."

My dad had said the same thing when I asked him to go back to the Wellness Community, the place that had helped him so much when my mom was sick and after she died.

"I'll do anything you want, but I know you wouldn't want me to do anything I really didn't think was helpful," he said, as if this were the most logical thing in the world.

So there it was: They'd do anything for me, except the one thing I wanted, which was for them to take care of themselves. I remembered those crushing days after my mom died. I remembered standing in the garage with my dad, looking for a can of something or other, both of us lost because my mom would probably have known where it was, both of us shyly admitting to our pain, trying not to cry.

Was the problem, now, that I couldn't handle their pain, or that they couldn't handle mine?

That night CC and I met our friends Pedro and Stephen at a new restaurant called the Blue Cow. We warmed ourselves beneath heat lamps outside, and I got quickly drunk on a rum Manhattan because I'd only eaten fruit and roasted fennel for lunch.

I ranted about my family and their refusal of therapy. I said, "I'm drunk and angry," and it was met with general approval.

This was me talking about cancer in a way CC could get behind. Not sad or scared, not by ourselves in bed or in the car.

Pedro had been taking meds and doing group therapy for anxiety and depression. The origins were unclear. Pedro was probably the most charming and best-looking person either of us knew. He had pale skin with dark eyes and hair. He said, "If I've learned one thing about therapy, which I really approve of, it's that you can't make anyone go. They have to want to go."

Stephen, who was quiet most of the night, shrugged. "Make 'em go. If they hate it, they don't have to go back, but this is your chance to make a demand."

Later CC and I agreed that we agreed with both of them.

CC was ovulating, so on Sunday we went to Pac Repro. Melodi, the nurse, was wearing USC sweats, her weekend gear. She hinted that CC might have polycystic ovarian syndrome, which meant long, frequently ovulation-free cycles, but a good reserve of eggs. She could have a baby in her forties if she wanted. Normally, I would have obsessed over another piece of fertility non-news. Instead it just felt like an errand. Plus some small and important proof that we were still trying to have a future.

That night we saw *The Sessions,* a movie about a man in an iron lung who sees a sex surrogate, played by Helen Hunt. I thought a lot about people in broken bodies, whose only close friends are paid staff. Those relationships were still real, the love was still real, and I supposed that was encouraging. CC complained mildly that it was a quiet movie and kind of a bummer.

"I'm a little depressed," I told her.

"Yeah, the movie wasn't—I mean, I knew it would be like that, but I'm not sure it was what we needed."

"I was a little depressed before," I said.

She said she wanted to go to Vroman's, the bookstore next to the theater. I sat in my car and cried for a while. I thought about my body being taken from me piece by piece until I was just a mouth that could hold a pencil to punch 9-1-1 on the phone, like the man in the movie. I thought about being the person people might love well enough, but whom they always needed breaks from. I thought about maybe already having ovarian cancer, and even if I didn't, giving my ovaries and uterus and tits to a lab and then a biohazard trash bin. I thought about having no nipples, which was intriguing and scary. My period was close and my boobs were swollen, the way they always got at this time in my cycle. Soon they would never do that again. I tried to see it in a Donna Haraway cyborg kind of way. I would rather feel like a cyborg than an invalid, but I might not have a choice. I might feel like both.

I wiped my face and walked over to Vroman's, where CC and I looked at 2013 calendars. Books seemed too loaded and hard to engage with. All those stories of people living harder and easier lives than mine, written by writers who'd live long enough to publish and publish again. When my mom was going through chemo, she'd napped next to our cat, Eliot, with copies of *Woman's Day* and *Family Circle* fanned out around her. She'd said books felt too challenging, and I'd resented her weakness.

Buying a 2013 calendar was a loaded act as well. I sort of felt like I might not see 2013, but in reality, it would just be full of doctor's appointments. *I want a Frida Kahlo calendar,* I thought. She was sick and lovelorn and had multiple miscarriages, but was there anyone fiercer?

I found one, because Frida gear was ubiquitous. It was too big and heavy and not the cheapest, but I bought it.

CC and I were both tired and irritable. She didn't want to leave Vroman's—she was like a little kid who never wanted to go to bed—but I wanted to go home and type up my notes from the IUI.

First we had to pick up my new Klonopin subscription for anxiety, but CC burnt out halfway to the pharmacy and asked me to take her home. I filled out a new-patient profile at the pharmacy, which asked about medical conditions.

For the first time, on a standard form, I checked "cancer." It felt incredibly depressing, so below it, I checked "depression."

CHAPTER 18: PRETTY

Visiting Dr. Max Lehfeldt, one of the plastic surgeons Dr. Hills recommended, felt like a reward for all the scary tests, for getting prodded and felt up by people looking for what was wrong with me. I'd never been that into my boobs, aesthetically or sexually, so I believed I was headed for an upgrade. Dr. Lehfeldt was youngish, blond, a little extra bright around the eyes. He seemed gay, but later I found out he was married to a woman, and they had a toddler.

I stood in front of a big camera-machine in a "before" pose, holding my stomach in, standing up straight, arms at a forty-five-degree angle, palms to the front. It was the first time someone photographed me naked.

The nurse pressed some buttons and made the 2D photo 3D. There I was, my boobs pale and veiny and not exactly perky, but lovely in their own way. Smooth-ish and symmetrical. They were like some shy English rose, or like Melanie Lynskey in *Hello I Must*

Be Going—a little doughy and prone to embarrassing behavior, but loveable. I realized I would miss them after all. Even though they'd always been burdensome. Even though they turned on me.

Since leaving MacDowell, where thick sandwiches and slices of pie literally appeared on my doorstep, I'd probably lost ten pounds. But my muffin top was still evident above my black jeans. Skinny jeans with metal studs around the pockets, knee-high black boots that could kick some ass. I wanted a look that said, "I care about how I look, but I'm no starlet in search of big tits."

Dr. Lehfeldt kept talking about how thin I was. I'd gone in assuming I would need radiation and would therefore be ineligible for implants, the simpler type of reconstruction. The other kind involved taking a flap of belly fat and pumping it into your empty boobs. It's a nice tummy tuck, but the pictures I saw online (one of the few things I let myself search) showed foot-long scars like a sad smile below a belly-button nose. With reconstructed nipples for eyes, my whole torso could try to put on a brave face.

When Dr. Lehfeldt finally opened my cheap-but-satiny black gown and looked at me, he grabbed my hunk of belly and said, "I could probably get a large B cup out of this."

We agreed, though, that a C-cup made sense: smaller than the English roses, but not so small as to make the rest of my body look huge. He said that, even with radiation, there was an implant option. I didn't quite understand the science, but the combination of silicone and radiation makes the body cranky and prone to forming scar tissue. But if he wrapped my radiated boob in muscle tissue from my back, like a fig in prosciutto, it would be protected. I would have a scar on my back, but other muscles would compensate.

CC and I found ourselves awake at three in the morning. It wasn't unusual for her, but it was for me. It was the first night I'd slept without an Ativan or a Klonopin in a while. We were cuddly and sweet to each other; the wee hours brought out her tender side and my worries. A world of shadow and catastrophe. So it was nice to have her there with me, rain falling outside.

She was reading the *New Yorker*.

"Can I talk about my surgery for just a minute?" I said.

I told her what Dr. Lehfeldt said, that I would lose feeling, including "protective sensation" in my boobs.

"Just for a while, right?" CC said.

"No," I said. "Forever. I'm not freaking out, but it's weird. Just, like, this part of my body I won't be able to feel."

"Yeah," she agreed. "Like just imagine if you couldn't feel your elbow. Although I guess that would be different. You'd always be hitting it on things."

"It's good I'm going smaller," I said. "Otherwise I'd always be hitting my boobs on things, or spilling food and not knowing it."

I would essentially be an amputee. I was amputating a part I didn't "need," and my prosthesis would be internal. But I'd be an amputee nonetheless. The thought made me uncomfortable. Along with "conjoined twin," I'd also played "girl with a fake leg" as a kid. Disability had frightened and therefore fascinated me. It was the convergence of neediness and exceptionalism. *Olympic gymnast* and *amputee* were somehow cut from the same cloth. In my college lit-crit readings about fetishes, I'd learned that they were fixations built from fear, pearl around sand. Hence the popularity of bondage and sadomasochism. Hence the thrill of Diane Arbus's world. When I thought about becoming an amputee—and there was such a thing as amputee porn, too—I felt like I was falling into one of her photos, half scared, half titillated.

Dr. Hills' office called with a surgery date: December 19. I exhaled.

I hadn't known I'd been holding my breath, but I'd discovered you could go for years thinking you were breathing normally, not realizing whole sections of your lungs were closed off.

I made a list of things I needed to plan for: Christmas, baldness, and my unlikely but possible death on the operating table.

Two big things happened in those weeks leading up to surgery: First, Kerry Sparks at Levine Greenberg called to say she liked my edits to *Family, Genus, Species* and wanted to officially represent it. At last, I had an agent. I felt like I was finally in the same league with so many writers I admired and envied, even as I worried that this would tip the scales negatively in the zero-sum-game, magical-thinking quagmire that was my brain. Second, I got the results of my genetic testing, which confirmed that I had the BRCA2 gene mutation. I knew the chances of me *not* having it had been slim. And apparently BRCA2 was a slightly less toxic mutation than BRCA1. But as I read about pancreatic cancer and contemplated, at best, a lifetime of risk and vigilance, I started to feel sick.

And then I went back to preparing for surgery. I asked our friend Kenny, a hairstylist, to come over and cut my hair short. I paid him his regular rate, but I thought I might cry, so I didn't want to go to the salon where he worked. We made dinner for Kenny and his boyfriend, Craig, and then turned the kitchen into a makeshift salon. I put my hair in a ponytail, and Kenny sliced it off so I could put it in an envelope for Locks of Love. Some young cancer patient or kid with alopecia would get a wig made of my thick, wavy brown hair. Boring in color, but healthy and low-maintenance. As it turned out, I didn't cry, and I looked kind of great with short hair. Clipped on one side with a shag of curls on the other.

Years later, Kenny and Craig would start their own adoption process. They would be required to get physicals, and Kenny would discover the cough he'd attributed to being around too many styling products was actually lymphoma. And still, he would be fine, and they would get a baby.

But because they'd decided to go through the foster care system, the first baby that was placed with them would be sent back to live with his grandmother. Joy and heartbreak, joy and heartbreak. Life resists tidy arcs.

CC took boudoir "before" pictures with my digital camera. On our bed, I struck smiling and serious poses wearing only a pair of blue bikini-style underwear, then studied the results. My body looked anxiety-skinny and my boobs looked, above all, familiar. Body parts and tumors and growing fetuses all get compared to fruit, and mine were grapefruits slowly giving in to gravity.

I told CC how surreal it all felt and fished around for reassurance that she would still find me attractive. I knew that the prospect of having to stay in on weekends would be more detrimental to our romantic life than the alteration of any body part. Maybe that's a way in which we were quintessential lesbians, falling for each other's minds more than bodies. We'd once talked about those gym couples—usually heterosexuals or gay men—for whom looking good together was the core of their relationship. We went running and attended yoga together, and we'd rather look in shape than out of shape, but our bodies were the side dish, not the entrée. "Can you imagine dating someone dumb, though?" she'd said. Neither of us could.

She answered my questions with a story. I was usually annoyed when people told me the plots of books or movies in detail; the only exceptions were my mom and CC. Now, she recounted *A Thousand Acres*. In the movie version, Michelle Pfeiffer played one of King Lear's daughters, one of the older ones whom Shakespeare had villainized. In the movie, CC said, she was unforgiving, but it was a point of pride, and the audience could see her point of view. The movie introduced her in a scene where she was getting a follow-up breast exam. As the camera panned her body, it revealed that she had one breast, one scar.

"It wasn't gross," CC said. "It looked really normal and it took a minute to register. Then it established her as this kind of wounded warrior."

She hadn't made an offhand promise to love me scars and all. She'd taken the time to tell me a story—about how she had encountered a breast-less body, how she'd taken in its strangeness and its beauty.

CC came with me to my pre-op appointment with Dr. Hills. We didn't learn anything new, but the same bad news always seemed to hit me over and over from different angles. I was covered in bruises, literally and figuratively. Dr. Hills explained that three things, discoverable in surgery, could open the door to radiation: cancer in three or more lymph nodes, cancer in the tissue outside the nodes, or messy margins on my tumor. If they found cancer in three or more nodes, she said, they would remove the first two layers of my lymph nodes. I knew radiation was a possibility; I hadn't known that losing my lymph nodes was, although I was glad to learn I would still have a few stragglers to clean my body, or whatever it is that lymph nodes did, exactly.

CC told me Dr. Chung had told us all of this already. Dr. Hills said, "Do you remember that diagram I drew you the first time we met?"

No, no I didn't. I had fifteen pages of notes in a document I'd labeled FreeBoobJob. I was not falling apart so completely as to drown out all practical information. But until a month ago, I knew almost nothing about breast cancer. And I was *in the process of being traumatized.* It seemed like I could miss something here and there and still fall into the Good Patient category. It seemed like I could freak out now and then and still fall into the Handling This Well category. I desperately needed to be in those categories.

In the car after the appointment, I told CC, "I'll be okay, but it's a lot. It doesn't seem fair that I have to wake up missing body parts *and* potentially getting bad news."

Dodging all three reasons for radiation seemed like a tall order. My bargaining mind couldn't hope for that much. So which would I choose? Messy margins, maybe, because it would mean, at least, that the cancer hadn't been working its way into my bloodstream. But no one was asking. I didn't get to choose.

CC murmured gentle things and then said, "We'll know so much more in a week."

I turned from her and pounded the window of my car. "That's not comforting! I thought we knew what we were working with! And now there's this big diagnostic component."

She said, "I know you have a lot of trouble dealing with the unknown, a lot more than I do."

Our moment of togetherness withered instantly. I was supposed to drive her to her car a block away, but she started to get out. I was making her feel helpless, and so she hated me. That was how it went with us.

"Just because you didn't make it all better doesn't mean you failed," I said. "I'm glad you're here."

I drove her to her car, and she said she loved me and I said the same. But then she got in her car and, in my rearview mirror, I saw her roll her eyes. I pulled over in front of her and rammed into the curb. I threw my arms in the air in a *what the fuck* gesture. I got nothing back. We both drove away—she to lunch with a former coworker, me to more fucking appointments.

Sunday afternoon I had lunch at Cathy's house with my dad and his partner, Susan. At the office Christmas party my dad had hosted, I'd asked Susan how she was doing. "Oh, I'm good except for, you know . . . " and she'd kind of gestured in my direction. I laughed because I didn't know what else to do.

I pulled my sister into her hallway and said, "Susan keeps making big pity eyes at me."

"I know," she said with the usual undercurrent of *We get each other*, but she was quick to slip back out to the mini-party in her well-decorated living room.

I couldn't quite put my finger on it, but she was looking at me differently, too. She didn't like my new haircut, I could tell. It was too butch, maybe, or too rebellious. It reminded her that things had already changed, and she did not like change.

Later, I mentioned my in-the-near-future hysterectomy, and a look of horror crossed her face. She had a genetic test coming up and knew this could be her, as well. She didn't have a partner, and she wanted to get pregnant someday. I assumed she did not have the gene. I assumed this would be another instance where I got to take the hard road and she got to be the good girl. I was glad for all the ways life had forced me not to be good, but I still craved all the pats on the head, all the gold stars.

We all sat in her living room around the pesto focaccia bread I wasn't eating because it was a simple carbohydrate. She and I sat on one couch and argued and cried. My dad and Susan sat on another and watched.

Cathy admitted she was scared for herself, and guilty because either way, her situation wasn't as bad as mine. At first she'd wanted to take cancer from me, she said, because I had too much to deal with already. But then, yes, she decided she was glad she didn't have it, okay? "It's okay to not want cancer," I said. "That's human. I don't want it, either."

"But I don't feel like I can talk about my fears to you," she said, "so I try to talk about other things. Maybe distraction is what you need right now."

"It's fine if that's what *you* need. I can respect that. I'll try to talk about it less. But don't pretend like you're doing it as a favor to me. I distract myself plenty—I go to work, and I write, and I go to fucking holiday parties. But, yeah, I also have four-hour doctor appointments. I don't really have the option of just hating it and enduring it. I have to walk into it and talk about it, and you're making it pretty clear you don't want that. So now I know."

I was snappy and bitter. I could hear it. At one point she asked if I wanted to see what she'd gotten CC for Christmas, and I rolled my eyes. Change the subject much? I called her on it, and she stopped.

I felt suddenly grateful for my dad, who was nothing if not predictably himself. He didn't treat me any differently, because he could separate the disease from the person. Cathy was more like me—steeped in voodoo and always on the lookout for signs that she was doomed—but also less like me. She would rather avoid things than confront them. And I felt abandoned.

That night, CC wanted to go out while we still could, so we went to the York and she drank two old-fashioneds and ate a burger. I had a sad little ramekin of kale and a club soda.

Drunk CC performed a monologue as Angry Cheryl: "I knew there was a beast stalking my land, and I went after it, even when people told me I was paranoid. I tracked it down and caught it before anyone else would have. And I hate it. I'm angry. I'm going to direct that anger where it's due. When they mark me up for reconstruction, I don't have to be a good patient. I can say, *I hate this.*"

My heart overflowed with love for her.

I checked into Huntington Hospital at 7:00 a.m. I wore the only bra I hadn't already put in the Goodwill bag, a raggedy brown sports bra that I left in the trash can in my hospital room.

People in scrubs asked me my name, age, and birth date over and over. Dr. Lehfeldt marked me up with a blue Sharpie: line down my sternum, dotted lines around the tops of my breasts, triangles over my nipples where he would cut out a wedge shape and sew the two sides together. He said that this pattern, the "reduction pattern," would have a nicer shape and not-too-noticeable scars, but more cutting meant more potential for healing problems. I went for it, big risk taker that I am. I was determined to get pretty boobs out of this.

My dad and Cathy hung in the waiting room, where my dad fired questions at Dr. Lehfeldt, including stuff about Cathy's theoretical preemptive mastectomy. Ever efficient, ever productive. Yet he reminded me of a cartoon computer overloading, spewing smoke and numbers. I didn't want to know how many questions he asked when I wasn't there. As I kept telling people, this was the one day that was more stressful for everyone else than for me.

I rode a gurney down to Radiology, where they would inject "a mild nuclear material," as Dr. Hills described it. They wheeled me into a tiny room with old-looking equipment. Three computers with green and black screens, a black stretcher-like chair patched up with masking tape, and a big, weird radiological-looking machine.

The woman who shot me up with the dye that would make its way to my lymph nodes muttered, half to herself, "How'd you find it? Because people keep telling me I should get a mammogram. You're my age, it's scary." I did not tell her that it was scary to be me, too.

Awesome comment number two came from the surgical nurse. Making small talk, CC had asked, "Is this a surgery you do a lot?"

"Yes," the nurse said. "And it's a sad surgery, but the reconstructions look very nice." She turned to me. "No one knows why God gave you cancer, but God also wants to make you very pretty."

"Actually," I said, "I don't think God gave me cancer, but I'm looking forward to being pretty."

When she left, I lost it. I didn't think God gave me cancer, of course—then I'd have to believe God gave my mom cancer and made children in developing countries die of malnutrition. But the same part of me that believed, in some deep place beneath my skin and bones and tumor, I was being punished for a crime I'd unwittingly committed also believed that speaking things aloud made them real. Fuck that nurse and her banal magical thinking.

The anesthesiologist said something reassuring and fatherly about it sucking that I had to be here, but that I would be fine. People can't help their vibes, I suppose. I liked his.

I saw a little bit of the operating room and met two assistants with funky Christmas-print hair coverings as the world started to blur. My veins grew warm and I had the sense of being held in giant, gentle hands. With my own very best magic, I conjured the image CC and I agreed we would both focus on: the two of us walking by the little lake full of ducks in Glacier National Park, future kid by our side.

CHAPTER 19: ON THE OTHER SIDE

I clawed my way back to consciousness, returning to my body and brain in layers. I was aware that something drastic had happened, but also—immediately and surprisingly—that I was still *me*. This was undeniably true even before anything else came into focus: the beige hospital curtains, my family, the beeps and echoes of the hospital floor beyond us.

I have vague memories of waking up and asking about my lymph nodes, voices telling me the biopsy was negative, then falling back to sleep, then waking up again and wondering if the news had been a dream. Later I asked Cathy if I'd asked twenty times; she said maybe two. It was probably more. When the Kleins weren't catastrophizing, we were prone to understatement.

I was wearing a hospital gown. I was clean and tidy. I wasn't even bandaged, just taped with neat sticky strips along my sutures. I silently thanked Dr. Lehfeldt for this, his perfectionism appeasing mine.

For years, I've had what I suppose is an enlarged pore between my left armpit and boob. It's nothing anyone else would notice, just a dot really, but I sometimes pick at it in an offhand way. It was there, and it was like spotting a loved one's old familiar car in the driveway of your new house, a house so new you still get lost on the way to the bathroom at night. I was still me. For all the dissertations to be written about the fluidity of identity, something was fixed.

I was curious, of course, about my boobs. Or foobs, as people in the community I was now a part of called them (or was that a weird goofy word that no one *actually* uses, like "Frisco"?). I was still covered in blue marker and my nipples were gone and I felt like I'd just done the hardest upper-body workout of my life. But it was a familiar and not-terrible kind of pain. They looked a little pancake-y, more like pecs than boobs. I didn't exactly have feeling in them, but I didn't totally *not* have feeling, either.

I showed them to CC and Cathy right away that woozy Wednesday night. When you can't feel your tits and there are no nipples, they become strangely PG.

I woke up long enough to hear that the biopsy had come back negative and to dry-heave into several clear blue barf bags that looked like they belonged in a dustbuster. I was officially cancer-free.

My dad and Cathy had the look of people who'd been awake too long, in the same clothes, eating from vending machines and drinking from Styrofoam cups. Someone called "Code Blue" over the loudspeaker and we paused, reverent and guilty.

Cathy read me people's good Facebook wishes from her iPhone and posted something on my page that said: *For friends and family of Cheryl — all is well and I read the fairly groggy patient your lovely FB wishes. They seem to have paid off nicely :).* The Facebook influx continued for maybe twenty-four hours, and then people started posting about gun control and holiday plans again and I felt, not for the first time, how they were with me in this experience and not.

Everyone left, and CC slept in the fold-out chair next to my bed, my partner in crime, my person who could sleep deeply anywhere.

I crashed out again, and woke up at 3:00 a.m. feeling strangely euphoric. There was a bright strip of light beneath the door. The beeps and announcements continued, just varied enough to never quite become white noise. But my room was still and bathed in blue light from the street. I was on the other side of the thing I'd been building my life around, and even though I'd been looking forward to it, I'd also been fearing it. Now the cancer was gone, my lymph nodes were clear, and I hadn't died on the operating table. I texted everyone who'd been waiting to hear, although CC had already been in touch with a few of them. I felt like anything was possible. But in a good way, for once.

CC got up in the morning to see a client. Dr. Hills and Dr. Lehfeldt stopped by to look at my boobs and agreed there was good blood flow. Dr. Lehfeldt wore a skinny gray suit with a yellow tie. He said I could even go home today.

I didn't want to go home yet. Home was a place where I would need to think about things, and I wasn't ready for that. So I decided to stay for the additional twenty-four hours my insurance had approved. My dad and Cathy stopped by during the day, and Stephen stopped by on his lunch hour. Apparently he and Pedro spent almost the whole day there on Wednesday, defusing low-level tensions between my dad and CC and making friends with Hobie, the therapy dog, whom Dr. Hills had declared too unsanitary to visit me.

The whole day felt twilighty, even though the anesthetic had worn off. It seemed to be taking place in a world next to the one I knew. I remember making a joke about not wearing underwear, which I wasn't, just a one-size-fits-a-four-hundred-pound-man hospital gown, with my drains pinned to the sides. Four tubes spilling bright red ooze from my body into grenade-shaped plastic pods. Our conversation was chatty and normal, and yet we were all here because I'd just gotten my breasts cut off, and we all knew I wasn't wearing underwear.

Friday morning I stepped into the baggier of the three tank tops I'd brought, pinned my grenades in a fold as the nurses had vaguely taught me, and felt a thousand times better.

A social worker stopped by. Because of some invisible gate opened by a cancer diagnosis, she'd been calling me at regular intervals. In our first call, I asked her about survival rates, trying to egg her into my favorite kind of pep talk: Can you spin medical facts in a way that makes it sound like all my dreams will come true? She could not.

She was a thin Asian woman with big coppery hair. She immediately sat on my bed and put her hand on my leg. She gave me some advice about stretching and told me to get a prescription from Dr. Lehfeldt for one of the sick-person yoga classes she taught. I did not like her.

But she also said, "Remember, from here on out, all the treatment you'll be getting is mostly about preventing a recurrence. The cancer is out of your body." And that I would take home with me.

Cathy agreed to stay at our place for three nights because, for all we knew, I'd need help wiping my ass. She and CC both had learned how to empty my drains in the hospital. But it became clear that I could do most tasks that didn't require lifting things that were heavy or up high.

I was terrible at waiting for test results but good at bouncing back physically. Because of the former, I almost didn't want to hear from Dr. Hills about my pathology report. But she called Friday afternoon, and it was mostly good: They'd gotten clear margins on the tumor. There was still no evidence of lymph node involvement. But here was the catch: The tumor had not been two small tumors after all, but two ends of one giant dumbbell-shaped tumor that was ten and a half centimeters in all.

I'd had a tumor that was bigger than many people's entire breasts, and none of the fancy imaging had predicted that. It sounded like Dr. Hills hadn't even known that after doing the surgery. It took people dissecting a former part of me in the lab like an autopsy. It bumped me up to stage IIB, Dr. Hills said, although I'd thought I was already there.

Once again, I felt like a bit of a sideshow. But weird news was not enough to numb out my good news. I spent the next day and a half resting and taking long walks with Cathy, who opened up about her own BRCA2 fears.

"I just hate the idea that I'm your worst nightmare," I said.

"You have CC," she said. "My worst nightmare is being single with no boobs or with cancer."

It made perfect sense that her fear of cancer or prophylactic surgery was tied up with her fear of being single. And because her fears weren't my fears, they seemed like just . . . fears. Meanwhile, it was excruciating to me that I was wearing new-mom clothes and burning through the days I'd saved for maternity leave and obsessing about my body. All without a baby, like *Garfield Minus Garfield*, an internet cartoon in which someone had cropped out the cat and left poor Jon sputtering existential nonsense to himself.

My dad and Susan came up Saturday night. Susan talked a lot about cats and her thoughts on the younger generation using the word "bitch." Sometime after a conversation about LL Cool J, Ice-T, the real meaning of "Cop Killer," and *NCIS: LA*, I excused myself to go rest.

On Sunday, CC and I were finally alone. It was a relief.

CC went to the clinic for an IUI. OC visited the litter box multiple times in an hour, pawing at the clay sand and meowing. I took six pills in the morning.

CC declared my new foobs sexy, probably because I was wearing a navy blue wife-beater, a boyish look she liked. But it made my heart swell—that she could adapt so easily, that she could step up and keep things clean and deal with my family. She deserved a break. We deserved a baby. "Deserve" meant nothing, but still.

The most concretely helpful thing anyone told me after my mom died was this: *Look out for yourself about three months from now. The initial grief and the outpouring of support will have faded, and it will really sink in.*

At the hospital, the social worker had said, "After about five days, the great feeling you have now will wear off."

Christmas Eve, exactly five days after surgery, was the first time I cried and started to think about my upcoming appointments and a third, mysterious lymph node test, which would look for "micrometastases" in the cancer-free-at-first-glance tissue they'd removed. My creeping fear and uncertainty was so familiar, it felt like a return to the natural state of things.

For Christmas, my dad gave me *The Red Parts* by Maggie Nelson, who started teaching at CalArts a few years after I graduated. The book was a memoir about the reopening of her aunt's murder case and being haunted by an act of violence that preceded her birth. She wrote about being sure she would find a body anytime she opened a jammed bathroom stall, about talking out loud to hypothetical burglars when she came home. All the good things in Maggie's life (beauty, publication) had not saved her from being stalked by fear. As such, she was one of my people.

CC and I took a long walk down York on Christmas Eve morning, past the yawning gastropubs and the older stores that were more like flea market stalls—where you could register your car and buy an outfit for your baby in one stop. I told her I was thinking more about my ovaries; I'd been thinking of getting them snipped out during my next surgery, which would be to replace the tissue expanders with more lifelike silicone implants.

"Are you sure you want to do all that to your body at once?" she said. "It would be one thing if it were really just the surgery, but it will have a hormonal impact, too. You should ask the doctor what he thinks."

I promised I would. "Maybe this is how we're different, in that I like to get things over with all at once, but when I think about going through chemical menopause with chemo, then getting back on track, then doing it all over again surgically, *that* sounds like a lot."

She could see my point, she said, but I could hear the wariness in her voice. We both knew what I was like at my hormonal worst.

But my real point in bringing it up, I said, was that I'd made a compromise with myself: The ovaries would go soon, but the uterus could stay for a while. That gave me a back-up path to parenthood: If I took hormones, I could implant my leftover embryos even without ovaries and become pregnant. My most important girl part is my clitoris, and no one had talked about getting rid of that, thank god, but my uterus was second. The Squeakies had lived there. It *could* be home to a baby, even if it probably wouldn't be.

"Remember," CC said, "your ovaries and uterus are fine right now. They're healthy."

"Probably," I said. "But thanks for reminding me. I feel so confused and crazy sometimes. Like, I was so scared of being sick for so long, and then I really was sick, but now I'm not really anymore, but I'm still being treated for that illness and I'm still scared, so is that really any different from actually being sick?"

My Uncle Robin and Aunt Connee were supposed to drive up to Tahoe to meet Connee's sons and their families a few days before Christmas, so we wouldn't be seeing them at our traditional Christmas Eve dinner together at Tom's Chinese Restaurant, not even the take-out version I'd proposed hosting at our house. I thought of Connee's sons, each married with kids and no cancer. I thought about how they were her real family, untroubled and successful.

But the trip was canceled at the last minute. "Long story," Connee texted. We waited for her to tell it when she and Robin arrived with dozens of little white take-out cartons. Robin reduced the long story to one word: "Snow."

Soon our living room and kitchen were strewn with paper-wrapped chopsticks and waxy bags of crispy noodles and plates piled high with all Tom's vegetarian dishes. My fortune cookie promised a wish would come true after a long wait.

Baby, I thought. A friend had taken CC to her IUI on Sunday, but the possibility of an actual pregnancy seemed less and less likely, or maybe just further away. When did the countdown start for the long wait? I wondered. If we'd started counting two years ago, maybe the wait was almost up. But if the wait had started when I cracked the fortune cookie, it was just beginning.

What are the rules? I always want to know.

CC and I were both tearful by the end of the night—from exhaustion, from the hCG shot, from too much time with our families. "Why can't it just be us?" she said. She was tired of my dad taking charge, tired of Elena hitting it off so easily with my dad, tired of feeling like a lesser hostess.

"Don't tell yourself you're failing at taking care of me," I pleaded. "Because then you'll get resentful and not try. That's what happened before. But you're taking great care of me, and I'm the one who gets to decide that. And I still need you. You can't give up yet."

When my dad and sister returned, with Susan, at 8:30 on Christmas morning, it seemed like ten minutes had passed. They stormed the door with bags and bags of gifts. I couldn't help thinking everyone had gone all out for Cheryl's Last Christmas. There was an untrustworthy audience for everything I did now; I got the feeling that I would get twice as many "likes" for anything I posted on Facebook, out of pity, schadenfreude, or excitement about simple proof of life.

My sister wore a gray pencil skirt and a teal sweater with impossibly tall shoes and eyeshadow to match. I wore the new Old Navy sweats she'd given me and no makeup. That morning, I'd finally tried out the dry shampoo, which had made my hair bigger but not cleaner.

When Cathy extended her camera to take a portrait of the two of us, I said, "Look, it's you and your sickly brother."

CC opened her gifts, then drove down to Orange County to see her family. Those plans had changed as well. The Ybarras were supposed to visit us in the afternoon, but CC's mom had come down with the flu. I talked to her on the phone later in the day and got a lot of details about how weak she was feeling. She did not seem self-conscious about sharing them with a cancer patient. This was the paradox of CC's mom: the natural nurturer whose own trauma history sometimes made her self-absorbed. The mother who will leave sweet notes in your lunch but repeatedly forgets what you're studying in grad school and doesn't really try to find out.

We opened presents for three and a half hours, with a short break for eggs and cinnamon bread. My family's tradition was for each person to pick out a gift and for the whole family to watch as the recipient opens it. By 11:30 a.m., I was fading.

I wanted people to stop giving me things. I wanted to stop taking things.

CHAPTER 20: UGLY

On New Year's Eve, Justine and Sam showed up at our door with two tote bags and an infant seat full of Ruthie.

Sam held up the bags. "We're going to make butternut squash pizza. We brought the pizza stone."

CC helped him set up in the kitchen, and I thought about the mess they would leave, which I wouldn't be able to clean up because I wasn't supposed to lift anything heavier than three pounds for another two weeks.

Justine scooped up Ruthie and sat in the armchair. It was a stately looking piece of furniture, upholstered with black and white vines. The front was wild with stray threads that had been plucked by cat claws, but it was still our nicest piece of furniture. I almost never sat there before surgery, because usually we kept it covered with a sheet. But during the past two weeks, it had been my throne when guests visited.

Now I sat on the Craigslist loveseat. Justine lifted her maternity shirt and black sports bra and pressed Ruthie to her pink nipple. Her exposed breast was white, full (compared to the A-cups she was usually so proud of), innocent, functional. There were no scars or gummy surgical tape or Sharpie marks where a plastic surgeon had sketched out a plan. Justine's was a breast living out its little breast dream.

"Ruthie *loooves* to eat," Justine cooed, looking into Ruthie's eyes, still newborn-gray. "It's the one thing Sam can't help with, unfortunately."

Sam had gotten his own bilateral mastectomy a couple of years before I met him. He got to call it top surgery. It was an *affirming* surgery, not a sucks-you-have-a-disease surgery. He had previously commiserated with me about the world of triple-clasp bras. Now he changed all the diapers in lieu of breastfeeding.

I supposed that if CC were pregnant right now, I would be on diaper duty.

CC and Sam clanged around in the kitchen while I tried to make conversation with Justine. She barked directions to Sam: what pan to use to roast the squash, where to roll out the dough. Why couldn't they have just brought premade soup and stayed for an hour like everyone else? It took our oven an hour just to preheat.

"Excuse me a minute," I said, and went to the bathroom for a long time. Let Justine think I was emptying the four grenade-shaped drains that extended like tentacles from my ribcage, filling with light red fluid, my body's visible grieving process.

Then I made a dash for my phone and shut myself in the laundry room, where I texted my sister. *Justine is sitting in our living room breastfeeding Ruthie & telling Sam she wishes he could help with that part. fuck my life. i'm hiding like a coward. they must think i'm such a sad sack.*

When the pizza was ready, I wiped my face, took a few breaths, and went to the kitchen. Justine—who'd once thrown away a gift subscription to *Gourmet* magazine because the recipes were too simple—was a great cook, even by proxy.

"This is delicious," I gushed.

CC asked about Ruthie's sleep schedule and the closet they were remodeling in their master bedroom. Sam and Justine were the only couple we knew who'd purchased a house in Los Angeles without any help from their parents. It was all hardwood floors and carefully curated art. I'd always admired their patient, deliberate approach. They spent years looking for a new couch.

The thing that crushed me—more than the breastfeeding, more than the baby—was that Justine and Sam were living proof that Plan A can work out perfectly. MBA and law school, respectively, followed by house, wedding, sperm donor contract, baby. They were perfect new-millennium power queers.

Sam poured beer for himself and Justine, who had drunk lightly and defiantly throughout her pregnancy.

"So, do you pump?" CC asked her. "Or are you going to wait till you go back to work?"

CC lived in a world where breastfeeding was something she might do someday. Maybe someday soon, I hoped. But this information was as irrelevant to me as a recipe in *Gourmet* magazine. I didn't even have nipples anymore. The chasm that had developed between us last year cracked open again, for a minute.

"I'm kind of tired," I said. "I'm going to go lie down."

I went to our bedroom and cried some more. I emailed Keely, my most rabid breastfeeder friend, for some validation, because she also happened to be long on empathy. The truth was, Justine and I had never had much in common. Once she told CC that she didn't understand why anyone would commit suicide, or even want to. "But homicide," she'd said, "that I can understand."

"Justine looks out for Justine," CC had said more than once, and not unkindly. Now Ruthie was an extension of Justine.

Eventually I heard dishes being cleared and murmured good-byes. CC came to the bedroom. I was never not glad to see her, even—especially—after all we'd been through.

"I should have thought about it," she said. "It didn't even occur to me. I just don't think of these things—"

"Stop," I said. "Don't make this about your failure, because I know what will happen next. You'll resent me because you didn't make me totally happy."

"Those things—breastfeeding and things like that—just don't set me off," she said.

"Of course they don't, because no one cut your boobs off." And then I was sobbing for our babies all over again. "I wanted to breast-feed them. I would have done it. I would have been a good mom. I would have taken such good care of them."

CC was probably flashing back to the time when I'd sobbed like that every day. She probably felt a little mad at me. I felt a little mad at her for not thinking there might be something wrong with Justine whipping out her tits and talking about Sam's lack of breasts. As if getting them cut off had been a minor, humorously rude act, like blocking someone's car in the driveway. Because what if there *was* nothing wrong with Justine's behavior that night? Then I was just an oversensitive girl who was perpetually Having A Hard Time.

There was a time in my life, in my lonely, post-college years, when the idea of having a tight-knit clique of queers would have thrilled me. But now our friends seemed like scheming yuppies. I knew they would talk in pitying tones about their unlucky friend who was Having A Hard Time. I existed, I was sure, only to flesh out their narratives, to add the touch of sadness that makes beautiful people more so. They would stick to Plan A while I spiraled toward Plan Z.

The truth was, I liked CC and myself better than I liked any of them. We were interesting and introspective! We believed in God and The Arts, in a God that could be found in a good book. We knew melancholy. We knew change. I liked our hard-won, scarred *Now*. And I wanted *them*—all those people living out the fantasy lives of my superego—to understand that our failures were also our triumph.

But they would never understand. Or maybe I would never kick my superego's ass. Same thing.

CC would not understand what it meant to have your body turn on you in a half dozen ways, to confirm the worst dark thoughts you'd had about yourself. But she put her head gently on my sore shoulder.

"Ow." I shifted carefully.

"Sorry." CC relocated her head to one of the two specialized pillows she'd gotten for my recovery. It made her feel good to go on runs for antibacterial hand lotion and dry shampoo and long-handled back brushes.

"Justine made Sam clean up," CC said. "I could tell she felt bad."

"That was nice."

"Do we need to go out somewhere?" she asked. "To wash this taste out of our mouths?"

Her answer was often to get out of the house. The fact that she'd cheerfully endured almost two weeks of not doing so was a testament to her love for me and her willpower, and maybe her own exhaustion. I wanted to say yes, because I knew it would be good for both of us, but I couldn't imagine showing up at the bar around the corner with my unwashed hair and a hoodie stuffed with drains, resembling a newly and oddly pregnant woman.

So we did what our couples therapist was always telling us to: We entwined our bodies without totally understanding each other. We lay there in the stew of our respective selves and held hands across the bed.

On New Year's Day, when CC's family drove up from Santa Ana to make potato tacos, I told Elena about Justine. As an alpha female with a fierce temper, Elena had a bit of Justine in her, but she'd been through a tough divorce a few years ago, and I counted her among my tribe, the Tribe Of Broken Plans.

CC's mom sautéed potatoes, and her dad brought in a case of bottled water from the car. Beverages were his thing, his practical and economic form of generosity, like CC with her lotion and pillows.

Elena perched on the loveseat. I was back in the armchair.

"I just hope that when I have kids, if I have kids, I won't turn into an asshole," she said. "When Canny and I got divorced, people kept saying, 'At least you don't have kids,' like that was this big consolation. And it broke my heart, because we'd really tried to have kids, and that whole timeline of my life was completely thrown off."

I hadn't known that. I'd known they'd tried, but I hadn't known that putting off kids was part of her heartbreak. But of course it was.

"I have another friend who went through a divorce," Elena continued. "She was like, 'Being there for my daughter really got me through the day for a while.' And I understand that. But I had to be there for myself. I had to get up every day and try to be strong, not because it was this heroic act for my kids, but because it was what I had to do, all alone."

Elena was only a year and a half older than CC, but the combination of her strong will and their parents' timidity had made her a sort of de facto parent figure. When CC was having trouble in kindergarten, it was six-year-old Elena who got called to the principal's office. What had the principal been thinking? Had he assumed that CC's parents didn't speak English? Alice and Ray were both born in the United States, but a certain deferential immigrant attitude lived on in Mexican Santa Ana.

CC often had been on the bad end of Elena's bossiness, but at that moment I saw Elena as a tough six-year-old with skinned brown knees, yarn ribbons around her pigtails, taking notes on how to help her little sister. She'd learned young how to take care of herself, and relearned along the way.

In a more charitable moment, I might understand that Justine had done the same—Justine who'd grown up with a single mom in rural Georgia, who'd lost her favorite aunt to cancer a few years ago. Maybe she wanted to protect her daughter, that little cooing extension of herself, from the jagged edges of life for as long as she could. It wasn't her fault I was one big jagged edge these days.

I wouldn't hear from Justine or Sam for months, despite sending a couple of conciliatory emails explaining my feelings using lots of "I" statements, explaining that I understood that hungry babies needed to eat and new parents had full plates. *Trust me*, I wrote, *when I say I'm tired of being the weirdo that people need to walk on eggshells around.*

At first, I assumed they were just marinating on the proper response, and we'd be back to dinner parties soon. But Justine told CC she "didn't think the time was right," and the time stayed not right, until it was clear I would never get to show them how okay I really was.

Elena reached for her mom's pico de gallo in the green plastic bowl and spooned chopped tomatoes, onions, and cilantro onto her tacos. CC and Elena's biological grandmother had died shortly after giving birth to their mom; baby Alice bounced back and forth between Santa Ana and Mexico before settling with family friends. Alice had loved her adoptive mom deeply and spoke of her fondly, but she would also mention—in passing, with laughter—how she had more chores to do than the other kids in the family, how she'd make stacks and stacks of tortillas that hungry uncles would steal, leaving her with the blame and more work.

Maybe Alice *wouldn't* have known exactly how a mother was supposed to behave when called to the principal's office about her shy kindergartner. But she was doing her best, for herself and by herself. With help and without.

CHAPTER 21: BALD

Dr. Chung prescribed Ativan when I saw him the day before my first infusion, to help with post-chemo nausea. The pharmacist at Target said: "Ativan is a controlled substance." Ativan was normally prescribed for anxiety, and she'd never heard of it being used for nausea. It wasn't listed in her big book even as a secondary, off-label use. "I will have to call your doctor," she said. She had a Russian accent and bright green eye shadow. "You would be surprised how often doctors make mistakes. And when I call them, they say, 'Thank you, thank you.'"

"But I *just* saw Dr. Chung. He told me he was prescribing Ativan for nausea, and it says so right there on the slip. He did everything he was supposed to do, so why isn't that enough?"

The question of my life.

I imagined her checking a mental or actual box that said "drug-seeking." Yet if Dr. Chung had written "anxiety" on his scrip pad, she would have poured pills into the red plastic bottle and sent me on my way.

"I'm starting chemo tomorrow," I told her, playing the pity card. "I really don't want to have to come back here."

"I could give you one or two pills, but that's it. I have to talk to him tomorrow. You have to understand my perspective: If something seems like a mistake, I have to investigate it. I could get in a lot of trouble if I gave you the wrong medicine."

We cycled through the same conversation three more times. I lost.

I was terrified of becoming Travis, one of my Grandma Jac's friends, who had a rare genetic condition that caused him to slowly lose feeling in his extremities, which led to progressive amputations. He loved nothing more than yelling at and about incompetent medical professionals and able-bodied people who used handicapped parking spots. When my mom got sick, she was scared of becoming Travis too, but she stayed herself: kind, engaged, scared, quietly brave. She became more assertive.

Every pharmacy visit was a crossroads: Who did I want to be?

I decided to do a fasting thing that Kim told me about. She was an old Art Center friend of CC's, who'd gone back to school for a PhD in public health. Her focus was melanoma prevention, but she kept up to date on all things cancer and shared both my hypochondria and, apparently, my belief in immersion therapy. Hence the health-care job. The fasting protocol had only been proven in mice so far, but the idea was that when healthy cells were starved, they kicked into survival mode, whereas cancer cells just died. And if mice did this a few days before getting chemo, the chemo was more effective and the side effects were minimal. So with Dr. Chung's stamp of approval, I refrained from eating for forty-eight hours before chemo, plus the day of chemo.

I arrived at City of Hope on Chemo Day hungry and nervous.

Before my infusion, I had consulted a radiologist. I was starting to see a pattern in the emotional waves that carried me from appointment to appointment. Even if there wasn't big news to be broken, I usually left feeling overwhelmed: *I am a cancer patient. I am a cancer patient for life.*

Dr. Helen Chen was mid-forties and goofier than I expected a female Asian doctor in her mid-forties to be. In a good way. Mostly.

She came charging into the room declaring that I was a perfect candidate for radiation, which I translated into, *Your cancer is extra sucky! No way are you getting out of this without every sucky treatment on the books!* She also remarked, gleefully and frequently, on how big my tumor was.

Yes! My tumor was big! Should we save it in formaldehyde and put it in a museum next to two-headed cows and deformed fetuses? I felt a new, tenderhearted kinship with two-headed cows and deformed fetuses.

Dr. Chen was also unabashedly positive about my prognosis. The tumor didn't spread, so she suspected it was slow-growing. Without radiation, I had about a twenty percent chance of recurrence, maybe higher. With radiation, it was more like ten percent, and hormone therapy should take it down another notch or two.

A ninety-something percent chance of cure sounded pretty good. Who *didn't* have an eight percent chance of something bad happening to them in the next ten years or so? They could get a disease of their own or get hit by a car. Then I remembered that cancer didn't inoculate me against getting another disease or getting hit by a car. There was a time when I thought it did—after my mom died, I decided my dad could never die, and I still sort of believed it.

But my sister had gotten into a terrible car accident just last weekend. She called me shaking and crying from the side of the freeway where her car spun out after another vehicle slammed into it.

Three days later, she found out she had the BRCA2 gene, too.

I left Dr. Chen's office feeling okay about radiation. The chances of it causing a secondary cancer were something like one in a hundred thousand. She downplayed permanent skin damage, calling what one website referred to as "woodiness" a "slight permanent tan." I wanted to kick cancer, but since my only consolation was looking cute in spaghetti straps, I suddenly had become vain about my upper body. I could live with a little extra tan.

Still, every day there was something new to surrender. Breasts, skin, ovaries. Hadn't feminism taught me that my body was the one thing I owned? But no matter how many consent forms I signed, it felt like *they* were taking them, and *they* felt fine about it, because it was their job and they did this every day and they were saving my life. All those things were reasons, but it still wasn't okay.

Two rows of recliners lined the second-floor chemo room. It looked a little like a nail salon; they should really hire someone to give pedicures and massages to people trapped in comfy chairs for three hours, I thought. CC, Nicole, and I played blackjack for a while. Nicole offered to teach us gin rummy, but I secretly hated card games at least twice as much as I hated being hooked up to an IV. I pulled the cancer card in order to not play cards.

Instead, I took an Ativan-fueled nap, Nicole headed home, and CC messed around on her iPad Mini until it was time for us to go home, too.

That night, CC and I went to see *This Is 40*. The main characters had problems like being in debt while driving luxury cars and living in a giant house, and being accidentally pregnant at forty.

The following week, CC and I drove to Pac Repro for her fourth IUI. The nurse on duty had long red hair and a friendly demeanor.

She looked at CC's ultrasound pictures from earlier in the week.

"*Great* follicles."

"Thank you."

Biology as accomplishment. Two identical follicles on the left side. The last two times CC had taken Clomid, she'd grown slightly uneven ones on opposite sides. The mere fact of difference seemed promising. The nurse told us that we had "magical sperm," with six million extra swimmers in this vial than in the last one we'd used.

Two perfect eggs and six million *extra* sperm. How could CC not get pregnant? Except, of course, we knew exactly how people didn't get pregnant. We were experts in not getting pregnant.

CC squeezed my left arm—the one not at risk for lymph-edema—while the nurse did her thing. She left the room and we waited for the sperm to swim, CC's pelvis in the air on the raised table. The other times, we'd been in the Baby Bunny room. Now we were in the Baby Penguin room, which also seemed promising.

"Bunnies take their fertility for granted," I said. "Penguins walk for months across icebergs with an egg between their feet. They go for months without eating so they can barf up a little bit of fish into their babies' mouths. Penguins fucking *work* for it."

I went to the window and looked through the mini blinds. The week had started out icy, but now it was sunny and clear. Beyond the tile roofs and treetops, the mountains were purple-blue. CC saw all this over her raised knees, covered by a paper sheet.

Earlier in the week, Cathy had texted me, *Want to come down here on Saturday? I need a reason to get dressed this weekend.* The last time she'd seen me, I was wearing a hoodie and not lifting anything heavier than five pounds. Today I'd moved furniture. I put on a sweater dress, leggings, and heels.

She was wearing a miniskirt and a wool biker-style jacket. She had great eyeshadow, as always. "Hey, we look like two non-mutant sisters," she said.

My inner eight-year-old, whose biggest frustration in the world was being copied by my adoring five-year-old sister, had experienced a strange, *Hey, this is my story!* reaction to her BRCA2 results.

We ate dinner at a restaurant called Tin Roof next to a fertility clinic at the Manhattan Village mall, seated inches away from a glum-looking couple in their early twenties.

Cathy's test results had pushed her out of her determined distraction, her safe world of yoga class and pedicures. She'd gone to a support group facilitated by a group called FORCE. The group had been good, she reported. The women were welcoming and pretty. The ones who had their ovaries removed didn't look like shriveled up shrews. She'd made an appointment with a therapist and seen a crisis counselor in the meantime.

Sometimes being the oldest made me so mad. I had to hash things out with our parents. I had to get cancer. *My* reconstructed boobs would have a weird circle where they'd take skin and muscle from my back to compensate for radiation-damaged tissue. I would literally have more scars. Other times, I was grateful. My sense of safety had been broken the minute she was born, freeing me up to fall in love and live in tough neighborhoods and make art.

We went to a late showing of *Django Unchained,* a movie full of the scarred backs of people who didn't get to choose their fates. We went back to her house, where I shimmied out of my sweater dress and showed her my boobs-in-progress.

On Martin Luther King Day, CC and I hiked the hill at Debs Park. The week had started out icy, but now it was springtime-sunny. We saw dozens of dogs and one thin cat darting into the bushes.

CC talked about her Saturday night with Justine and Sam. CC

mentioned me more than usual, she said, to open the door for one of them to say, *How is Cheryl?* or *We got her email.* They didn't take the bait.

"Justine was talking about someone she knew who'd had a kid really young, like at twenty-one. Now she's forty and married to a different guy, and they just had a baby. Justine was like, 'That's ridiculous! Who would want to raise a kid and then have another one as soon as the first is out of the house?'"

CC was irked by Justine's judgmental tendencies, and my heart swelled with gratitude. I tried to let her have her own moment with it, but I couldn't stop myself from saying, "Fuck you, Justine!"

"There are lots of reasons someone might do that," CC said.

"Someday Justine's plans will fail." My voice was full of venom. I wanted to be there when they failed.

"Then she'll just switch tactics," CC said. "And her new way will be the right way."

We headed down the hill toward the 110. I tried to give a little speech about how it was fine to be an old parent. "As long as you're there for your kid's early childhood, you will have had a real influence on them, no matter whether you die when he or she is eight or—" That's when my voice broke.

I couldn't imagine raising kids to adulthood. And if I couldn't imagine it, how could it be true? I remembered an essay CC had once sent me, by Emily Yoffe of *Dear Prudence* fame, about her husband's first wife, who had died of breast cancer and left no children. When Emily's daughter found a box of photographs or some other memento, Emily had explained.

"So she was sort of like my other mom," the daughter said. Yes, Emily agreed, she was.

I retold this, sputtering. "Sometimes I imagine you with your next girlfriend, the one you'll have kids with," I said, my heart shattering all over the trail. "You'll have nostalgic memories of me, like you do of Jake." Jake was Ferdinand's tabby brother, hit by a car when he was barely past kittenhood. "I think of your kid, and I want her to think of me as her other mom. Sometimes even that much of a connection seems like enough."

"Baby, we're going to have *our* kid, together."

It was what I wanted her to say, preferably a thousand times. I'd learned that her reassurance wasn't inexhaustible, so when she offered it, I tried to savor it. I wanted to dip it in bronze and make it true and endurable.

Late one weeknight, while I was pulling into the parking lot of Trader Joe's, I tugged absentmindedly at the wispy hairs above my ears. A small handful came loose. I did it again and again, six or seven hairs each time. They came loose easily, like when I put Nair on my bikini area. Later that night, I went to the bathroom and pulled loose fingerfuls of pubes, no Nair required.

It was yet another thing—like waking up without nipples— that seemed impossible and unimaginable, yet so simple when it happened. It was yet another thing that whispered in my ear, *You have cancer.*

I got teary in bed late that night. I didn't want people to look at me with pity. I wanted people to think I was just like them, my future a buffet of choices. I wanted them to know just enough about my suffering to think I was brave and enviable, but not enough to recoil from me and thank the god that favored them.

I told CC I wanted to shave it off.

"Are you sure?" Her eyes looked a little glisten-y, in a way they never had for my boobs. "Your curls," she said.

I ran my hands over my hair, then opened my palms to show her the dark brown globs. She got it.

She had plans with Pedro, and said she'd ask him to come over after, with his clippers. We owned no such tools.

CC, Pedro, Stephen, Nicole, and I gathered for a mini head-shaving party in the kitchen. I was so grateful for these people who'd become my family, who were about to see the little spots on my scalp that are always red and flaky and picked-at, a ritual that used to be between me and my commute.

Pedro tried to use one of the longer clipper settings to take off the top layer, but either my falling-out hair didn't have enough resistance, or my naturally thick hair had too much. He and CC took turns with the scissors instead.

"Stop giving her a style cut," Nicole instructed. "CC's living out her childhood Barbie dreams here."

I was determined not to feel ashamed of having cancer, even though sometimes I did, even though there were parts of cancer culture (and parts of queer culture, for that matter, like embarrassing rainbow jewelry and certain types of shoes) that I resisted fiercely.

"Now you have kind of a *Tank Girl* look," Nicole said of my partially shaved head.

CC was recording it all on her iPad Mini. "Is there a video message you want to send to your enemies?" she asked.

"Oh, I've got a list," I assured her.

We all agreed I looked particularly dykey. "This is the first time I've seen you look scary, like you could really kick some ass," Nicole said.

"See, I associate the shaved head with really femmey dykes," CC said. "I go the opposite direction—it's always the girls who wear dresses and are really petite."

When they were done, I looked in the mirror. It was a *little* bit *Les Mis*/Nineteenth Century Poorhouse Chic, but not as much as I'd worried. My eyes looked bigger. Maybe I could pull off the femmey-punk-dyke thing. I'd assumed I would be a hat-and-scarf girl, but suddenly I wanted to rock my new bald head.

CHAPTER 22: THE WOMAN IN THE NEXT BED

"It's hard to say what particular good it did me to learn about [my cancer's] higher recurrence rate in the third to fifth year," wrote Joewon, a friend of a friend, in a December 2012 blog entry.

What did me good, on the other hand, was the things I learned from other women with cancer. During my first chemo infusion, the woman in the next bed, who looked about my age, almost determined the ways in which I took my own chemotherapy . . . "Eat whatever you want and keep your strength up. It's a cycle of good days and bad days. You'll be fine on good days, fine enough to go out with friends and stuff." The nurse gave me a lot of helpful general information, but this co-patient's first-hand report was in fact much better than the nurse's noncommittal "every patient can react differently" spiel . . . . She wasn't invading my privacy. She was instead forgoing her privacy to help me with what I was in for. In the end, she told me that it wasn't easy but "bearable" (her exact word) and showed me that it was possible to carry on with life, with the chemo as part of it.

There is a somewhat famous story about storytelling. It goes roughly like this: Scientists wanted to warn future generations about hazardous nuclear waste buried deep inside a mountain. The reactive materials would take ten thousand years to decay. In that time, signage would crumble, technology would change, language would evolve, the earth around the mountain might shift. Carving pictographs in the rock face seemed long-lasting, but vague. Eventually, a team of experts decided on oral tradition, the most ancient and flexible practice. Each generation of storytellers tells the next.

I think this is one of the things that scares me about death: No one is alive to tell me how it will be. But as an unwilling member of an unpopular club, I was privy to mentorship from the other unwilling members who went through it before me, and lived, at least for a while. *Lived to tell the tale.*

Joewon was a grad school friend of CC's friend Kim, and she referenced me in her post, too, before I even emailed with her. Now she was the woman in the (virtual) next bed, and I was taking in her wisdom. This would be bearable. I was already bearing it. Joewon lived in Seoul. She was anxiety-prone, a literature professor, and a woman who chose not to dye her graying hair while living in the (other) plastic surgery capital of the world.

She'd gotten cancer just in time to ruin her sabbatical, during which she had hoped to travel. So she was traveling now. She and Kim and CC and I met for brunch at the Coffee Table in Eagle Rock. Burritos and eggs and coffee on a table inlaid with tile in the shape of a dragonfly.

I was a little nervous; I'd emailed Joewon at my most panicked, sent her paragraphs and paragraphs about my tits and ovaries and deepest fears. She'd answered promptly and at length, full of empathy and reassurance. Internet friendships are like bonding on a long road trip with someone you don't know well. You're shoulder to shoulder, looking at the yellow line or the rows of crops ticking by, and you're free to speak all kinds of truth. Then you get to your destination, stretch your legs, have to make eye contact and joint decisions. Things get a little weirder and harder after all that disembodied intimacy.

We talked about museums and massages and grad school and bedbugs and lice. Even without cancer as a common denominator, Kim and Joewon were my people.

And we talked about illness, too. Joewon had had a rough time with chemo: She'd been quarantined in the hospital twice because of her low white-cell count, which sounded like a scary and lonely fate, not to mention boring. She'd gotten terrible insomnia (hence the title of her blog, Eternal Insomnia) and bad bone pain. But it was all bearable, she said. And when she told me radiation was nothing, I believed her.

"The only awkward part was being shirtless in a room with two young, male lab-tech guys," she said in her slight accent. "Just lying there half naked with a mangled boob."

She pulled the collar of her blue sweater down to show me the inch-long port scar. I told Joewon I worried about all the worrying I'd do when treatment was finished.

She got it, immediately and totally. "When you're a hypochondriac, it's hard not to go crazy. But you do get to the point where you don't think about it every day. Or, you do, but not *too* much."

She told us about the time she'd flagged down her surgeon in the middle of a conference to make her feel a new lump. She grabbed Kim's hand and pulled it to her boob to demonstrate.

"She said it probably was nothing, but I needed to wait ten days to see her. It was a long ten days."

I knew that if Joewon was truly as anxious as I was, and it sounded like she was, and if she admitted she still thought about cancer every day, then she was also telling the truth about being mostly okay now. Teaching and living her life.

Molly was another woman-in-the-next-bed. The first time I met her in person, I was coming off a morning spent roaming the aisles at Target, contemplating that, depending how you sliced the statistics, there was a ten percent chance I would be dead in five years. The possibility of death kept finding new inroads. I'd think, *Okay, ninety percent is decent odds. Not perfect, but I don't have to* cheat *death, I just have to be average.* Then I'd realize some little nuance: Those were five-year survival statistics. In ten years, there was a higher chance I'd be dead, though making it through the first five years was a good indicator that I'd make it through the next five. I couldn't quite wrap my head around it—it was like I was staying alive to face more risk. Which, I suppose, is how life works.

Then I remembered that coffee existed, and I got some from the Target Starbucks, and dried my eyes. I drove down the street to Swork Coffee for a second cup and waited for Molly to find me. It wasn't hard to do because I was the only bald woman in the place.

She told me her story, which is to say her cancer story, which was, of course, only a piece of her story. She'd reached out to me at Poets & Writers about a Poets & Writers thing, and in the process she'd come across my blog, so she added a "P.S." to her email: "If you ever want to talk to someone who went through the same thing at a similar age. . . ." So here we were, talking. About fake boobs and prognoses and the same, overly perky social worker who'd crossed both our paths.

I admitted: "I just feel so old and creaky and uncool."

Molly was more than a year out of treatment. Her blond hair had grown back. She was starting a new micro fiction collective.

"Are you kidding?" she said. "I think we're the coolest."

The way she talked and wrote and moved through the world was undeniably cool.

For a few months, we were fast friends. I joined her collective and hung out a couple of times at the loft she shared with her husband in Atwater Village. I had some kind of art/cancer/sister crush on her. Navigating a world most people tried to avoid, I had finally found someone aspirational.

And then she slowly drifted away, admitting in an email that she was struggling with depression. I circled back to her blog and her Facebook page now and then. One January day she shared a long, unflinching, un-self-pitying Facebook post: She was living with metastatic breast cancer.

She wrote beautifully. I hadn't seen her in a few years and so she became Molly The Story, even as she was Molly The Writer and Molly The Person. Death is the process of transitioning from Writer to Story, whether you are a literal writer or not. Story is a kind of earthly immortality, although I hope there are other kinds. Writers try to trick death by telling our own stories.

Six years after I finished treatment, my coworker Lalayna was diagnosed. She had just returned from a trip-of-a-lifetime to Cuba. The last day before the holiday break, a group of us went out for drinks, and she talked nonstop about dancing with Cuban guys, the cab driver who wanted to marry her, cigars, sex workers, arroz con pollo, tamales wrapped in banana leaves. It was her MacDowell. She'd had cancer the whole time.

Lalayna told me about her diagnosis, sounding cool-headed.

She wondered why her family was making such a big deal. I reminded myself that other people were not me. We made square loops around our building, traipsing a patchwork of sleepily gentrifying storefronts and low-rise apartment buildings. The sidewalk was strewn with scooters you could rent on the spot using an app, and homeless people sleeping in the open.

"My mom thinks I should get a double mastectomy," she said, "but that's not what doctors are recommending. She's just like, 'Why wouldn't you do it? Don't you want to live?' And I'm like, 'We're all gonna die.' My family hates when I talk like that."

Her older brother had died in a motorcycle accident in his twenties. Her mother knew death, knew the dark secrets no parent wants to know, knew what I knew post-miscarriage but multiplied by a black hole.

Around the same time, I learned that Molly's cancer was in her bones. There was another round of chemo and a preemptive surgery to stabilize her hip and femur. She was still and always cool. In the years after we lost touch, she created a darkly comic, darkly hot, radically honest Instagram account called @dying4sex, in which she posted photos of herself in lingerie alongside statements like *I wish someone would give me a hard time about my handicapped placard so I could take out all of my frustration about this disease on a stranger.*

In December, she posted a picture of herself naked on a hospital bed. Instead of lingerie, she wore a blue latex glove on her hand, which she used to cover her private parts. In March she tweeted that she had entered hospice. She had hoped it wouldn't take this long, but she thought it wouldn't be much longer.

Around that time, Lalayna was prepping for surgery, and I had my semiannual checkup. Lalayna got a second opinion from a doctor who wanted to look more closely at a couple of her lymph nodes. "Squishy," the doctor called them.

We had a staff meeting at Roosevelt High School, where our organization maintained a presence. Teenagers in hoodies and tight jeans milled about among murals honoring Chicano history. On the other side of a chain link fence, bulldozers pushed dirt to make room for a new building.

"This new doctor wants to think about chemo," Lalayna said. "I should rephrase that. She wants to do chemo."

She still spoke calmly, but a layer of cool had fallen away since we last talked. I'd taken her defended presentation at face value out of respect and for lack of other information, but, of course, it was denial. Of course it was.

Now she said, "This is vain, but I'm worried how I'll look without eyebrows." We walked from the gym to Building C. Roosevelt was a hodgepodge of architectural styles, from deco to brick to the glass-and-concrete projection for the new building, like a body that had been through a lot.

Lalayna was a planner, a scheduler, a bit of a control freak. She had thick brown eyebrows and short hair that was naturally textured and unnaturally blonde. I told her that was a perk of chemo versus, say, the flu. I tried to be the Woman in the Next Bed I thought she needed. I confessed I still got nervous before appointments, but I downplayed the degree. "Nervous" was such a quaint word; it brought to mind ladies fanning themselves in parlors. If I was reading Lalayna right, she already knew anyway.

At our staff meeting, we applauded the promotion of Beatriz from Program Manager to Program Director, and I felt a twinge of envy and wondered for the zillionth time just how much I cared about my career. During a break, I stepped outside and checked Facebook, where I saw a photo of Molly, lit by late afternoon rays, a flower in her hair, hands together as in prayer or applause.

I have died. I no longer walk the earth like you. In a body,

that is a blessing when it works, and, when it stops working,
I assure you the dropping of it is an equal blessing.
That's all I can tell you about where I'm not.

It was a post I'd been waiting for, holding vigil as I went about my everyday life. And still it knocked the wind out of me, a testament to the power of Molly's writing, or the power of death, or both. There were a handful of people—Nora Ephron was one, another was a Black police officer who wrote about his fears and frustrations heading into a Black Lives Matter protest at which he was ultimately killed—who wrote about death and the world in ways that were so honest and wise as to form, I believed, a force field of protection around them. Wasn't that the purpose and power of knowledge? And then, no, they weren't protected at all. They died anyway. And I—in my greedy, lazy, meandering quest to know (the meaning of life, whether I had cancer at this particular moment, etc., etc.)—would, too.

I stood in the shadow of a temporary bungalow and sobbed as students rolled past me, as uncurious as a stream parting to make room for a boulder. I reminded myself that I hadn't talked to Molly for years, we weren't *friends,* I was just projecting my feelings and fears onto someone who was a full and real person, and wasn't that unfair to her?

I wiped my eyes and returned to the meeting to discuss our strategic plan. I avoided Lalayna for the next few days. I wanted to be an example of someone who'd emerged strong, scarred, kind, and real. A beacon. If she saw what I really was—crumpled, terrified, ten pounds overweight—how would she muster the hope she needed?

I thought of Molly as the death doula I hoped I wouldn't need. It strikes me as horribly unfair that the living can help us be born, but the dead can't help us die. Or maybe they can. I hope they can.

But if that's true, then it seems like they only appear in the last few seconds before they cross over. Maybe they're there the whole time, but we can't see them.

Molly made me feel less alone. And even as she appeared cool and *perfect*, that dirty word, I know she left her husband and struggled with anorexia and bitterness and frustration about all her body kept her from doing. Those things could exist alongside all the admirable stuff.

I am an agnostic believer. A person who seeks knowledge but knows how much she doesn't know, while feeling—most days—a deep somethingness that is both profound and hard to unearth. Molly talked about returning to "the great oneness." It made me think of "The Origin of Love" in *Hedwig and the Angry Inch*, which describes humans as half of ancient, two-headed creatures scissored apart by an angry god. We wander the earth trying to return to each other. And we can't sew ourselves back together in this lifetime, but we can hold hands and walk next to each other. That's all. That's everything.

CHAPTER 23: **MOTHERLESS**

I was pulling a flouncy eyelet sundress over my head when my sister called. The dress seemed right for a Mother's Day tea, and thanks to the spaghetti straps, it meshed with my current favorite look, Things I Couldn't Wear Back When I Had Real Boobs And Had To Wear A Serious Bra At All Times.

"I'm leaving now to come pick you up," Cathy said. "Adam and I went to brunch and neither of us had a watch. I'll probably get to your place at about noon."

She'd been dating Adam for a couple of months. He was a firefighter with sad eyes and a beaky nose, not the beefcake calendar variety, but heroic enough for Cathy's tastes. Her last serious boyfriend had been a cop—funny and good-looking, but prone to cryptic, slightly mean texts, and ultimately kind of a mama's boy who couldn't decide if he wanted to get married and have kids immediately, or if seeing Cathy twice a week was moving too fast. Adam was more categorically Nice. They were in the long-brunch phase of courtship, and I resented them. I was certain they'd get married and have kids immediately.

It was 11:45. Adam lived in Long Beach, and I lived in the very opposite corner of Los Angeles County.

"It takes more than fifteen minutes to get from Long Beach to Highland Park," I snapped. "Don't bother picking me up. I'll meet you in Echo Park, at the party."

Adam represented a world of no watches, no disease, no disagreements. Where bodies were only used for hot sex. When she made me look at a "rash" on her hip, it seemed like one part hypochondria, one part humblebrag—because it was clearly a bruise and, yes, now that she thought about it, she and Adam *had* had thrashing sex the night before.

When Cathy and I were kids, we gave our mom the standard construction-paper art projects and gold-plated *#1 Mom* charms for Mother's Day. But our real present to her was being nice to each other for one whole day.

This year, our mom had been dead for almost ten years. Nicole and her sister Vanessa were hosting another Motherless Mother's Day for all us saddies.

Adam did yoga and went backpacking and sent Cathy sweet, goofy texts. After their second date, she told me, *He has a gay brother.* Homophobia was a dating deal-breaker for her. *His brother is HIV positive, and we had this amazing conversation about how neither of you let the stuff you're going through keep you down.*

She meant it as a compliment, and maybe she wanted it to be true, but despite keeping up a busy schedule, I was undeniably down. I'd felt demoted to the status of Queer Friend Who Dies Nobly To Make The Main Character Seem Deep And That Much More Beautiful. A B-plot, a bit of inspiration porn to spur on the Real People.

"I'm glad we're going to this," she said on the phone. "I think we could both use the distraction."

Things had been civil but tense between us lately. I'd avoided calling her for a few weeks. How long would it take her to call me? When she started contemplating a preventative Angelina Jolie–style mastectomy, she'd wanted to compare notes on types of implants. I felt like I'd been sentenced to prison, and *she'd* shown up wearing a striped Sexy Jailbird uniform from a costume shop, wanting to talk about our matching outfits.

The residential streets in Echo Park had been developed before street-grading was common. They were some of the steepest in the country. If you weren't careful, Google Maps could send you up Baxter Street, where buses and stretch limos had gotten stuck straddling its apex. I meandered lower hills while complaining about Cathy to my dad on the phone.

"Does she really think it takes fifteen minutes to get from Long Beach to Echo Park?"

"Cathy can be a little unreliable, especially when she's busy," my dad said. This was not actually true—no Kleins were truly unreliable—but I heartily agreed. "But she's going through a lot, and I'm glad Adam seems like a good guy," he said.

"I know Mom didn't like it when we fought, but I just feel like she's taking up all the space. I can agree she's going through a lot, but it's not the same thing as what I'm going through, and I wish she'd stop pretending it is. She doesn't have cancer. Why do we have to treat this as an emergency?"

"She has another appointment with a geneticist and a surgeon coming up, and we'll see what they advise, but I strongly think she should get the surgery as soon as she can," my dad said.

"Obviously she can do whatever she wants and needs to," I said.

"It's her body. But now you're stressed out, too. And I know this is the little kid in me talking, but I'm mad at her for taking all your attention."

"I can pay attention to both of you," my dad said reasonably.

My car was hot, and tears were streaming down my face. I had no mom, and now, because of Cathy's not-her-fault needs, I had only half a dad.

I parked on the steep hill next to the little yellow house Nicole's sister shared with her Austrian cameraman boyfriend. Vanessa had orchestrated her usual perfect spread. I made a fruit salad to her exact specifications (mixed berries and fresh mint leaves), but she immediately emptied it into a better bowl. There were buttery scones, a tomato and prosciutto tart, tea, prosecco.

I helped myself to the items that seemed the most vegan. I put butter on them so I wouldn't feel deprived. When Cathy finally got there, she asked me if anything was wrong. I gave my head a slight shake and hid beneath my floppy straw hat, determined to suffer mysteriously.

Vanessa and Cathy traded stories about teaching high school. Nicole and I often commiserated about how our little sisters sidestepped family obligations and avoided confrontation, but somehow they'd both ended up teaching teenagers in tough, confrontation-heavy neighborhoods. It was not uncommon for Cathy to begin a story with, *So, we were on lockdown the other day* . . .

"What are you wearing to prom?" Cathy asked with only a touch of irony.

"My friend is loaning me a dress," said Vanessa, who was long and lanky and had worked as a fashion publicist before getting her credential. "She's actually bringing it by today."

Today Vanessa was wearing a short jumpsuit and a chunky

necklace that had belonged to her and Nicole's mother, who died of breast cancer in 2009. Nicole was still mad that Vanessa had raided her jewelry box the day after their mother's death, while Nicole was sleeping off the death vigil.

The party moved outside to a brick patio amid flowering trees. The table—handmade by an artist friend of Vanessa's—was set with her mismatched vintage teacups. Nicole was complaining about the girl she was dating.

"She gets high every night, and then she makes insensitive comments, like a drunk person, and won't have sex with me," Nicole said. "And the sex is my only reward for tolerating the insensitive comments. Actually, sex is the main reason I got back together with her in the first place after she was so thoughtless to me the last time, so what's the point if I'm not even getting laid?"

This was why I loved Nicole. She could be so brutally honest about someone she was in fact completely smitten with.

Vanessa's other two motherless friends—a brother-sister pair who'd lost their mom just a month ago—smiled abstractly. They had the stunned look of the newly half-orphaned. The look of, *Wait, so the world is still here?* Cathy sipped her tea. I was sure she was thinking about sex with Adam.

Cathy had spilled her BRCA2 news to him early on, just in case he wanted to dump her right then and avoid getting to know her small natural breasts only to lose them. She tended to be reserved, and it was a rare moment of disclosure. For a minute, she'd been scrubbed raw by life just like me, she'd had nothing to lose just like me—only she was sharing it with Adam, and not with me.

Adam had responded kindly: "That's such a hard thing to go through. We'll get through it together. I'm into *all* of you, not just one specific part."

How fantastic it must feel to have a firefighter rush in, all sirens and ladders, to save you from your fears of dying alone and boob-less.

"Is there anything you *like* about this girl?" the sister half of the brother-sister pair asked Nicole.

"Yeah. When we *do* have sex, it's hot. And when she's not high, she's really thoughtful and sensitive."

Cathy ate another one of the Trader Joe's rugelach bites she brought. She'd put on some weight in the past few months. I chalked it up to the constant dinners out that came with a new romance, but maybe, I thought now, she was also indulging in a favorite family habit: comfort eating. I was no stranger to it, but the combination of anxiety, side effects of my antidepressant, and a hyper-obsession with my health had landed me at my skinniest adult weight. Sometimes I felt smug, sometimes extra vulnerable. The world could see my skull and the ladder of my sternum and my soul. Cathy was creating a soft layer of padding between herself and its cruelties. The bumpers of her hips pulled her green dress tight.

The prom dress arrived. The butter melted in the sun. Cathy thanked Vanessa for a lovely tea and excused herself. She gave me a feather-light hug and promised to call soon. I complained about Cathy to Nicole and then left as well.

As soon as I got in my car, I called Cathy on my cell. I couldn't stand giving the silent treatment to someone who welcomed it.

"I'm mad at you," I said.

"For being late?"

"Well, that was the final straw. But I'm mad at you for not calling me and for being fake when we do talk."

"I'm not being fake," she protested. "I just try to talk about other things, things we can agree on. But then you act like I'm shallow."

"I never said you were shallow," I shouted. (And while that was true, hadn't I sometimes comforted myself with that thought? That maybe she owned a house and was on her way to domestic bliss, but wasn't I an artist who listened to more NPR?)

As I made my way from the 2 freeway to Eagle Rock Boulevard, past the Rite Aid and the emergency vet and the homeless encampment, Cathy unleashed a years-long list of grievances. After our mom had died, we'd made an unspoken pact to support each other unconditionally, but now that the treaty had been broken, she let me know how mean I was. I was dismissive of her last boyfriend, she said, and unsympathetic to her best friend's fertility problems.

"Because she *already has two kids*," I said.

She ignored me, she said, because she didn't want to get yelled at. She didn't want to talk about her own surgery because she didn't want to *think* about it.

"And there are some things about your health I don't want to talk about, and I don't think I *should* talk about with you," she said.

"What, that you're afraid I'm going to die?"

"Yes," she said.

"You think I don't know that? You think I haven't thought about it? Not talking about it just makes me feel those terrible emotions all by myself, which is really lonely."

"When Mom was sick," she said, "she tried to talk about death with me, and I turned her down. It was the right choice then, and I'd make it again. *No* one talks about that stuff."

"Yes they do."

"No they don't! Whenever Dad brings up financial stuff, you tell him you don't want to think about him dying."

"I'm trying to tell him that our priority is *him,* not getting a tax-free inheritance after he dies. But yeah, maybe he could use someone to share those thoughts with."

"Well, I'm glad that you're at that point," she snapped, "but I'm not."

Maybe I had to be the crazy one, but I would be the crazy one who was Brave Enough To Look Death In The Face.

Then I remembered the meeting I'd attended at our church in the early, raw days soon after my diagnosis. I remembered Susan with stage IV pancreatic cancer, who'd said, "I'm putting things on my calendar. I wasn't even supposed to make it this long, but I figure why not make plans? I'll either be here for them or I won't."

The pale green prayer shawl from Zelda had hung in my bedroom for months, a symbol of the night I'd seen God's love and my mom in Susan's ailing form. Touching it made me feel sick and heavy, but I was too superstitious to put it away. I never went back to the group.

I told my sister fuck you. We both said I love you and hung up.

CHAPTER 24: ITCHY

In April, I went to Houston for work. As I waited for my flight
home at the George Bush International Airport, I leaned into my
exhaustion and bought a dark-chocolate-covered pretzel and a
giant peanut butter cup at Rocky Mountain Chocolate Factory. I
ate them on the plane.

The night before, CC's voice had been thick with sleep by 8:00
p.m., and she hadn't gotten her period. I let myself daydream she
was pregnant. Then I actually dreamed she was pregnant, but for
some reason *I* could pee on a stick and find out for her.

As soon as I passed through security, I got a text saying she'd
started her period.

I felt myself sliding from anxiety and despair into a low-grade
depression. I'd heard a report on NPR about how willpower waned
throughout the day. The more tired I was, the more likely I was to
pop malted milk Easter eggs into my mouth.

My dad picked me up at the airport, and I drove straight from his house to dinner with CC, Pedro, and Stephen.

"So you're almost done with treatment," Pedro said. He'd taken to posting relentlessly positive, Malcolm Gladwell-ish things on Facebook in recent months. Infographics about the benefits of volunteering, vaguely embattled *GQ* articles about masculinity.

"Well, there's radiation and another surgery or two," I said. "But radiation isn't that bad, from what I've heard."

"It makes you kind of tired," CC said.

"Don't remind me of how tired I'm going to be." It came out more snappishly than I intended. I was already so tired.

Later she said she was annoyed with Pedro and Stephen for trying to push a positive narrative on us. I felt a belated affection: She understood that this wasn't over for us.

We went to bed grouchy. I was still sad that she'd gotten her period, but too tired to talk about it without falling into a bid for adoption-related reassurance.

I finally broached the subject, driving back from her parents' house on Easter Sunday. She'd had two cups of coffee and was in a good mood.

"What are we going to do about having a kid, baby?" I asked.

"Before we do something about it, shouldn't we just talk about how we feel about me not getting pregnant this time?"

"Right. That's what I meant. You know me, I jump straight to the doing."

How we felt: sad, tired, like it wasn't fair. Like maybe pregnancy was waiting for us on the magical sixth try, like it was all a big scam and we'd never get pregnant.

"After I didn't get pregnant the first time," she said, "I remember talking to Sam, and he said after four times I'd be pregnant, and I really took it to heart," she said.

"Yeah, because nobody really knows, so you look to voices of authority wherever you can find them." It was the same way I looked at lucky numbers and the faces of people who knew someone who knew someone who had cancer for clues about my own fate.

Our thoughts on what to do next weren't all that different: I thought we should relaunch our adoption page and/or look into trying to get her pregnant with my frozen embryos. Neither option was easy. Both came with learning curves and phone calls and paperwork. She was still unenthusiastic about adoption, how it made all our private stuff public, how it made us dependent on an agency and some random knocked-up chick, how it removed all control.

For me, life had removed all control. I might as well get a baby out of it.

CC thought we shouldn't even start investigating those steps until June, when she'd be finished with school and I'd be done teaching my online writing class. That seemed fair, even though I was impatient as always.

She said some things about feeling restless, about having the urge to engage in some "destructive behaviors."

"I guess I'm really sad about Justine," she admitted. "I've known both of you too long to throw either relationship away."

I hadn't seen or heard from Justine or Sam since New Year's Eve, until she showed up for a scheduled book club at my place the previous weekend. Again, she took the most comfortable chair in our living room and popped out her tit to feed Ruthie. My face, and CC's, must have registered some incredulity, but she seemed to ignore it. Later that night, I wrote an email with the subject line "the end"—as in, the end of our friendship—and saved it in my drafts folder.

"Do you want me to make up with her? I'll do it for you, baby. I'm still mad at her, but she's been a great friend to you, and I don't want your friendship to be a casualty of this."

CC said she understood why I was angry, but she needed a friend. My problems were only a part of her problems with Justine, but they were a big part. But, she said, she couldn't ask me to make peace—because I was the sick one.

"I'm glad you're asking this," I said, "because what terrifies me is that you'll want something from me and feel too guilty to ask, and then you'll resent me, and we'll be back where we were last time."

When I thought about talking to Justine, I could only imagine being cold or mean or guilt-trippy. I couldn't summon anything charitable. But I knew from experience that seeing someone in person usually melted away a lot of those feelings. And CC was worth the leap of faith.

The next morning, I walked while CC ran. Same route, different paces. I still went jogging sometimes, but it was getting harder. Now, I cried out loud as I walked past sleepy bars and verbena-scented boutiques, muffler shops and party supply stores bursting with piñatas. I cried because I wasn't running, because at this time two years ago, I consoled myself that two years out, I'd finally have a kid. Now that prospect seemed at least two more years away, and I didn't even know just how alive I'd be in two years. I cried because I could taste how close a life of stagnation and bitterness was, and the only thing I could do was put one foot in front of the other.

That night, CC and I celebrated my thirty-sixth birthday with a night of comedy at a Silver Lake bar that, two bars before, was called The Garage. I'd gone there in 1999 for Francesca Lia Block's book party for *I Was a Teenage Fairy*. Then, it had felt dark and magical and full of promise, the way everything east of Western

Avenue did when I was in college. This April night, it was full of smart, lightly cynical, philosophical comedians.

David Huntsberger speculated that what made humans the dominant species was our sadness. We weren't amazing fucking machines, he said. We sat wrapped in blankets feeling bad that no one had liked our YouTube videos. That sounded about right.

In May, I had my sixth and final—knock on wood, a forest of wood, always—chemo session. I was still working and writing and seeing friends. But when I went running, I couldn't make it up hills without pausing to rest. I had no pubic hair, no leg hair, and only the faintest whisper of eyebrows. Sometimes, after driving the long stretch of 10 freeway to get to the Westside, I pulled over to the side of Overland, reclined my seat, and took a nap. My eyelid twitched for no reason. Well, not for no reason.

I knew I'd gotten off easy. I hadn't had neuropathy or bad nausea. Maybe it was the fasting; maybe it was being thirty-six; maybe it was luck. Every new treatment came with a horrifying list of possible side effects. When asked to divine the future, all doctors would say was, "Everyone is different."

I picked up a pamphlet called *Radiation Therapy and You,* and it was so terrible-sounding that I wrote a parody of it and posted it on my blog.

Hi! You're reading this because you have cancer. Just wanted to remind you. In this guide, you'll find many facts that will help you through your treatment.

Q: What is radiation therapy?
A: Radiation therapy is a cancer treatment that uses radiation to do therapy. Against cancer.
Q: Who gets radiation therapy?

A: You do. Because you have cancer.

Q: What does radiation do to healthy cells?
A: Nothing good. It's fucking radiation.

Q: What type of radiation will my doctor prescribe?
A: Your doctor will prescribe the type that he or she feels will work. Sorry, we don't want to get all science-y here.

Q: What side effects will I experience?
A: You will experience the type of side effects that you will experience. Remember, every patient is different, and we don't want to get sued. Also, your psychotherapist is discouraging you from having expectations.

Q: But really, what side effects will I experience?
A: Diarrhea, fatigue, hair loss, mouth changes, nausea, vomiting, sexual and fertility changes, skin changes, throat changes, urinary and bladder changes, and other.

Q: Other?
A: Have you seen Spider-Man?

Q: How should I take care of myself during my treatment?
- *Don't wear lotion or deodorant to your radiation therapy session.*
- *Don't use sunscreen.*
- *But don't get any sun, either.*
- *So, just stay inside. It's not like you're the life of the party these days anyway.*
- *Stay away from children, as you are basically a walking Superfund site, not to mention depressing to small innocent people who don't yet know about all the shit life has in store.*

- *To combat fatigue, try not to do anything.*
- *But make sure to exercise, cook healthy food, floss, quit smoking, bathe frequently, and grow your own aloe vera.*

Q: Are there any extra humiliating things I should do?
A: Use a saliva substitute to moisten your mouth, wear a wig, clean your rectal area via something called a "sitz bath," and purchase some adult diapers.

Q: Are there any permanent side effects of radiation?
A: Permanent and long-term side effects include:

- *Skin that looks like Megan Brockelsby's mom's—you know, who used to chain smoke in her tennis skirt and cracked bare feet while waiting for Megan after school?*
- *Super powers**
- *Cancer***

Q: What happens after I'm finished with radiation?
A: You will need to meet with your radiation oncologist for the rest of your life to check for cancer—the one you were treated for and also new, ironic cancers caused by cancer treatment. Oh, you're in the system, honey.

Q: Um, this is all kind of terrifying. Is there anything I can do to cope with the emotional effects of cancer treatment?
A: Try taking a walk or closing your eyes and imagining a peaceful meadow.

*Rare.
**Not as rare as you'd like.

Every weekday for a month and a half, I drove to City of Hope before work, changed in a dressing room that played *Good Morning America* on a small screen, and lay topless on a padded table while a massive machine—tan and utilitarian with a big staring eye— rolled over me at this angle and then that angle. There was a video screen in that room, too, a bigger one, which played footage of oceans and birds. At some point they must have tattooed me— three black dots that told them where to position the beam—but I don't remember the gun or any pain. (At my second reconstruc- tive surgery, Dr. Lehfeldt would offer to remove the tattoos, but by then I was proud of my war wounds.)

Radiation didn't feel like much. Nothing like the full-body chemical aftertaste of chemo. But my skin reddened and peeled in a perfect square despite having worn nothing that would create "tan lines." It itched and then hurt and then itched again as it healed. It was impossible not to think of Hiroshima or Chernobyl and to feel, once again, like the victim of a crime, yet too fortunate to complain about it. Radiation was coming at me in small, calculated doses. It most certainly hadn't melted my hometown or killed my family, and it couldn't be traced to a world war or neglectful government. I was burning and peeling because I had access to the best health- care in the world.

Despite all of this, I hadn't been looking forward to the end of treat- ment. Chemo and radiation offered me a six-month vacation from worrying about getting cancer. I'd been on active duty, inhabiting a tiny world carefully structured around doctor's appointments, and now I wondered how I would reenter civilian life. How was I sup- posed to plan vacations and work events when follow-up cancer checks stood in the middle, threatening to divide my life, *again*, into Before and After?

I was beset with the idea that Everyone Expected Me To Be

Fine now. I didn't feel fine. And in reality, no one lost much sleep over how I should be feeling one way or the other. But my internal voice always sounded like a middle school teacher's warning: *High school won't be like this. In high school you'll have no excuses. No one will baby you.*

I daydreamed about what post-treatment life would be like, even as I dreaded it. I would have hair. That was the one thing I was unabashedly excited for. I wouldn't be a true civilian ever again, but I wanted to look like one. Being bald hadn't been horrible, and maybe I'd grown fiercer as I faced down people who thought I was brave or pitiable, but the option to pass was as appealing as it was problematic.

The summer after I graduated high school, I talked to my future roommates at UCLA on the phone and dyed my hair red and lost a few pounds. My friends and I had long been making fun of Manhattan Beach's yuppie obsessions, and the idea of the big city glittered abstractly in my periphery. But I confided to my mom one morning in the Ralphs parking lot: *It feels like I have three months to live.* Then and now, my excitement was threaded with dread.

CHAPTER 25: STERILE

Dr. Yessaian was a gynecological oncologist. She was youngish with a wide, open face and dark eyes. Like my many other doctors, she never suggested that getting rid of my ovaries was optional. I knew it was the right choice, but I wanted to be reminded that it was my body, my choice, that I was going above and beyond by excising them. I wanted to be congratulated for taking a bold preventative step, not treated like a disaster site awaiting cleanup.

She told me it was probably fine to keep my uterus. *Gosh, thanks.* But first, she recommended a colonoscopy—because colon problems were linked to uterine problems, and the results of the colonoscopy would hint at whether a uterine biopsy might be in order. As far as I could tell, my colon was three degrees removed from my actual cancer. I was a BRCA2 breast cancer patient, which meant I was *at risk* for ovarian cancer, and my uterus was *near* my ovaries, and my colon was *related* to my uterus. I was all for just-in-case tests, but this seemed extreme even to me.

I asked her what the effects of going through menopause at thirty-six would be.

"Hot flashes, night sweats. Sometimes they last for a couple of months, but one patient of mine has been having them for five years. Mood changes, but some women say they feel better because they don't have premenstrual syndrome anymore."

So it was like everything: Everyone was different, no one could tell me what to expect, other than it would probably be bad. Although I did hold out a little hope that sending my estrogen levels from sixty to zero would be different from my wild fertility ride.

"Bone density issues—you should do weight-bearing exercises and take calcium and vitamin D. Lowered sex drive, vaginal dryness . . ."

I'd heard it all before, but my eyes welled up at the last symptoms. It seemed *extra* unfair to take my sex life from me. More than my boobs, more than my colon, that was private. That was personal.

"Will I still be able to have orgasms?"

"Of course. You'll still be a sexual person."

She stuck a finger up my vagina and one up my ass and said things felt okay.

The world of babies, sex, and tampons was Not For Me now. It felt like a violation, I told my therapist.

"It is," he said. "When you have surgery, they literally strap you down. And your body doesn't know the difference between a violation that's for your own good and one that's not. Little kids howl when they get shots, for good reason."

My poor ovaries. They never did anything but work hard for me. I wished I could keep them in a little jar, like my great-grandmother had allegedly done with her fingernails. The museum of lost body parts. The things you try to keep when you barely escape "the Indians." (There was another family story, about my great-grandmother hiding under her covered wagon when the local Native American tribe attacked.) When you're brave and stupid enough to think the Wild West belongs to you.

The summer after fifth grade, I was more than five feet tall and had tipped past one hundred pounds. My best friend, Bonnie, was short, eighty pounds, blond, and confident. My mom had gotten her period in fourth grade, so she had made sure to provide the birds-and-bees basics early. When I was in third grade, she'd started asking me if I wanted a bra. My answer was a shudder of humiliation.

She plied me with YA books about girls going through puberty, but the protagonists, like Margaret in *Are You There, God?*, were usually flat-chested and sweet, praying to get their periods and become women. The girls with tits were bitches and sluts.

I managed to acquire tits without becoming remotely sexy, but I didn't want to become a woman anyway. Not that I wanted to be a man, either; I wanted to be a *girl*. Being a kid meant that, when I achieved something, I could be a prodigy. Being a girl also meant not having to date.

That summer, I went on vacation with my family and got sick, as I always did the minute school was out. I sat on the mustard-yellow plastic toilet in our mustard-yellow plastic bathroom and moaned as my dad drove the motorhome. My stomach had been cramping for a while, but now there was a small streak of red in my underwear. I called out to my mom. It had been years since I'd undressed in front of either of my parents, but in moments of crisis, I could still hand my body over to her.

She gave me a thick pad to use as the motorhome rumbled forward. It was one of hers, not the purple-wrapped Always for

Teens I would use later. It was bulky to straddle, certainly not something you could forget about.

"Do I have to wear it at night?" I asked. It seemed like your period should stop at night, the way other activities did. It seemed to me there should be rules, based on what was fair and not fair.

Wearing the bulky pad, I sat between my parents in the cab of the motorhome. My dad drove and my mom sat in the passenger seat.

"I can't do gymnastics anymore," I sobbed.

"Of course you can," my mom said.

But I knew what gymnasts were supposed to look like: small, muscular girls who didn't need to wear bras beneath their leotards, who didn't worry that their leotards would get pulled to one side on the uneven bars and reveal pubic hair. Already I was not one of them.

I dreaded getting home from that trip, because that meant telling Bonnie. *Not* telling Bonnie wasn't an option. All the YA books said you weren't supposed to have secrets from your best friend. All the slumber party discussions revolved around who had pubes or not. Truth or Dare always involved getting naked.

"I have something gross to tell you," I said. "Like, really gross."

Second Street, where Bonnie lived, cut east-west across a north-south hill. We walked past retaining walls and mounds of ice plant.

"I started my period," I said.

"That's not gross," she said. I don't know what I'd expected her to say—*Ick? We're not friends anymore?*—but I hadn't for a minute contemplated that she could be so charitable. Relief flooded over me.

Eventually the other girls got their periods. Eventually they grew boobs. I stopped feeling like I had a freakish body and believed instead that I had a fat one. I started feeling like a freak for other reasons—because I'd never kissed a guy, because I wondered if I liked girls.

I'd been hoping to do both surgeries at once: implant exchange and oophorectomy (a squirmy word like *lobotomy*). At first Dr. Yessaian said fine, no big deal, but then she learned I might be doing a latissimus dorsi flap procedure—one of the more complex reconstruction options—and said, "It could work, but that's a real surgery. And some doctors don't like anything associated with the dirty vagina to get near their pristine environment."

There was always a new depressing fact to get used to, and when I thought about going to sleep with ovaries and waking up in menopause, I wanted to scream. Grieving had become part of my daily to-do list, as routine and annoying as putting gas in my car.

What body part would I lose today? What plans would evaporate? In what new ways could I feel like an ugly sixth-grader with tits and terrible hair and bloody underwear in a room full of sleek gymnasts?

We told our adoption agency we wanted to start the adoption process again. Before they would repost our profile, they asked for a letter about my health status. Dr. Chung wrote: *While this diagnosis certainly increases the chances of death, I'm hopeful and confident that Cheryl will continue to do well.* That summed up the mindfuck I'd be living with for the next five years. Or more. Or less.

The letter talked about how well I'd handled treatment. I'd been both compliant and strong. It said that, based on my stage, my chances of long-term survival were seventy to eighty percent. I'd thought they were eighty to ninety percent, based on what Dr. Chen said in my first meeting with her. Eighty percent because I was stage II, ninety percent because I'd done radiation. But seventy percent? That was one in three people like me dead within five years.

How was I supposed to just go through the day knowing that? How was I supposed to walk into my office and care about issuing fifty-dollar grants when the only logical things to do, it seemed, were to kill myself now or steal a baby so it could love me for a minute before I keeled over?

I recited reasons I wouldn't be in the unlucky twenty to thirty percent of stage IIB patients. That group would include people with non-hormone-positive cancers, people who received less treatment, people who didn't exercise and eat right, old people who died of other things, and people who were diagnosed ten years ago when treatment was less advanced. I felt like I was elbowing them aside in my rush to escape a burning building.

I pushed and called and emailed and forced my doctors to talk to each other, and eventually pulled off the not-small feat of scheduling my two surgeries for one day. Dr. Lehfeldt decided I had enough extra skin from my previous boobs, which apparently he'd tucked away like pants hemmed for a growing child, that I could skip the lat flap procedure and get regular old silicone implants.

The night before my surgery, I got a call from Ana in Dr. Yessaian's office.

"I'm calling because you need to sign your consent forms, acknowledging that this procedure will make you sterile."

The word was barely out of her mouth when I said, "Oh, trust me, I know." As if the real point were my knowing. "I was going to sign the forms at my pre-op, but there was some kind of mix-up with the faxes, so the nurse said I could sign them the morning of my surgery."

"But I don't want you to run into any trouble at the hospital," she said. "Could I email it to you now?"

"I don't have a scanner at home."

"Can you drive over to our office and sign them?" she asked.

"I *could*, but why can't I just sign them tomorrow morning?"

"You need a signature seventy-two hours in advance for sterilization," she said.

Recently, there'd been a news story about the coercive sterilization of female inmates. In the wake of eugenicist rulings like 1927's Buck v. Bell decision—laws to wipe the "feeble-minded" off the earth—it had become illegal to sterilize inmates unless "medically necessary." It seemed that, now, doctors had colluded with patients—often women who'd just given birth—to fudge medical necessity. It was hard to say whether the women had really wanted not to have any more kids, or whether the doctors saw them as feeble-minded welfare queens. It was hard to say whether the doctors thought they were doing the women a favor, or society.

And now I was caught up in these laws. I had to assert that this procedure was entirely voluntary, even though it felt anything but.

"Well, even if I sign tonight, it won't be seventy-two hours," I said. My voice was rising, shaking. I wanted to yell at someone for taking my last little shred of fertility and youth, and it looked like Ana drew the short straw. "Look, I'm already mad that I'm having this surgery. I don't want to be sterilized. I don't want to jump through any more hoops than I have to."

"I understand," she said, putting on her Dealing With A Difficult Patient voice. "I guess I can call the hospital."

Ana called back a few minutes later. "I talked to the hospital. You don't need to do the seventy-two hours thing, because you're not doing this for sterilization, but to prevent ovarian cancer."

This was very theater-of-the-absurd. "But the result is the same."

"Right, but the reason is different."

I decided I liked knowing that somewhere there was a piece of paper saying that "they"—I imagined a stern-faced committee of Nazi doctors and eugenics proponents—were trying to save me from cancer, not prevent me from reproducing. I wanted it on record that

I did not want to be sterilized, because it was too easy for me, in all my queerness and defectiveness, to believe that others did.

I asked CC to pick up pads and Jell-O on her way home. Buying pads for my last period ever was too depressing. Vons was out of Jell-O, and I was supposed to be eating nothing but clear liquids. I felt sorry for myself, and CC was so upset that she hadn't gotten me the one thing I needed that she pounded on the bed with her fists.

Thursday morning, my dad and sister beat us to the hospital by twenty minutes. My dad was having a nice chat with the woman processing my co-pay, which he paid, which I didn't try to stop him from paying. He told her she was very professional. She said she loved her job. I was glad he didn't seem as stressed out as he'd been last time, but I was in no mood.

Huntington was a huge peach building spanning a block, with a turnaround island and two towers connected by a footbridge over the entrance. An easel held a sign listing maternity ward visiting hours. A promotional photo showed a new dad cuddling a dark-haired baby.

Someday, I thought, maybe, *maybe* we would be here—or at another hospital—to visit our baby and their birthmother. That was the closest we'd get to that sign being relevant to us. Today, it was cruel.

I sat quietly with CC in the little room where they did my pre-op stuff. A blond, middle-aged nurse named Becky asked me to pee in a cup so they could make sure I wasn't pregnant.

"Is there something I can sign instead?" I asked.

"I think so, but I'll have to ask your doctors. They might refuse to do the surgery."

"I mean, I'll do it if I have to, but I'd rather sign something."

CC piped up. I sort of wanted to give my spiel, but it was also really lovely to see CC so supportive of my little symbolic protest.

"Just to clarify," CC said to Becky, "would they say she has to take a pregnancy test *or else* they'll cancel the surgery? Or would they just cancel it without even giving her the chance to do it after all?"

"I'm just saying I've seen it happen," Becky said. She had a Midwestern accent, the type of voice that had both apology and toughness built into it.

"So they might be divas?" CC said, incredulous. "They might just be like, *No, I can't!*"

"Here's the thing," I said, as calmly as possible. "I haven't had my period since the chemo. My partner is a woman. And I'm here to have a procedure that ensures I will never, ever, ever get pregnant. It just seems kind of cruel to take a pregnancy test. And I'll do it if I have to, but just as, like, a symbolic thing, I'd rather not."

Becky tried to explain lawsuit culture: "It's just that, if they did the D&C, and they found something—"

"They would be finding a miracle Jesus baby," I said, and Becky seemed to like that phrase.

The anesthesiologist, a good-looking gray-haired guy named Dr. Yarian, came in and explained lawsuit culture to me. He was cheerful, with what CC described as a cocky-pilot vibe.

And I could hear it from him, sort of. At least he wasn't the one who would actually be taking my ovaries. So I peed in the fucking cup.

Dr. Yessaian came in, also cheery and animated, wearing stylish drapey clothes and a chunky silver pendant around her neck.

She, apparently, had also been assigned to explain lawsuit culture to me.

"So much paperwork," she said, flipping through my binder.

"For a fifteen-minute procedure, there is an hour of paperwork. You know, other countries don't have consent like we do. Where I used to practice, twenty years ago, you just trusted that the doctor would do what they thought was best."

"Where did you practice?" I had a hunch since I'd looked her up online.

"Baghdad," she said. "And granted, it was a very backward system. The only consent they had was for hysterectomy and tubal ligation. But then it wasn't even the woman who had to give consent—it was her husband."

So yes, it could be worse. A lot worse. I could be a woman in Iraq being sterilized for whatever reason my husband saw fit.

And yet.

We also saw Dr. Lehfeldt, my plastic surgeon, during this time, in his fitted greige suit and butter-yellow tie. He gave us hugs and drew some tribal-looking sketch marks on me with his purple Sharpie. I remembered that I was here for a fun reason, too.

And then they gave me the good drugs—the moment I'd been waiting for, that rush of heavy warmth, and it wasn't till I woke up that I remembered how crappy coming out of anesthesia could be. For the next few hours, I puked and woke up and fell asleep and puked and woke up and tried to listen to instructions from a tough nurse named Rose, who had heavy eyeliner and long nails and scolded me for being fidgety but clearly knew her shit.

I ate saltines and drank 7Up and thought vaguely about how I was supposed to stay away from soda and simple carbs. The crackers were dry in my mouth. I wasn't chewing them in a ladylike way, and it seemed that every time someone came in the room, I was puking into those little blue vacuum cleaner-style bags.

Rose said the anesthetic was probably out of my system, and

now it was the synthetic morphine pain meds that were making me sick. Best to get home, eat something, and take a Percocet for pain, she said.

So I pulled on my sweats and button-down plaid shirt and told my dad to stop asking questions CC had already asked. I grabbed a blue bag and climbed into the wheelchair that appeared before me, and it felt like we were in an action movie, where the patient has to be whisked away, although we were probably bumping along quietly.

I sat there in the lobby with the maternity ward sign and puked some more, trying to hide my face from anyone who didn't want to see someone puke in the lobby, which would be everyone.

But I'd done it. I'd finished active cancer treatment and reconstruction. I'd dealt with my troubling genes and landed on the other side of menopause. And my boobs looked great.

PART III

CHAPTER 26: HOME

Poets & Writers gave me the gift of space, literally and figuratively. Sometimes when Jamie was working from home, I locked the door at P&W, balled my jacket into a pillow, stretched out on the rough institutional carpeting, and slept hard enough to dream. The work I did was easy and administrative, or amorphous and optional ("outreach"). In my ample downtime, I sent stories to literary journals, updated my blog, read poems, and made fashion collages online.

In the evenings, I went to readings that P&W sponsored, drank wine from flimsy plastic cups, and bought books I would never read. I got to roll in late the next day because P&W believed in comp time.

I knew how good I had it—working at whatever pace suited me, answering to a boss who never demanded more than a weekly phone call, assuring him that everything was going smoothly. What I only half knew was that, for eleven years, I was getting daily validation that writing was not just a reasonable but a *noble* use of my time. As much as my mom had initiated me into a world of words, I'd also been raised by people who believed in productivity and utility, in saving dessert for retirement. If the puzzle pieces had been arranged differently, I could be one of those people I sometimes met in the workshops for seniors that P&W sponsored: the ones who'd "always wanted" to write, but never found the time or confidence. Somehow, my mom and grad school and P&W had conspired to trick my brain into believing that writing *was* productive and useful.

As my doubts about the reach of storytelling, at least *my* storytelling, have increased, so has my confidence that it has saved my life. This is the clarifying nature of middle age, I suppose.

At P&W, I enjoyed a director title, meetings with my favorite writers, and long lunches in the courtyard of the church next door, where I punched that log. But I was increasingly bored and angst-ridden, sick of having only one coworker, and unconvinced that a cushy job was the same as a satisfying one.

When I saw a job listing for a grants manager at Homeboy Industries, I remembered the book we'd read by Father Greg Boyle, his interview with *Fresh Air* host Terry Gross about his own cancer diagnosis (the gist: "I'm too busy caring about homies to care about cancer, but yeah, I'd like to get better. Who wouldn't?"). So I applied.

I know now what I was looking for: Instead of a boss who demanded little but didn't want to hear anything negative, instead of a coworker who recoiled politely when I talked about cancer or my relationship or my fucked-up ovaries, I wanted to be surrounded by other people who'd fallen apart and picked themselves up again and were both better and worse for it.

I did a preliminary phone interview with Jacki, the chief development officer, in the stairwell of P&W, my voice echoing against the tile. I barely knew what to ask, but I must have said something about work culture, because she said, "Well, I don't want to say that we don't have *boundaries,* but the homies are kind of all up in each other's business, and that filters up. It's a busy and boisterous place."

It was a red flag. It was also exactly what I wanted.

I interviewed in person a week later. I met Jacki at Homegirl Café, where I made a show of being unfazed by the face tattoos on the people serving up scones.

"Ugh, I hate this part," Jacki said of interviewing in general. I appreciated her candor. She did not seem like the kind of person who would just sigh quietly when things got hard.

We slid into a booth, and I wrapped my hands around a ceramic mug and talked about implementing a new database at Poets & Writers. Soon we were joined by Tom, the CEO, a breezy white guy. They asked me to talk about "a time I'd handled a stressful situation."

There was so little stress at Poets & Writers. Should I talk about how we sometimes lost power when the acupuncturist next door ran too many space heaters? About the stress of constantly being surrounded by writers who were more successful than me?

"This one comes from my personal life," I ventured, "but I recently went through treatment for breast cancer. That was stressful. But I kept working the whole time. I just took some sick days for chemo."

They both nodded in appreciation. Their faces said: *Yep, that sounds stressful.* Their faces did not say: *Holy hell, why are you saying that in a job interview, you unprofessional over-sharer?* Their faces did not say: *How horrific! You poor thing, you're going to die. Sorry, but we can't possibly invest in you.*

Our waitress moseyed up, a tall Black woman with a waist apron, a badge that said *Ta'lia,* and eyes that kept darting to other parts of the café.

"Hey y'all, what do y'all want today?" Half warmth, half apathy.

"Nothing for me, I've got to get to another meeting," Tom said. "Nice to meet you, Cheryl."

"Can I get a blueberry scone and scrambled egg whites?" Jacki said. "Ta'lia, how've you been? How are your boys?"

"They good. Anthony started high school."

"No! Oh my god. He was this big last time he was here. Can you believe my oldest is in middle school already? Look—" she pulled out her phone "—he's got *peach fuzz*."

"What do you want?" Ta'lia asked me.

"Maybe just some more coffee?"

"How's your job search going?" Jacki asked. "Has José hooked you up with any good interviews yet?"

"Nah. I thought I was gonna get this one thing at the Marriott, but it didn't work out. My eighteen months is up in two weeks. I ain't sweatin' it though."

"Ta'lia. That's just wrong. We've got to get you a job. Write down your number." Jacki shoved a paper napkin toward Ta'lia, who pulled a pen from her apron and wrote ten neat, bubbly digits.

She left and returned with a dessert we hadn't ordered, mango cornbread, sweet and sticky and crumbly. I'd just met Jacki, but we shared it with two forks.

I returned to talk to Jacki again, and Tom again, and finally Father Greg. His office was, intentionally, closest to the glass doors that opened onto Alameda Street and the Chinatown Gold Line stop. The walls were covered with jailhouse art and photos of clients and old friends from the neighborhood. Some dated back to the nineties: overexposed snapshots of young Latino men in enormous white T-shirts, bandanas wrapped around their heads, tattoos on their arms, chests, stomachs, faces. None of them smiled. There were also

Sears-style portraits of families and babies, all smiling. War and peace.

Gang violence in Los Angeles and across the country peaked in the eighties and nineties. In the Boyle Heights housing project where Father Greg first gained notoriety as the young priest who would ride his bicycle into the middle of shoot-outs, there were four gangs. Things had settled down considerably since that time. Depending on whom you listened to, it was the result of a better economy, zero-tolerance policing, empathetic community policing, the outlawing of lead paint, or Father Greg. Homies filled the chairs in the lobby every time Father Greg was in his office, and multiple generations of gang-war vets wandered around with PTSD.

I sat across from Father Greg, who resembled a business-casual Santa Claus. On the train ride over, I'd imagined saying all the things I couldn't possibly say in a job interview, about cancer and soul-searching and God. About a grief and anger so wrenching it could only emerge as violence.

"I'm a little star-struck," I said.

I don't remember much about what we actually discussed. He probably asked why I wanted to work there. I repeated something I'd read recently, about how a medical model was useful for looking at trauma.

"Right," he said, agreeing, but a bit tired. "Hurt people hurt people."

I was in his office less than fifteen minutes. He had a unique ability to be uncannily present, to make you feel like he *saw* you, while also rushing you out the door. But I guess whatever I said was okay—or maybe I just didn't set off any alarm bells by talking about wanting to save people—because I was hired.

In the mornings, I stepped off the train at the elevated Chinatown stop, a skeletal pagoda in the sky, and saw the homies gathered.

Trainees in official organizational parlance, *homies* unofficially. They wore gray and blue and Homeboy T-shirts. They smoked and talked in the cool mornings. Maybe they were anxious to leave wherever they were leaving, or anxious to prove they knew how to show up for a job early. Or maybe this was where their new homies were, the ones who Got It.

Trauma colored everything at Homeboy. Each morning opened with a Thought of the Day: Case Manager Natalie on hoping to get her children back, Café Manager Arlin on fucking up and moving on. Staff, trainees, tattoo removal clients, and visiting school and church groups packed the lobby and lined the stairwell.

One morning, a woman named Esther asked people to pray for her. I'd already felt a shy affinity toward Esther, who had a job that involved sitting at a desk at the top of the stairs. She was wide and butch, with hair slicked into a braided ponytail. She told me I had a nice smile. This morning she said her sister's cancer had spread, her voice breaking.

After Morning Meeting, there was a small line to hug her, and I waited patiently behind a white woman in a purple sweater. I felt my own excitement—I wouldn't have known how to comfort a homie whose friend had been shot, but I knew cancer, even as I knew that cancer, like everything, was made worse by poverty. Still, I could say with confidence, "I went through that last year, and I know how hard it is on your sister and on you and your family."

My Story glided right over Esther, but she opened up to me and the woman in the purple sweater. "They took a big tumor out already," she said, gesturing vaguely to her abdomen. I said a silent thanks that it wasn't a case of breast cancer spreading. "But then I guess it went to her lymph nodes, and now her liver and back. The doctor is worried because she's lost a lot of weight, and he thinks maybe it's because the cancer is taking over. My sister is so strong, though, and she's gonna fight this thing."

I didn't know whether that meant Esther didn't understand her sister's prognosis or was in denial about it. Or maybe this was one of those transcendent things that the non-traumatized couldn't fathom: that you could simultaneously accept and fight death. That you could fight for each moment to matter.

I went upstairs to the tiny office I shared with Jacki and Lauren, a tall divinity student who nominally worked in fundraising but spent most of her time counseling trainees. I cried a little bit. I thought, *I'm sorry, I'm sorry,* which was what I always thought when I was really sad in a way that went beyond logic.

One of the GED tutors popped her head in and asked if I was okay.

"Just . . . Esther's story," I said.

"Esther," she nodded. She asked me about getting funding for iPads, since the GED had recently moved online. Trauma one moment, business the next. It made perfect sense to me. The *most* sense.

There was an Excel grant calendar that my predecessor—who'd left for the quieter, stuffier office of UCLA's fundraising department—had carefully maintained. Jacki quickly got me working on a proposal to The California Endowment, I updated a website called Global Giving, and I felt good about my first week. The calendar listed a handful of deadlines that fell between my start date (January 7) and the day of my work-plan meeting with Jacki (January 16). I wanted to ask her about them, but she was always running out the door or shouting into her iPhone at one of her kids.

No one really expected me to write four or five grants during my first two and a half days on the job, right?

Jacki did, as it turned out.

"This is a fire," she said. "Something you have to fix right now." Actual fires were burning all around Los Angeles in our oddly dry January, turning the skies a stunning ombre orange and everyone's lungs asthmatic. This was not a fire. This was not cancer.

Twenty-four hours after our work-plan conversation, I'd drafted a Nathan Cummings Foundation proposal, done damage control with four funders, and gathered the information I needed to write an overdue report to some rich people. When I gave Jacki a quick breakdown of my plan and priorities, she seemed mildly impressed, and I felt good.

I went on to work at Homeboy Industries for almost four years. It was a place where, if I needed to collapse in panicked tears three days before a cancer check-up, there was a row of therapists' offices with open doors. It was also a place of chaos and bluster, where one nerdy white girl's opinions got crushed beneath the politics of bigger personalities. Two years in, I burned out on Jacki once and for all when she fired a hardworking member of our department to save her own skin in the eyes of two meddling donors. I nursed a theory that, in the same way that people start to resemble their pets, nonprofits look like their clients. Homeboy was too crisis-ridden to believe in a real future and never saved its money for one. It simultaneously fronted like a prisoner at a parole hearing and, like that same prisoner, secretly believed it was worthless. The truth was neither. It was fine and flawed. It was exactly what it seemed those first frenetic weeks. It was exactly what I needed, until it wasn't.

CHAPTER 27: MAKING PROGRESS

I was in my second year at Homeboy industries when, four days before my thirty-seventh birthday, I opened our adoption Gmail inbox to this:

Hello Cecilia and Cheryl. This is a relatively new idea for me so I am in no way decided on adoption unless I find a perfect fit. Your profile stood out for many reasons tho. I love the diversity and openness of your family. Also the positive things you are doing for people who have made some not so great choices in life touches a special place in my heart. About me: I am a mother of three who is leaving an abusive relationship. In that process of being stalked, left on the streets with me and my kids, I had to ask for help from my ex's parents. Due to refusing to be with him when he got out of jail I am no longer allowed to see my children. I am currently going through the process of becoming independent and starting over from scratch. The pregnancy: This baby was planned with a man I met at a time that I was weak and missing my babies. The father is in jail and will be there for a long time. I am currently 24 weeks along. He or she will be a mix of half Ukrainian (me), half Hispanic (father). Why adoption: This choice is a new thought and I have not been able to shake the feeling that as a mother, who is having a hard enough time with the babies I currently have, bringing another into a VERY unstable environment may not be the best choice. I've had to give up my children (who I raised day in day out) once in the past. I promised them I would bring them home. That is something I do not feel I will be able to do while taking care of a newborn. I do however feel the right thing for this child may be parents who will be able to provide a loving environment from the get go. This is not a choice I am embarrassed of or feel that the child should not know about. I just know that I have NO help or support and what kind of mother is okay with her baby struggling day in day out. This kind of sums things up although I am sure you have a ton of questions if you're interested in getting to know more. Like I said this is the first time I am responding or talking to anyone regarding this. Hope to hear back from you and I wish you both the best in fulfilling your dream of starting a family. A child would be blessed to have such amazing parents. —Anya

It was the first time a birth mom had actually referenced something about our profile—and the thing she'd responded to was the truest, most intimate thing I'd written, the part that alluded to my own brokenness and my faith in faith itself. Even more than with effusive, bipolar Crystal, I thought, *Yes, she's the one.*

Her email seemed so open and honest that I wanted to respond to her in kind. *Fuck the rules,* I thought. I gave her a piece of my heart and my story immediately.

Hi Anya,

Thank you so much for your email. CC and I (Cheryl writing here) were very moved by your story, and by your commitment to your three children. The choices you've made for your own safety and theirs sound incredibly difficult, but also like the right and necessary thing to do. We also really admire how much you want a safe and stable home for your baby-on-the-way.

I appreciate your honesty in letting us know that adoption is a new idea; it's a big choice, and one you shouldn't rush. We're working with a really great organization called the Independent Adoption Center (IAC), which helps pair birth moms and adoptive parents, and provides counseling for both. They've supported us through all the ups and downs that come with being a hopeful adoptive parent, and I know they do the same for birth moms—they're very no-pressure, and they understand that the decision to place your baby takes time.

If you can tell me where you live, I can pass along the phone number of the closest IAC office.

We would love to get to know more about you—your life, your kids, your hopes for starting an independent life. (Kudos to you for making that step—I'm sure it's unimaginably hard, but all the challenges you're going through will pay off.) As for us, we've had our own challenges. We always wanted to adopt, but we both also tried to get pregnant for a while, and I had a miscarriage that we grieved really hard. In 2012 I was diagnosed with breast cancer, which was another big hurdle. Luckily, they caught it early and I'm in very good health now, but it was scary. I'm sharing these things because I sense that you understand firsthand how difficult life experiences can actually make you a stronger person.

I hope you'll let us know any other questions that are on your mind, about us, the open adoption process, or anything else at all. CC is Mexican and my background is Eastern European (mostly Latvian), so even though we're open to all ethnicities, it sounds like your baby would blend perfectly in our little family. We chose open adoption so that our child could know his or her birth mom and be proud of the choice she made.

Thank you again, and we look forward to getting to know you! (You can email, or also call or text us.)

Warmly,

Cheryl and CC

CC and I shared a quick *yay!* and she left for work. It was Cesar Chavez Day, and an ironic furlough day for Homeboy, which was always in some stage of a budget crisis. I hiked off my nervous energy at Occidental College. If you followed a skinny path along the ridge of a hill behind the Environmental Studies building, you could see most of the city: the stripe of the Ventura Freeway that bisected the San Gabriel mountains, the cluster of skyscrapers downtown, the ribbon of brown smog at the base of the blue horizon.

I let myself daydream. I knew, now, that telling myself not to get my hopes up just meant I would yell self-defeating things at myself inside my head while still getting my hopes up. Better to spiral into fantasy and pick up the pieces after my heart broke. I imagined our baby born a month after Jamie's second and Piper and Lindy's first, and the close friendships we'd develop because of it. We would run into Justine and Sam eventually, and they'd see how perfectly imperfect I was, the Relaxed Mom Who Knew The Truth About Love And Loss.

And then a day passed, and I knew the truth, that we weren't going to hear from Anya again. She'd responded to our story with her story, which was a beautiful moment of connection, but it wasn't the same as wanting us to adopt her baby.

If you only knew, I said in my head, a silent prayer to the struggling birth moms of the world. *If you only knew what you do to us, how much you hurt us.*

I tried blaming myself for disclosing the cancer thing, but my heart wasn't in it. Self-blame was as narcissistic as it was tempting. This was about Anya and her kids and her baby, and I was just a blip, an idea she had that had passed or been eclipsed by the various emergencies of her life.

CC, who was usually reluctant to try to fill my bottomless need for reassurance, said, "Don't blame yourself. You're a good writer, and that was a nice reply. Whatever you said about cancer isn't going to make us or break us."

The moms in my online adoption support group said hush, twenty-four hours is nothing, she's in crisis. But another twenty-four hours passed, and another. I turned thirty-seven childless, cursing myself for thinking this way. I'd spent birthdays thirteen through twenty-two feeling self-conscious about my lack of a boyfriend and sexual experience. And eventually I'd gotten a boyfriend and then a girlfriend and plenty of sexual experience, and all that worry seemed like a waste. I caught up. So what if our kid was six or seven years younger than our friends' kids? Would that be such a tragedy? We'd make new friends. We'd have a different story in some ways, the same story in others.

The less optimistic part of me thought the next exam would reveal cancer, that I'd spend the last six or seven years of my life acutely aware of what I didn't have, wrestling hard to love my life anyway, arriving there eventually and yay, woo-hoo, what a triumph. I would sit in a hospital bed holding the hard-won wisdom that would be my sad little consolation prize.

These competing narratives spent their days wrestling in my head and stomach, teetering one way or the other based on stupid things like whether I've had coffee yet or how many grant deadlines lay in front of me or what someone said on the internet. This seemed like the truth of thirty-seven: You know how meaningless and arbitrary it all is, and you have to do your best to keep going anyway.

Easter arrived, that time of eggs and miracles. Cathy and I argued on the phone about how often I opted out of going to Grandma Jac's for holidays; for once, I felt the weight she carried as the younger sibling. If it was the oldest kid's job to forge ahead in the world all alone, it was the youngest's job to hold the pieces of the family as it was.

My cancer check-up loomed like an enemy ship on the horizon, closer and closer until it passed. It was my third check-up since finishing treatment, and a pattern was emerging. I would successfully refrain from falling into acute anxiety—which I defined as a fluttering in my chest and a flirtation with Google—until a few days before my appointment, at which point I would succumb to the evil sirens of the internet, look for reassuring statistics, find the opposite, and fall into a pit of tears and terror. Then Dr. Chung would breeze into the exam room saying, "Your blood work is fine. How's it going with the medication?" and I would ride that high for days before returning to the world of the mundane. The world of the mundane was also the world of the living. Here, I would get annoyed about office politics and traffic, but I also ran full force into life. I hadn't found a cure for my anxiety, but maybe I didn't need to. Maybe I just needed to make the most of the space in between flare-ups, like a suspension bridge over deep water.

In May, Elena told CC she was pregnant. She and Brian had been trying since getting married in a tiny ceremony at park in Orange, right before I shipped off to MacDowell. Elena hadn't been hopeful. She and her ex had tried to get pregnant, with no luck. Now she was thirty-nine, and the fertility specialist she saw had been discouraging. They signed on with IAC and plugged away at their home study. But she had the advantage that all straight, marginally fertile couples had: free sperm and endless chances. They'd been vacationing in the sequoias when she started feeling sick. They made a detour to a Kaiser, where a doctor confirmed her good news.

I told my adoption Facebook group:

> My sister-in-law is pregnant. She's been trying for a while, and they had actually signed up with our same adoption agency. She knows and partially shares our story, so she's being super nice about it, and eventually it will be cool to finally be an aunt. But the feelings of When Is It Our Turn are louder than ever. We've been in this game (pregnancy attempts + adoption attempts) for four years. We've been proactive, we've worked on our relationship, we've tried to stay in the present and be grateful for all the great people and opportunities in our lives. But lately every day is a struggle against hopelessness.
>
> It wasn't easy for my SIL, so I'm closer to being happy for her than for most people. But in a way, it also makes me sadder— it's taken us so long that even people who've had a hard time are finally pregnant, and even people who had to wait a long time to adopt have adopted.

It was a zealously supportive group of people who were all a little crazy in their own ways; who, like everyone at Homeboy, were not scared of a little drama. Robin had adopted the daughter of her son (also adopted), who had something like nine children with nine women, all of whom he'd abandoned. Allie had a ten-year-old biological daughter and four kids between the ages of three and five, whom she'd adopted from foster care. She added to her brood whenever the biological siblings of one of her kids needed a home, temporary or permanent. Katie had adopted Native American sisters who were related to one of Allie's kids. The two families met up for vacations and rez visits. Kristina was a fierce, gun-toting Alabaman who had almost killed herself when she'd been required to return a baby to foster care. Now, after swearing off adoption for a bit, she was in talks with a wildly unstable birth mom.

Just keep swimming, they told me. Your turn *will* come, they told me. We'll pray for you, they told me. There were plenty of people I would not have wanted to pray for me, but from these ladies, it felt like being held by a dozen warm hands.

Elena, I knew, would understand if I couldn't be happy for her. I wasn't fond of the word *happy* as a rule, because it was so simplistic and distracting and unfair. But I wanted to feel something other than envy and resentment. So I worked it like a ball of putty in my pocket.

Of the many reasons I lost my shit when friends got pregnant, high on the list was the fact that it signaled abandonment. They turned, quickly or slowly, to the world of snuggling and sleeplessness and good reasons for wearing yoga pants. I got to keep attending poetry readings on weeknights and thinking about death.

But if a new baby was my niece or nephew, it might be different. Elena couldn't leave me. (Here, I hear my therapist's voice, reminding me how abandoned I'd felt by my mom when my sister came along. Every friend was a stand-in for my mom. Every infant was my sister.) I wouldn't be a mom, but I would have a role in their story. Part of my frustration with the process of trying to become a parent was that there was no incremental progress. Sure, I suppose you could count our home study, but we were still categorically Not

Parents. (Except that because of the Squeakies, I still felt like I was. It was a secret I carried, not entirely unlike being gay. I knew who I was, and even though the world told me I was wrong, and I took in shame by the armload, I also knew I was *right*.)

With writing, there was incremental progress. Maybe it had been years since I'd published a book, but I had essays and stories in little journals here and there to remind me that, yes, I was a writer. Even if only five or six people read my words, that was a lot more than zero. So maybe, I considered, being an aunt was the parenting equivalent of having a story run in an indie journal. Not my ultimate dream, but not nothing.

And then, just a week after learning she was pregnant, Elena started bleeding, and then she wasn't pregnant anymore. Her doctor ran tests and found a chromosomal abnormality. I thought of all those babies out there in the great wherever, with their imperfect bodies and brains, still doing their very best to grow.

She found a small wooden box and filled it with what she had: an ultrasound with the baby's presence marked by a dot, the congratulatory card we'd sent, which reached her the day before she lost the baby.

Meanwhile, CC and I were planning a trip to New Zealand. After I finished treatment, my dad encouraged us to celebrate on his dime. I had and have so many feelings about him giving me money. On one hand, I'd done nothing to earn it, and *he himself* had raised me to despise freeloaders. On the other hand, it made him happy. He desperately wanted me to be happy—that word again—and after losing both his parents and his wife too young, it was painfully clear to all of us what money couldn't buy. So if it could buy two plane tickets to New Zealand to visit our friend Emily on her year-long teaching residency, why not go?

Two days before we were scheduled to leave, we got an email from Zoey, who was thirty-one and pregnant, she said, with twins. "Twins" was on IAC's list of birth mom red flags, a way to lure hopeful adoptive parents with the promise of two-for-the-price-of-one. But if Zoey was running a scam, it fell into the very convincing, non-financial genre. I talked to her on the phone Thursday night, and it was like talking to an old friend: She was funny, straightforward, and down-to-earth. She was baffled by the behavior of her roomie at the hospital where she was on bed rest, who'd fractured her pelvis while Jet-Skiing at twenty weeks.

"Who Jet Skis when they're twenty weeks pregnant?" Zoey said.

I agreed. I didn't add that there were birth moms who did hard drugs while pregnant. Zoey was refreshingly responsible, a stay-at-home mom of two in a stable relationship who just couldn't handle two more kids.

We ended the night with a goofy text exchange about popsicles. But maybe her judgmentalness about the jet skier should have been a red flag.

Friday afternoon, I had four grant deadlines and the annual Homeboy Family Picnic before our red-eye flight. Between those tasks and texting—more small-talky, get-to-know-you stuff—I felt like I had reached Peak Adulting.

When I took a couple of hours to reply to her inquiry about my favorite movies, she texted again: *So I know I'm cranky and hormonal right now, but if you're having trouble prioritizing this conversation, I don't know how I'm supposed to think you're going to manage parenthood.*

I replied immediately, my hands shaking: *I'm so sorry! I have a ton of stuff to wrap up at work before leaving town, but that's no excuse.*

It was such a big and sudden shift that I was more surprised than devastated. The next thing I knew, we were kind of text-fighting—both of us trying to be mature and acknowledge our shortcomings, but both of us being super sensitive and continuing to engage when we should have called it a night.

Maybe the problem was that we were too much alike.

Maybe she had borderline personality disorder.

Maybe she wasn't who she said she was at all.

We left things on a conciliatory "talk after the trip" note. I told myself it was over.

And it sucked, because I had behaved so well that whole day! CC and I were communicating so excellently the whole time! I multitasked like a motherfucker (or just a mother)! Where was my gold star? Where was the person who would swoop in and take care of *me* now?

Somehow we arrived at the Tom Bradley International terminal in decent, if exhausted, shape. I shed some tears over taquitos and a michelada at Border Grill, and popped a Klonopin after boarding, but still.

We took a cab to Emily's apartment in Auckland. She and CC had known each other since early adulthood, when they lived in a tight-knit community in Lincoln Heights. Emily, who had a Japanese mother and an ex-Mormon, Swedish-American father, had earned her PhD in Japanese history just in time to enter a terrible academic job market that took her to the Washington/Idaho border. She hated the job. She hated the town.

In Auckland, we could see the happiness roll off of her—not annoying giddiness, but true, hard-won happiness. The best incarnation of that word. She dressed like an older, updated version of Daria, the angsty nineties cartoon, in jewel tones, down fitted jackets and artsy T-shirts. Her apartment was sparse but charming. A kiwi bird made from salvaged fabric perched on the back of her couch. A small tag on his gray foot said his name was Sean Finnegan.

"I can't wait to take you to my favorite food court," she said as we plunked down our suitcases next to her futon. "Not like a mall food court, it's this whole outdoor place. It's good, you'll see."

She seemed to have declared Auckland her safe space, where only good things happened. Over tapas at an outdoor table, we talked about being on the other side of trauma.

Mine was miscarriage and cancer; hers was Rachel's death. I asked Emily how, exactly, the aftermath had shaped her.

"It's a cliché," Emily said, "but it all happened so fast with Rachel, and I realized that life is way too short to spend it doing something you don't like. I didn't want to just fuck around, but I was also kind of trapped in Idaho."

A coworker who had also lost a good friend told her: "This kind of experience gives you a clarity not everyone has access to. But it fades—the challenge is to keep it close to you and let it inform your life."

So Emily had bided her time and gone to therapy and the gym, and made herself the kind of person who will be ready to take full advantage of better things when they come along. I wanted the whole baby/cancer experience to inform my life in the same way. I didn't have the luxury of dreaming my life would be perfect and waiting until then to enjoy myself. I did have the luxury of an opportunity to leave my old perfectionist thinking behind.

Emily showed us the two tattoos she'd gotten above each shoulder blade: a tiger for Rachel and a plum-colored, abstract flower, for herself.

Three days later, we rented a car and made our way, on the left side of the road, through the sheep and cattle pastures of the New Zealand countryside. From the little town of Thames, we headed into the parkland of the Coromandel Peninsula to begin a two-day backpacking trip through a ferny forest. New Zealand is famous for long hiking tracks that thread both islands. We were only doing a snippet, but it was plenty. We made our way up, up, up, taking turns wearing Emily's too-big backpack, whose straps dug into my collarbone. As we crossed skinny rope bridges, I thought of Zoey on bed rest, and how lucky we were to be able-bodied in New Zealand. It was rare that I compared myself to a pregnant woman and counted myself lucky, but that day I did.

Back in Auckland, we went to a fancy souvenir shop called Paunesia, where Emily had purchased Sean Finnegan, the vintage fabric kiwi. The woman who owned the shop talked about the stuffed kiwis as though they were her little buddies, wrapping everything in colorful tissue and stickers.

We bought a handmade bird rattle for the baby we hoped to adopt. It felt audacious. It felt like a necessary act of faith, a little totem of hope.

Our next stop was Rotorua, a spa town two hours to the south. It was an adventure hub, with all kinds of manmade joyrides to fill up your free time between nature-based adventures. We spotted ads everywhere for Zorb, a human-sized hamster ball in which to hurl oneself down a hill, and Wet Zorb, which was the aforementioned plus water. But Rotorua's main draw was its geothermal pools; the whole town smelled like sulfur, but in a comforting, spa-like way.

We unpacked at Crash Palace, our graffiti-art-decorated hostel, and went straight to the Night Market. There, a girl with a guitar played nineties songs and made me want to cry with aimless gratitude. There was manuka honey, mussel fritters, kebab, Chinese dumplings, and a "Mexican" food booth selling a dish my mom always called "chili-mac."

When we got back to Crash Palace, I hopped on the Wi-Fi and saw an email from a woman named Kay who "felt a connection" with our adoption profile—or she *had*, fifteen hours earlier, but that was a year in internet/birth mom time. I replied twice over the next two days ("We're traveling so our connection is a little spotty, and just in case you didn't get our first reply . . .") and didn't hear back.

On our last full day in New Zealand, we visited Huka Falls, a highway-wide river whose white and pale-blue rapids generated fifteen percent of the country's power. I spent most of the visit on a park bench journaling and crying because of all the baby stuff (or lack thereof) waiting for us back at home. That morning, CC and I had whisper-argued in bed at our hostel while Emily pretended not to hear us.

"I think Zoey's tactics are messed up," CC said.

"But if you hold out for the perfect birth parents, we'll never adopt," I said. "I feel like my destiny in life is to weather heartbreak."

What I meant was: That was one of the stories that my brain projected, and the film reel was getting thin from so much play. What CC said was: "That makes no sense. I feel like you're playing the victim again."

I knew she didn't see things as black-and-whitely as she once did. I knew she trusted me to bounce back, and would therefore take more risks with me. I knew that I could trust her to move on from a mood, that if I waited out her feelings and mine, we were usually okay.

But the shitty thing about adoption, and the reason I couldn't see myself as ever being polyamorous, was that it's not enough for two people to be on solid ground, to love each other and to have worked through their shit. Three or four people have to be there at the same time. And that seemed like yet another way that doing what worked for other people wasn't enough.

Back in Los Angeles, I sent Zoey a last-ditch text, tentatively proposing another phone call. *Thanks,* she replied, *but we're not interested.*

CHAPTER 28: A SUPPORTING CHARACTER

I can't necessarily recommend exposure therapy—and I am sure I don't even really understand it in a clinical sense—but it does wonders for increasing your faith in your own resilience. It reinforces the notion that "[Thing You're Scared Of] is not the end of the world, because, look, it just happened again and the world is still here, as frustrating and annoying as ever."

I was sitting cross-legged on the floor of our office talking to Chelsea, a twenty-year-old aspiring chef from Sacramento who was *one week* pregnant, when I saw another message pop up in our inbox. Somehow, Zoey had set off a Huka Falls–level cascade of expectant-mom contacts.

The new email was from Harmony, a thirty-one-year-old woman living in Houston. She'd been in the military and now worked as a nurse. She had dated a married man with no intention of leaving his wife, and now she was three months pregnant. With twins.

Here we go, I thought, but she wanted to talk, so we set up a phone call for the next day, which I took from the hallway outside my therapist's office. I stared out a tiny window at Westwood, my college stomping ground. I could see the domed Euro-Chinese restaurant that used to be The Wherehouse and the Indian restaurant that used to be the only grocery store within walking distance of campus.

Harmony was friendly, Southern, originally from Greenwood, Mississippi. CC had grown up on a Greenwood Street, and I took that as a good omen, then chastised myself for looking for omens. She didn't deliver a lot of new information, and our conversation was disjointed because of background noise on her end. But at least she was a real person.

"I keep thinking that everything happens for a reason," she said, "and maybe I'm having these babies so someone else can become a mom."

As much as I disagreed with the thesis, I desperately understood the sentiment. If there wasn't a silver lining, what was the fucking point of anything?

I gave her the number of IAC's case manager, and she said she would call. They always say they'll call.

But then she *actually did.* I said a silent prayer of gratitude for military-grade follow-through.

Bianca, a staffer at IAC's Houston office, called Wednesday morning and confirmed what we knew so far. "We just need her proof of pregnancy," Bianca said. "She said she'll ask her doctor to fax it to us at her next appointment."

Wednesday night, CC and I both spoke to Harmony on the phone. She talked breezily about her big family and her own identical twin sister, Harriet.

"I didn't know that identical twins ran in families," I said. I was suspicious. I was pretty sure they did not.

"They do," she said. "I just moved into the same building as my sister, so my niece and nephew are over all the time. I'll send you a picture."

Soon, one appeared on my phone: a car selfie of Harmony—strong cheekbones, short sculpted hair—with two elementary-school-aged kids making faces behind her.

"Y'all do Google Hangouts?"

I said I'd try to figure it out. Had she said "Y'all ever send things by carrier pigeon?" I would have rushed to a pet store.

"My brothers and sisters and I do it all the time, there'll be, like, ten of us on a call. It's so fun. Anyways, in a few weeks I'll be doing my anatomy appointment, and I'll get to find out if these babies are boys or girls. Y'all could come with me and we could set up a Google Hangout, so we could all find out at the same time."

"Oh, wow, that would be—" The words that came to mind were "boundaryless" and "presumptive." It's hard to explain, but even though I thought about babies all day every day, talking about Harmony's babies as if they would be ours was like a spell I wasn't ready to invoke. And how could she possibly want us there?

"Y'all, I'm getting so fat. And when I was working, I was working the night shift, so that's when these babies are awake. I'm like, *You throwing a party down there? 'Cause your mamas aren't going to like being up all night.*"

We joked around some more, and when we hung up, CC said, "She was so nice, but that girl cannot be serious for one minute." Later I described CC to Harmony as "a hard worker, but she always makes time to goof around and have fun." Harmony said, "like me!"

The next day, Thursday, I didn't hear anything from her. My heart sank a little. Contact from potential birth moms was a hope drug, and my tolerance was quickly building up. Now a single text didn't make my heart flutter. Now I needed a phone call or a promise. But I had been wrong to assume she didn't reach out. On Friday I belatedly saw her good-morning text from Thursday. Not only had she checked in on Thursday, she hadn't held it against us when I didn't get back to her immediately. Take that, Zoey.

Friday night she called as I was on my way to meet CC at the fingerprinting place, which would turn out to be closed. "Guess whose profile I got in the mail today?" she said.

"Um . . . ours?" As usual, the connection was a little bit bad.

"Uh-huh. You all so cute!"

"Oh, cool, did they send you a whole packet?"

"Nah. They asked me if I wanted that, but I said no." Her voice was a little dreamy.

"Oh, that's nice to hear." My voice was a little dreamy, too.

It felt like dating in this way, too: not just the rejection and the getting-to-know-you, but also the way that, after a good date, you wanted to know a second was in the offing, but not for a few days. You (or at least I) wanted to bask in the enjoyment of the first date, or that good kiss, and in knowing that you were now a Person With Someone. You were in no rush to get back to a place where you could mess it all up again, where, at the very least, you would feel nervous and pressured and stumble around for things to say.

Saturday afternoon, Harmony texted that she was going to the hospital. Her blood pressure was high. I immediately looked up preeclampsia, naturally, which I knew as the condition that Keely had had during her first two pregnancies, and which had recently killed a woman on *Downton Abbey*. The women on the Adoptive Parent Support forum—who had a habit of commenting "(((hugs!)))" and "Praying!" and did not always make me feel better—assured me that they or their children's birth moms had had preeclampsia and done fine.

The same group called me out when I asked about a polite way to tell Harmony we didn't want to "accompany" her to her twenty-week doctor's appointment.

Why not? they demanded. Sure, it might be a little intimate and feel a little risky, but turning Harmony down might hurt her feelings. She was sharing with us! That was good! That was what expectant moms who ended up placing did!

It was a little bit of a reality check. I'd genuinely kind of forgotten that friendly behavior could be something other than a birth mom exploring her options or acting out some pathology. And, the online moms said, if this leads to an adoption, you'll be glad to have been present for that moment. The moms who adopted nine-month-olds and five-year-olds said they would kill for those early ultrasounds. We decided it was a risk we could take.

"They got me hooked up to two fetal heart monitors," Harmony said. "Wires everywhere. But I'm doing okay. They gonna put me on some medication."

She checked out of the hospital later that day, and returned a day later, where she tried to video chat us. We caught flashes of a tile wall and Harmony's body, and then the picture broke into choppy rectangles.

What's up? I texted after. *Is everything okay?*

This time I'm here with my nephew, she replied. *He jumped off his bike like a fool and broke his leg.*

Oh no! I replied. But I was hugely relieved. I'd never been so happy to hear a child had broken a bone. *Well . . . better his leg than his head, right?*

He act like he broke his head.

I typed *lol* and did, in fact, laugh out loud. I let myself start thinking of baby names.

And then we didn't hear from her for a few days. Had she flaked like the others? She had been in the *military*, I reminded myself. She'd been to Iraq and sewn up bleeding soldiers. She had been trained to face things head on.

If she hadn't flaked, if she wasn't busy denying her pregnancy, was it something more catastrophic? What if her blood pressure had shot up again? What if she was in the hospital? What if she'd lost the babies? At work, I tried to focus on a social enterprise grant. I needed to save up whatever crisis capital I'd accrued for a possible preemie birth. Or for mourning.

I googled thunderstorms and power outages in Dallas. She'd mentioned summer storms. She'd mentioned going to Dave & Buster's, so I located the Dallas one to try to figure out what part of the city she was in, and if it was near any of the flagged spots on the power outage map. It seemed like such a sad long shot, the equivalent of a stood-up girl checking her phone for a dial tone. I wanted to hold my tongue, but I told the women of the Adoptive Parent Support group. They freaked out every time one of their kids back-talked or didn't grow the right amount of teeth at the right time. They would understand. And they did. They had stories of birth moms who'd fled from them in parking lots or not called for three weeks.

But the morning of her twenty-week anatomy appointment, as Fabian was reading off the day's twelve-step meetings at Morning Meeting, my phone lit up.

"How you doing?" Harmony asked, as if no time had passed. So I pretended it hadn't. I couldn't exactly say, *I'm freaking out because your communication doesn't follow the clear pattern that would put my mind at ease.*

"How are *you?*" I made my way to the stairwell everyone laughingly referred to as "Gervaise's office" because he didn't have one.

"I'm okay. My doctor's running late. I'll call you when he gets here, 'kay?"

"Okay. Thanks for checking in." *Thanks for giving me a reason to live.*

At 9:30 a.m., I was sitting on the floor of the creative writing class I led at Homeboy, trying to write to the day's prompt. I always wrote along with the students. I often read what I wrote out loud. In the code of Homeboy, it wasn't centering myself; it was being vulnerable so they could be, too. They all knew I was trying to adopt. I secretly daydreamed that one of them would take me aside and confess that she was pregnant and looking for someone to raise her baby. Adopting really was like dating: The One might be in any room full of new people (but usually wasn't). It was such a blatantly opportunistic and borderline predatory fantasy that I didn't dare take the smallest step—and I wasn't even sure what such a step would be—to act on it. So I felt less guilty than I might have otherwise.

A green bubble popped up on my phone: *two girls!! CONGRATULATIONS.*

Congratulations to all of us!! I replied.

Then I texted CC She replied with a thought I had not forgotten: *Remember that movie we saw,* Brothers? *I always think of those little girls and how cute they were.*

I called Harmony after class. She talked about us visiting in October for her birthday (and her twin, Harriet's). She talked about all the food her mother would cook us. I thought I might take a vacation from vegetarianism, I was so grateful to Harmony's mom—a woman who, oh, by the way, was "very open-minded" and had two gay daughters and one gay son. I glowed and bounced through the day. I made lists of girls' names. I let the Adoptive Parent Support moms congratulate me and assure me that "African-American female preemies" had the best chances, if it came to that. I told them that congrats were premature, so to speak, but if anyone knew how things could change on a dime, it was them.

When Harmony was five months pregnant, her aunt passed away. Breast cancer. The whole family would be coming out to Los Angeles for the funeral. "We could all visit you," Harmony said. Plans like this felt impossible to take in, like trying to understand the Earth's roundness by watching the sun sink into the ocean. Meanwhile, Harmony and CC texted about a meme that seemed to be making the rounds on Black social media. In the meme, Kermit the Frog drank Lipton tea and made side-of-his-mouth comments about people taking welfare checks out of Gucci purses or having too many babies by too many men. Things that white people definitely, definitely couldn't say.

"A lot of them are about pregnancy," CC said. "I think Harmony's working some stuff out."

On Friday, CC and I walked around Highland Park feeling floaty and coming up with names we both liked. She liked traditional names like Eloise and Nora. I, on the other hand, had once thought about naming my future child Candle. But we landed—or landed for now—on Anita Josephine and Luciana Walker. Nita and Luz for short. Bear (in Choctaw, because Harmony was part Choctaw) and light. Writing those names on a postcard felt like calling up the spirits.

One day, Harmony's mom, the one who was going to make Mississippi barbecue for us, wouldn't wake up. Her blood sugar was up to 500. Harmony's dad rushed her to the hospital, where the doctors determined she had a kidney infection. I called Harmony as soon as I left Homeboy to go get my fingerprints renewed at a shabby little insurance office in Koreatown. Even before I got in my car,

I thought: *Of course she's going to keep the babies. It would hurt too much to lose her mom and her babies all in the space of a few months.*

I also thought: *But maybe if she sees CC and me as caring, supportive people in this process, she'll have more confidence in our ability to parent.*

There I went again: opportunistic at best, predatory at worst. As if Harmony's very true and present story was just another tally mark in the "likely to place" column or the "likely to parent" column. But of course that's life—you are the star of your own novel, a supporting character in certain other people's, and wacky background in the rest. And Harmony took my phone call. Whatever happened, she seemed to consider this a ride to take CC and me along on. That had to count for something. I thought about anxiety and how it could be a kind of addiction. I'd never been addicted to any substances, unless you counted food, but I always related to addiction and recovery stories. The simultaneous feeling of surrender and control was intoxicating.

CHAPTER 29: **AN EMOTIONAL OLYMPIAN**

Harmony's mom stabilized and went home. But then Harmony told us *she* was in the hospital with back problems. She said she'd be sleeping a lot, but her sister would keep us posted. Monday afternoon—more than two weeks after our first phone call—I texted that, oh, by the way, why not have her doc send proof of pregnancy to our agency while she was there? She said sure. Tuesday I didn't hear from her. Had I pushed too hard? The adoptive parent support forum started calling "scam," and I started hating them in a "Why don't you want me to be happy?!" way.

Then Harriet called and said Harmony was doing okay, sleeping a lot, had had an emotional night the night before—because, hey, pregnancy. I felt great again—loving and full of generosity toward the world—until Thursday morning, when the forum ladies started recommending internet image searches. I relented and gave them a few photos of Harmony. I felt dirty and paranoid again. And, at the same time, trusting. Harmony *said* she'd be out of touch for a bit, CC reminded me.

Then I got a call from Bianca in the Houston office of IAC: A Harmony Morris had called that day—not realizing she was already in their system—because she'd been talking to a couple in New York.

We knew Harmony as Harmony Johnson, but her Google Hangouts name was Harmony Morris Johnson. Lots of people went by different last names under different circumstances. But things were starting to add up, or not add up.

"Are they straight?" I asked. I could imagine Harmony's family talking her into placing with a one-mom, one-dad household.

"No, two women," Bianca said.

I hung up, more despondent than I'd been in a long time. I cried at work and hit up two of the Homeboy therapists for free therapy. They made sympathetic noises and one of them named a foster-to-adoption agency she'd heard of—as if the lack of an agency was our problem.

I called CC, talked super quick, and spent a lot of the day imagining the fights we'd get into because I was too sad, and that was a trigger for her. I texted Nicole and Cathy, called my dad and therapist. All my usual self-hatred just felt tiring. I felt like an old alcoholic who lost the taste for alcohol but hadn't found anything to take its place.

On Friday, I reluctantly signed up for a Homeboy beach trip. I almost called in sick, but I remembered running off my nervous energy on the Hermosa Pier the summer CC and I were separated, how I would run to the end and look out into scary gray-blue infinity. I knew nature and homies would do me good, and as I watched a white guy with an Aryan Nation tattoo and a Black guy with a Black Power tattoo toast with silver bags of Capri Sun, I congratulated myself on my instincts.

But my brain buzzed with questions that couldn't be answered. *What do those New York women have that we don't? Are they better looking? Rich? Black? Is it because I had cancer? Is it because I'm clunky and uncharming on the phone?*

For nearly a month, I'd let myself look at baby clothes and think of names. I still had a shred of hope, which was as annoying as anything.

I lay on a towel with the sun at my back, brushing sand off my journal as I wrote. A homie named Naldo made his way back from a surf lesson, which was led by a woman who'd started a nonprofit after becoming Instagram-famous for her #AlopeciaPride posts. Naldo had a teddy-bear face and a scar running from his eyebrow to his cheek. I'd recently learned that he'd spent two years in solitary confinement, among other horrors.

"Are you journaling? I always wanted to do that," he said a little wistfully.

"You should," I said. "I'm sure you have lots of stories."

"Not stories. Experiences."

"Exactly."

Shading the screen of my phone with my orange hoodie, I sent Harmony a last-ditch text.

Hey, haven't heard from you in a bit, just wondering what's up. Whatever's going on, I hope you remember that it's fine to have mixed feelings about adoption. We're here for you if you want to talk, but if not, that's okay too.

Authors of management books about how women shouldn't use undermining language in emails would have a field day with every bit of communication I sent expectant mothers. The vibe was always *Hey, I am one-hundred percent fine and casually here to support you, a person I barely know, through your drama. I have no needs!*

I couldn't divulge to Harmony that the agency had ratted her out. She seemed to like us so much. Had I imagined that? When you've diagnosed yourself with a thousand diseases you don't have and one that you do, you don't just second-guess your judgment, you second-guess the fabric of reality. Having studied just a touch of poststructuralist theory in grad school doesn't help.

To my surprise, she texted back.

Hey, sorry I been out of touch I been feeling emotional. I don't know why. I'll call you when the nurse leaves my room.

She finally called as I was driving a carload of homies through the Santa Monica Mountains. Reception was spotty, and white David and the David with devil horns tattooed on his forehead were bullshitting each other in the backseat. Also, white David had just gotten his first smartphone and kept yelling things at it: "Google! How far from Zuma Beach to Homeboy?" Our conversation didn't solve any mysteries.

Sometime after that, CC got a text that said: *Please pray for us. She has a UTI that's been making her emotional and her medicines aren't mixing.* It took CC a while to realize the text was from Harriet, since it came from Harmony's phone and Harriet didn't identify herself until several texts in.

"There's some serious Samantha/Samara stuff going on," I said, referring to the sci-fi book we'd both read recently, in which identical twins shared an identity and took turns jetting off to another plane of existence.

On Saturday, I texted with Harriet.

I'm glad Harmony has such an amazing family, I said.

I'm glad you are becoming part of it, we're blessed, she said.

That didn't seem like they were choosing the New York couple. Harmony and Harriet loved us! We loved them!

Sunday we got more explanation from Harriet: It wasn't the urinary tract infection that was making Harmony emotional so much as the rude nurses who'd been asking intrusive questions about adoption. Every time Harriet would leave the room, Harmony would be unhappy when she returned. *Are you sure about this?* the nurses wanted to know.

I burned with righteousness. It was hard enough being a hopeful adoptive parent on my feet, in the world, armed with literature and statistics about open adoption and surrounded by liberals who loved the idea of a queer, multicultural family. We heard stories about people whose friends had adopted! Did we want to talk to them? Their experience had been bliss! Or a nightmare! (Either way, no, it didn't do us much good to talk to them at this point, did it?) Why don't we just adopt an older kid? (Why don't *you*?) What about foreign adoption? Closed adoption? (As if we could just switch horses that cost tens of thousands of dollars midstream because we were grumpy, never mind the moral factors I barely even cared about anymore.)

So I could only imagine what it felt like to be a single, pregnant Black woman with gnarly back pain, who was a captive audience, who was thinking of placing her kids for adoption. Who probably had some guilt and doubt already. Fuck those nurses. I bet half of them were anti-abortion. Did they want to cut Harmony a check and offer to babysit? More importantly, wasn't there some sort of nursing oath they had to take about not judging their patients, just providing care?

Harriet went to bat for Harmony, convening a conference of doctors and getting her her own room far away from those nosy bitches.

CC was outraged too. Getting mad at staff was CC's love language.

Later, I texted Harmony to ask for the name of her hospital and room number so I could send her a card. And so I could do a little research at the urging of the chatter on the Adoptive Parent Support group. They wanted to know why why why didn't we have proof of pregnancy yet?

So I called Baylor Hospital in Dallas, nervous what they might say. I didn't want to catch Harmony in a lie—I didn't want that for her or for me. I flashed back to second grade, when Brooke Wilson claimed she had long hair because she was Hawaiian. I knew that long hair was not a genetic trait (although I did not know, then, that there were substantial other clues that blond-haired, blue-eyed Brooke—who flew to Hawaii periodically because her mom was a flight attendant—was not an indigenous Hawaiian). I told Brooke as much. But then I added: "You mean long hair is a Hawaiian tradition, right?" "Yes," she said gratefully.

There was no one named Harmony Johnson or Harmony Morris or Harmony Morris Johnson at Baylor Hospital, the woman at Baylor's central dispatch said. Harmony replied that they had her listed as private because of a long-ago domestic violence situation, in which her abuser had come to her at the hospital. I was grateful for the opportunity to keep believing. Part of me thought this whole thing was a pleasant if uneasy dream, and I just wanted to keep it alive as long as possible. It was a strange side effect of my newfound ability to occasionally, kind of, live in the present.

I called CC to share this information at exactly the wrong time. She'd gotten locked out of the house, sawn through our bedroom screen, and had a crappy therapy session. Then her car wouldn't start. She exploded at me.

"Doesn't this situation make you mad at all?" she yelled.

"It does make me frustrated, and anxious," I said. "But not mad, exactly. Aren't you always saying we don't have to feel the exact same thing at the same time?"

I could feel myself talking in a sort of hyper-verbal, hyper-calm voice that no doubt sounded condescending.

CC always saw right through performances of calm. "You're so nervous and terrified."

"How can I help having some kind of reaction to your reaction?" I asked. "When you're angry like this, it makes me feel like you might pull out of the adoption process. Or our relationship."

"Fuck you, Cheryl," she said. When she used my name that way, it became a weapon. "Stop playing the victim."

I was tangled in the shifting rules of our communication, which seemed to unfold in equal parts therapy-speak and raw emotion. Was I playing the victim every time I admitted to feeling shitty or weak? Am I playing the victim now by asking that rhetorical question? Was a victim anyone who was negatively impacted by an event or circumstance? In that case, sure, I was a victim of plenty of things. So what? "Playing" the victim implied a kind of performativity, though, and I suppose CC was getting at a certain amped-up helplessness that I put on sometimes, even as I veered wildly in the opposite direction, casting myself as a villain in just as many situations. I've always wanted to be the sort of level-headed person who knows the size of things. Who internalizes the serenity prayer and says "X is hard. Y is easy. I have control of A, but not of B. Onward." But my brain is too Shakespearean.

I was two hours into my work day and hadn't done anything productive when Bianca at IAC reported that she'd gotten a call from Harmony, who was, at least, *trying* to send them her proof of pregnancy.

CC texted something resembling an apology, I took the small half of a Klonopin, and things seemed mostly okay. In therapy that afternoon, Dr. Schmidt confirmed the complete plausibility of Harmony's situation, even if it had not been fact-checked. Who wasn't slow with paperwork? Of course hospitals would be cagey about giving out patient info if there had been a domestic violence situation.

I confessed my doubts about my own sense of reality, but he assured me I wasn't delusional. I felt a kinship with Harmony. We were smart women with good heads on our shoulders but a lot of self-doubt that could be stirred up by the haters, as Dr. Schmidt called them. In my journal, I wrote: *I'm going to have faith until I have reason not to, and I hope she does the same. I love that girl.*

On Tuesday, Bianca emailed to say that Harmony had sent IAC a typed document that wasn't proof of pregnancy, but hey, baby steps! So to speak. Harmony also called the agency and confirmed that she wanted to match with us. Bianca asked her about the New York couple. Harmony was confused. Then she said, "Oh, them? That was a long time ago, before I talked to Cheryl and CC."

On Wednesday, Bianca emailed to say she'd spotted a posting on one of the adoption scam boards about "Harmony from TX." She immediately contacted the lawyer who'd posted it. The woman's replies were short, but the gist of it was that no one was saying Harmony wasn't pregnant, but she'd contacted a *lot* of that lawyer's clients. Bianca called the New York couple. They'd gotten a text from Harmony as recently as August 1—fifteen days after we'd begun our talks.

I texted CC from work: *You want me to get angry about stuff? Did you see Bianca's email? I've got plenty of anger.*

She replied: *Let's go for a walk or get drinks tonight and feel our separate feelings.*

Over the next few days, my head spun with possibilities. Had

Harmony been spooked by the reality and finality of providing proof of pregnancy? Was she playing us against other couples? (That thought made my chest ache, as the competitive, elementary school gymnast in me vied against the adult empath, who imagined dozens of people who had wanted kids as long and as badly as we did.) Was she even pregnant? Didn't those pictures she'd sent of her dog and her bedroom at her new house seem a little lifted from the internet? But on the other hand, wouldn't it be easier for me to think she was a full-blown criminal than to imagine her as a preemptively grieving, confused birth mom who liked another couple better than us?

Suddenly everything that wasn't right in front of me seemed suspect. Was CC really seeing patients at the clinic that night? Who was to say she wasn't having an affair or gambling at a seedy underground . . . something?

"I'm just not very good at dealing with dishonesty," I told CC when she got home from the clinic at a reasonable hour, smelling like Del Taco and offering me her leftover fries. "It's why I could never write a novel with an unreliable narrator."

Even someone who lied to other characters or to herself needed to tell the truth to the reader. And here I am, doing my best in this non-novel, even though truth is as shifty and subjective as they told us it was in grad school. But then it was an intellectual exercise, and reality as I knew it was pretty straightforward. Then, I didn't know what a wild, postmodern ride I was in for, or how terrifying it would be to live through so many glitches in the Matrix.

There is an episode of *Friends* where Chandler breaks up with someone—maybe Janice, maybe not for the first time—and drowns his sorrows with Monica and Rachel. They teach him feminine heartbreak rituals, handing him a tub of chocolate ice cream and a spoon.

"This ice cream tastes like crap," he says.

Monica shrugs, resigned: "After a while, you switch to low fat."

The first date I went on after Bari and I broke up was with an androgynous, Ivy League hipster-screenwriter I'd met on MySpace. She was witty and sarcastic but kind, and had a great asymmetrical haircut. Her mom had died young. Her dad's family was among the rich white people who fled Cuba after the revolution, which gave her an intriguing air of both privilege and oppression. When, after two ambiguous date-type things, I confessed that I liked her, she called me up and told me she'd gotten more of a "friend vibe" from me.

It would have been a nobler gesture if she hadn't already told me a story about a friend of hers rebuffing a girl using that exact phrase. Still raw and sad about Bari, I took the day off work to lick my wounds.

But now, heartbreak felt like a lifestyle, and I had to keep working.

That night, CC and I walked to the bar around the corner and drank old-fashioneds and discussed the maddening nature of the adoption process.

"I'm mourning how, for a little while, I didn't worry about growing apart from all our friends with kids," I said. "I mean, I love them anyway, but it was nice to not have that feeling of working myself up to enjoying their family-ness. It was nice to, like, see it as a point of connection instead of distance."

"I know," CC said. "Me, too."

The next night we went to a Spoon concert at Hollywood Forever Cemetery. I lay on the grass next to a mausoleum, looking up at the black palm trees against the gray sky, as the band played songs that were upbeat but urgent and achy. I was melancholy, half removed from the world, thinking of the dead. CC was irritable—

annoyed at honking drivers, at the woman who scanned our tickets, and at herself for not immediately handing the ticket-taker the proper things to scan. "I'm kind of angry tonight, aren't I?" she observed. "And you're probably kind of sad."

There was a time when I would have seen her irritations as shallow and mean, and she would have seen my sadness as Debbie Downer-ish and standing in the way of enjoying life. Now we knew better, even if it didn't always help in the moment. Now, unfortunately or fortunately, we'd had practice.

My friend Wendy invited me to her apartment for poolside drinks on Thursday. We studied our toenail polish in the aqua glow and discussed philosophy and psychology and baby-mama drama.

"Open adoption is like constantly breaking up with someone you might not have wanted to date in real life," I said. "And when I land in this place, where I'm oversharing all the time and crying at work and having all this drama in my life, I feel like people—I'm not sure who, so I really mean my superego—are saying, 'Well, she must seek it out.'"

"I took this class on psychology and literature, and I mentioned the idea of the id, ego, and superego," Wendy recalled, "and the professor completely shushed me, like those ideas were so out of vogue."

She thought of her dad, who volunteered with the dogs at his local shelter and whispered in their ears that they were loved, but who wasn't so great at expressing love with the humans in his life. "So oversharing is probably good," Wendy concluded.

"I wish people or my superego or whatever could know that I'm not a mess because I'm a mess but because this is varsity-level emotional shit. To put yourself out there over and over, to enter a stranger's life when both you and she are in this really vulnerable place, and try to plan a child's life and make this kind of arranged marriage. And then when it goes bad, to do it all over again, and put your best foot forward again. That's such a mindfuck!"

Wendy, who was a hearty agree-er, heartily agreed. I thought about Homeboy's Restorative Justice program, in which people who'd committed violent crimes met with the family members of violent crime victims. The perpetrators take responsibility for their actions while also linking those actions to the terrible things that were done to them. The family members forgive them as surrogates for the people who actually hurt or killed their loved ones.

"Okay," I conceded, "maybe open adoption isn't quite the emotional Olympics. But it's at least the emotional Gay Olympics."

On Saturday, CC and I went to a comedy show at an art gallery, where the audience sat cross-legged, shoulder-to-shoulder on a tile floor. The opener did a set in which he recounted the plot of *Dawn of the Planet of the Apes* in excruciating, not especially funny detail. The audience laughed indulgently. He kept going. Ten minutes, then twenty. Maybe because we were at an art gallery, I decided it was an experimental piece, where the point was seeing how far the audience would go based entirely on the belief that we were all here for the same thing.

We sweated from heat and discomfort, and then some more traditional comics—the kind who told jokes—came on stage and we sweated only from heat. I kept my phone in my hand—because hope, because addiction, because addiction to hope—and when it vibrated and showed Harmony's name, I stepped outside into the cool night.

"Oh my god, it's been so crazy," she said. "So, last weekend, my friends and my family kidnapped me and Harriet for our birthday. They took us to this really nice hotel. And there were stylists and make-up folks and nail ladies. We were like, *whaaat.* So we get all fancied up, right? Then they blindfold us *again,* and they take us to this club."

I paced up and down a hilly side street while she talked. She was Brooke Wilson, telling me about her amazing life in Hawaii. She was a stand-up comic telling me about *Planet of the Apes.* I was a willing idiot.

I studied the lit windows of small homes and the black silhouettes of palm trees against a Los Angeles sky that never quite blackened.

"Oh my goodness, it was so much fun," Harmony said breathlessly. "There was dancing and they gave us all these presents, and you know Michelle Williams?"

"The actress?"

"No, the one from Destiny's Child. She was there! And she sang 'Happy Birthday' to us! And you know Dez Bryant?"

I did not.

"From the Cowboys. He was there, too, and we started talking. And we been talking this whole week."

I sensed that I was supposed to be impressed, but I barely knew that the Cowboys were a football team. I looked him up later and discovered he'd been arrested two years earlier for hitting his mother.

"He is so good to me," Harmony gushed. "He bought me this big old ring, I don't know how much he spent on it, but that's not who I am. I'm not into material things like that. He been saying he wants to pay for my nursing school, but I wanna be independent. I'm not supposed to drive because of my blood pressure, so he's been having his driver take me places, and I am grateful for that."

"How have you been feeling?" I asked, trying to steer the conversation back to pregnancy.

"I been okay. Trying to take it easy even though so much is happening. And I know what you're thinking, but don't worry, I talked to Dez about the babies and the adoption, and he's supportive of whatever I want to do.

Oh good, her boyfriend of one week had given his blessing. This twenty-six-year-old professional football player who was hot for a thirty-two-year-old pregnant nursing student with high blood pressure. Who was I to think he was anything other than a big-hearted guy who was uninterested in whatever nineteen-year-olds in tiny dresses had gathered around him that night at the club? What kind of stereotyping jerk was I?

Awkwardly, exhaustedly, I repeated my spiel about proof of pregnancy.

"Oh yes, that's important," Harmony agreed. "But we should check with Bianca, because I *sat* there on Thursday while my doctor faxed the paperwork."

We were trapped in a crazy-making cycle of We Need That Fax/ Okay, I'll Send It Today/What, You Didn't Get It? Okay, I'll Send It Today. Nevertheless, it was nice to hear her voice. I'd missed her.

"Did it occur to you that she made all this up?" CC asked on our walk home.

"Yes. Of course. I think she might be a pathological liar. But I guess I hope she's a pregnant pathological liar who might still place her baby with us?"

Both CC and my therapist placed their money on Harmony genuinely being pregnant, but thought that just about everything else, from her perfect supportive family to her Prince Charming boyfriend, might be a fantasy to comfort herself during a rough time.

"Women with a lot fewer resources than what she claims to have parent their children," CC observed.

I trusted them, but I no longer trusted myself. I didn't trust reality to be reality. Later that week, I found myself thinking about the time I'd given a teenager I mentored a used laptop and it had gotten stolen from her house a few months later. *Had it really been stolen?* I wondered. Then I caught myself. As far as I knew, my mentee had never once lied to me. I mourned Perfect Birth Mom Harmony, although I supposed it was my own fairy tale, a honeymoon that was bound to end. I mourned Innocent Cheryl, who trusted and was almost always rewarded for it.

On Monday, Bianca confirmed that she had not gotten a fax from Harmony's doctor and found a lot of her behavior "very concerning," but stopped short of saying we should cut her off. I texted Harmony that she might need her chauffeur to drive her to her doc's office. I didn't hear back, and we never heard from her again.

I still have a voicemail she left during our summer love affair on my phone. I haven't relistened to it, but I keep it in my queue— Harmony Johnson, July 14, 2014—to remind me that I didn't make any of this up.

CHAPTER 30: **POPULAR**

This seems like as good a place as any to insert the dating montage where the protagonist meets with a rotating cast of romantic prospects, each of them comically wrong. But even though I am the protagonist in this story, (almost) each expectant mom was Ms. Right, as far as I was concerned. Of course, it all depends where you position the camera. CC and I were making comedic cameos along with other hopeful adoptive parents in the dating montages of pregnant women searching for The One (or The Two). Picture her: serene, distressed in the way movie heroines—carrying it all in her eyes, never complaining—hands folded over her belly. Picture us: goofy, desperate, old.

But this is my story, and so the camera sits just over my shoulder, watching the women file by. Between Crystal and July of 2014, we heard from:

- Tina, a Baltimore mom of three, whose fourth child was with a guy she was divorcing.

- Kay, the college student from Detroit who was studying in Israel and wanted to have her baby in the United States. A few weeks into the process, she miscarried. "I'm handling this really badly," she wrote. If there was a good way to handle it, I certainly didn't know. "This baby came out of nowhere and left out of nowhere."

- Shannon, another newly pregnant woman, who sent us and other families a long questionnaire with items like: "Science or religion?" and "What do you want for your child—to be rich and successful, or poor and happy?"

- Chelsea, the twenty-year-old chef-in-training who lived just outside of Sacramento. She was easy to talk to and super responsive, but she'd known she was pregnant for *one week,* and her fiancé really wanted kids.

- Laura, who'd learned a few hours before emailing us that her twenty-one-year-old daughter was pregnant by a one-night-stand and had kept it from her parents for months. Laura kept telling me how tall and thin her daughter was, and a model! She was beautiful and talented, but stubborn and made reckless decisions!

- Reggie, an alleged Washington State University college student who was pregnant with boy-girl twins. The first thing she let me know was that she had blond hair and blue eyes, and her ex-fiancé had black hair and green eyes and was six-foot-five. I was insulted that she thought Aryan dream babies were the way to our hearts.

- Dawn, the woman who called us in the middle of the night from the East Coast, asking if we'd take her three- and five-year-old kids. A TV blared in the background. Her voice was blurry and exhausted.

- Cassidy, a high school student in Louisville who loved her two cats and didn't think much of her parents. She texted that she worked "at an eggplant." We figured out this meant a chicken farm, but as CC said, "I like imagining that she's very, very small and she goes to work each day with a walnut shell as a helmet."

- Elizabeth, a thirteen-year-old who wanted to know if we would adopt *her*. I was alarmed, imagining an abusive situation. When I talked to her on the phone, I asked lots of questions about her parents, and they sounded okay. Elizabeth said she wanted to go to UCLA and thought it would be smart to establish residency with a California couple. I talked her through some other ways to go about that.

I joked that I had become a "junior case manager" for IAC. I knew how to listen, gather basic information in a casual and friendly way, empathize with the challenges of an unplanned pregnancy, and present resources and next steps. When I thought about skills I wanted to cultivate, I thought about writing, of course, and skiing and cooking rice that didn't turn out like glue. But I suppose that most skills—the ones that develop the fastest and earliest—are born of survival. We didn't need to adopt to survive, of course. But my need to be a mom came from having one. And then not having one. If I'd learned how to win her attention the first time I lost her—when Cathy was a cooing pink thing in an infant seat—by going forth into the world independently, that was about survival. Those skills bent and twisted over the years and here we were.

CHAPTER 31: HOLDING IT LIGHTLY

Fabian made his way between the tables in Classroom A, handing out glass pebbles, the kind you'd find in a planter or fishbowl. They were rounded on top and flat on the bottom. Fabian was Homeboy's resident artist and director of recovery programs. He'd found his way out of a heroin addiction through street art. Some old Chicano muralists saw his tags and told him to stop ruining his life. Father Greg also told him to stop ruining his life. Eventually Fabian sobered up, although Alexa pointed out that he still had some addict behaviors, like thinking he was more special than everyone else. He liked to wax philosophical and talk about himself in the third person.

Another homie trailed behind him, handing out bits of colored paper and Sharpies. Fabian shared a long story about a recent trip to Mexico City with a cohort of homies. They had met with a local church group and an impoverished indigenous tribe that, as he told it, fell in love with Fabian and begged him to teach them art.

"For them and for me, art is a very spiritual thing," he said. He clasped his hands together. "Now, I want you to think of a mantra. Close your eyes. What words come to you?"

I'd been at Homeboy almost a year. The proverbial Kool-Aid was still sloshing around in my stomach, but I could joke about its idiosyncrasies now, and its hypocrisies were starting to scratch at me. We were still years away from Fabian telling my female coworker that he understood the sexual harassment she endured daily from fresh-out-of-jail dudes because, once, a female trainee had put her hand on his thigh. Fabian was a talented artist, though, with a cover-story-worthy backstory. All these truths. All these stories.

Dutifully, I closed my eyes and tried to tune out the 3:00 p.m. Gold Line train that squealed as it rounded the bend of our building.

The thing that came to me—the phrase that had been padding quietly around my head in stocking feet for a few weeks, but which now put on shoes and formed itself into words—was, *hold it lightly.*

What was "it"? So many things. And especially one thing. Or, two, or three things. But now, most urgently, one thing.

It sounds like a fortune cookie, but every now and then a fortune cookie hits you in just the right way and becomes sacred. That sacredness is difficult to translate. Why is any liturgical practice calming? Why does the smell of waffle cones take me back to the Old Town Mall of my youth, the one with the two-story carousel, and transform that most banal of American spots—the mall—into a fairyland?

But if you can apply meaning to a fairyland or a dry wafer, the thing behind the thing I wrote in pink Sharpie on yellow paper that day, it's this: I always thought that giving something my all was to give it my greatest effort. To apply the weight of every cell in my body. But hadn't I learned—and I know I'm mixing metaphors here—that some cells are cancer? What if, instead, I cupped my hands and let The Thing I Cared Most About perch there? What if I let it breathe and rest its wings?

I shellacked my pebble with clear glue and kept it on my desk next to the paper monkey that my predecessor had made as an homage to MailChimp. Eventually I lost it.

IAC's policy was that after a year of waiting to be matched, families would become eligible for the "Hospital List." That meant that if a mother decided, shortly before or after giving birth, that she wanted to place her child for adoption, an IAC social worker might be called to the scene with a binder of "Dear Birth Mother" letters in hand. Sometimes this happened because the mother tested positive for drugs (and who got tested? Women who seemed poor or distressed or young or not white or were already in The System). The System would activate (or reactivate), and she would face the "choice" between surrendering her baby for adoption voluntarily— to maintain a shred of agency by working with an organization and choosing the family herself from the binder—or letting foster care make all the decisions.

Usually I follow the best practices of adoption-speak and talk about "placing" a child for adoption. Don't say "give up," the adoption people insist, because that diminishes birth parents. They're not *abandoning* their children, they're *making a plan*. That is one hundred percent true. But there is a kind of giving up that happens, in the sense of surrender, in the sense of raising a white flag to life's circumstances. It was like with my ovaries: I "chose" to have them removed, but I made that choice with a gun at my back.

CC and I went around and around about the hospital list. If either of us were acting on brand, you would think Spontaneous CC would be okay with a "Surprise! You're parents now!" scenario, while Planner Cheryl would need a month or two to get a crib ready. But our current brands—Hesitant About Baby and Desperate For Baby—had infiltrated our old ones like body snatchers. Our compromise was to revisit the issue every few months, a conversation that, so far, had felt both heavy and fragile, and which led to us saying "no for now" repeatedly. Because fruitless efforts always struck me as life's most unjust reality, I hoped that if agreeing to wait was slowing our process of acquiring a baby, it was at least winning me points with CC. Look how patient I was. How amenable to her wishes.

In November, someone in the IAC Facebook group mentioned working with a facilitator—a kind of professional adoption matchmaker, one of the many professionals who could grease the wheels of the process while costing less than a lawyer. This woman was named Jeanna, pronounced Gina, and by all accounts she was warm, attentive, and matched people quickly for $3,000.

We scheduled a call with her, CC and I pacing around her phone, on speaker, in the kitchen. Jeanna ran a small agency in North Carolina called Hope Embraced, a name I found both cheesy and clunky, with a website full of cursive fonts and purple backgrounds. But maybe that was what we needed. IAC was professional and bursting with Best Practices, and where had they gotten us?

Jeanna was effusive and impossible not to like. She told us her life story, which she'd undoubtedly recounted to dozens of other hopeful adoptive parents and birth parents, but it didn't sound rehearsed. She'd gotten pregnant in college. She freaked out, prayed about it, and sobbed on her sister's futon for hours. Someone mentioned adoption, and from there she'd navigated her way to open adoption like someone pulling themselves along a rope in a snowstorm. She hadn't known it was possible to "give up" her child and also to know him. But once that door opened, the decision became clear. Since then, she'd had two biological children and adopted two. She had been every kind of mother. It gave her deep and genuine empathy, not to mention a perfect marketing device.

If that sounds cynical, well, I had come to consider stories as hurricanes that could be harnessed to power a city or instead, if untethered, could flatten it. I posted homies' stories online regularly, next to a button saying *Donate Now!* I tried to hang onto their humanity and mine. I wasn't telling just any old story for profit (or for nonprofit), and later I would attend workshops about how not to exploit clients, how to avoid "poverty porn" and "inspiration porn." I didn't exactly disagree with these sentiments, but the attitude I observed among most of the homies, and which I felt myself, was that telling someone's story was a kind of seeing. And after so many years of feeling like nothing, having a witness was a relief: *You see what I went through? You see why I'm so twitchy and scarred?* We'd already shown our wounds to the world, so why not wield that story for something useful?

With my dad's financial help, again, we signed a contract with Jeanna and mailed a check. We kept up our online profiles on Adoptimist, Parent Profiles, and, of course, IAC's own site, but I felt like we'd pressed a button for expedited shipping, which made the waiting a little more palatable because it felt like we were waiting for *something* rather than possibly nothing. It was an approximation of the incremental progress I craved.

The next expectant mom who emailed was a straightforward twenty-five-year-old named Eve, who had a four-year-old daughter and was living in Oklahoma with her grandmother, who needed to move by the end of the month. We talked once on the phone and texted periodically. Eve was not having twins, asked questions about us, and shared stuff about herself but not too much. She seemed to have more pressing concerns than becoming besties with random lesbians from California. She called IAC when I gave her the number. She did not send in her proof of pregnancy immediately, but I believed she might.

I held it lightly. I was able to do so because we had Jeanna in our back pocket. Writers recommend sending out lots of submissions so that when you get a rejection, there are still potential acceptances out there in the universe. Another version of this is, I think, the idea of heaven. Father Greg and Ed Bacon at All Saints talked about heaven not as a reward for a life of good works, but as the guarantee that allowed us to spend our lives living rather than fixating on death. I fixated on death plenty, but the rationale did make sense.

So Jeanna was our promised land, I guess—a reason to believe that this wasn't all an embarrassing exercise in futility. I couldn't shake the feeling that we'd come so close to adopting, I could taste it. (What does adopting taste like? A short list of names. A borrowed crib. A slow walk past the glass window of a Mommy & Me class.) If not Harmony, maybe Eve, but if Eve turned out to be no more real than Harmony, then Jeanna—the heavy hitter, the professional buffer between us and the world of flaky birth moms. If she was heaven, then we'd secured a spot by buying indulgences, à la pre–Martin Luther Catholics. I wished I could Hold It Lightly without her. I wished I was so secure in my own goodness as to believe I didn't need help getting to heaven. But my desire rattled windows and shook the earth. It was the one thing about me that refused to wait in line politely. It scared me and fueled me.

CHAPTER 32: PULSING

I was lying in bed speaking my cancer worries in a small voice. "When are your next appointments?" CC asked, only a little tiredly.

"In a week."

"Oh—well, no wonder you're anxious. This is just your usual freak-out."

Maybe that wouldn't be comforting to everyone, but it was to me. Grow up in the same house for eighteen years, eating the same breakfast cereal on weekdays and the same waffles each Sunday, and routine becomes a sign of rightness, of health. I wasn't freaking out because I had some deep intuition about my body, but because this was my routine.

As my therapist put it more than once, anxiety about the future is really about the past.

Over Thanksgiving weekend, CC and I watched an Australian horror movie called *The Babadook* about a woman whose husband dies in a car crash while driving her to the hospital to deliver their first child. Six years later, she's a single mom struggling to raise a son who sees invisible monsters. She's frazzled. She wishes he would just go the fuck to sleep.

One day, a spooky children's book about a particular monster called the Babadook shows up in their house. The book promises a terrible fate for anyone who ignores it and reveals that the monster never goes away. At first, only her son sees the Babadook, and he seems like one of those classic creepy horror movie kids, crazed and possessed.

Then the mother begins to see it. Her son promises to protect his mom, even as she swallows the amorphous monster like so much black ink, becoming angry and cruel, eventually admitting she wished her son had died instead of her husband.

At this point, the film's point of view flips. She's the monster, and her son is sweet and brave.

The Babadook, the audience knows by now, is nothing more and nothing less than grief embodied. The film's simple but cautionary message? *Don't ignore it, or it will come after you and eat you and your loved ones alive.*

In the movie, the mom faces down the Babadook in a scene that had me clutching CC's arm and bawling. Yes, yes, yes—this was what the ball of grief and fear inside me felt like. I knew I wasn't alone in having a personal Babadook, and yet the nature of the Babadook is to convince you that you are utterly alone.

That week in early December, my Babadook felt big. By Wednesday night, I was crying in my car, trying to get myself to the gym for some endorphins. Halfway down the staircase, it occurred to me that my big fear might mean *there was something big to be feared.*

The body can be its own trigger. Your worry and your accelerated heart rate and the clench in your stomach remind you how you felt when things were very bad, so your brain concludes things must be very bad right now. And the feedback loop continues.

I sent CC a flurry of texts against my better judgment—knowing, as I did, that my anxiety triggers hers. I went to the locker room, changed, and shut myself in one of the green Formica-doored bathroom stalls. My eyes were damp. I felt unmoored. Should I call my therapist? About what, exactly? A jolt of an idea hit me: *I'll email Joewon!*

I told her I needed a pep talk, that my own fear was freaking me out, but hadn't she had some bad brushes with intuition, too?

The next day, her reply came, and it was exactly what I needed to hear, from a literary scholar and anxious person whose breast cancer Babadook bloomed and shrank.

> *Let's worry about something else, Cheryl. All these scans that we go through for our five years, these frequent exposures to radiation, couldn't they cause thyroid cancer later—when we are sixty-eight, for instance? But twenty to thirty years will surely bring groundbreaking new cancer treatments, right? So there's no worry then. In the meantime, we'll be busy having fun living a healthy life, often nursing our fear and occasionally ignoring it. And to our joy, we'll have our fearful, intuitive knowledge about our own bodies proven groundless each time we go see our doctors.*
>
> *In loving solidarity,*
> *Joewon*

Eventually, Joewon would have a recurrence. Not stage IV, but a local recurrence that she was (so I tell myself) more prone to because she'd had a lumpectomy instead of a mastectomy the first time around. She had to go through chemo again. She said that even though it was her worst fear come true, it was also easier because she knew the steps. She knew which stair creaked on the way to the basement, and she knew what was *in* the basement, and it helped and didn't. She was okay, for a second time.

December 4, the day before my appointment with Dr. Hills, was almost too busy for me to fixate—almost. I did find time to poke at my boobs every time I went to the bathroom. I went to a Lions Club luncheon, at the gorgeous old Biltmore Hotel downtown, to accept a donation for Homeboy. The event opened with a pledge to a nonexistent flag, and everyone called each other "Lion." Lion Carol. Lion Gilbert. Lion Luz. I took a break to call my dad from the steps between the ionic columns outside the hotel.

He rattled off all the reasons I could never get cancer again, and I held each fact like a rosary bead. No lymph node involvement, maximum treatment, etc., etc. Sometimes his scientific orientation irritated me because it had limits and it could be a kind of denial, but right then, I needed it and I needed him. Solid and predictable and loving.

Later that afternoon, in the Homeboy stairwell, I had my first conversation with Erica, a bubbly twenty-nine-year-old hairstylist from Santa Barbara who was thirty weeks pregnant. She called when she said she would, and she placed a baby for adoption three years back. Her father passed away shortly before this pregnancy, and her family—the ones who were already born and still alive—needed her. I told her I'd lost my mom, too; I got it.

A couple of awkward pauses aside, I thought it went well. But I was never sure. I didn't have the rest of the day to obsess over it. "Perfect" was as dirty a word as "deserve," but Erica seemed perfect. *Hold it lightly,* I told myself. If Erica didn't call IAC, if she didn't make good on our follow-up conversation with CC, we had Jeanna.

That night, Homeboy hosted a reading for students from my creative writing class. I had no idea what to expect. Five people in the audience and a dozen readers? Fifty people in the audience and two readers?

When I saw Devon, a butch, cornrowed girl who'd asked me to type up her short, terribly spelled essays, dressed up in khakis and a blazer, my heart swelled and broke.

CC sent me encouraging texts, and that made my heart swell, too. She'd been the one to say *DO IT!!* re: teaching the workshop. She knew what was good for me. She loved me.

Five students turned out, and our partner organization, Street Poets, showed up with a spray-painted poetry van, a sound system, and drummers. Homegirl Catering brought pretzel bread sliders, pesto pasta, little squares of coffee cake, and watermelon mint agua fresca. The event quickly became bigger than me or my class, thanks largely to Street Poets and its tendency to break into freestyle rap and impromptu break-dance parties.

But also because of all that came before: the hard lives and anger that went into our words, love and vulnerability trumping violence and toughness. We closed the night in a circle, holding hands. Mariela, the throaty-voiced student who made me tear up every time she wrote about her dead mother, squeezed the hand of the person to her right, and the pulse went around the circle. We were a living creature, stronger than the sum of our parts, defying death and darkness. It felt like nothing short of the meaning of life.

I was barely to the parking lot, still vibrating with the adrenaline of the day, blurry in the wet sparkling night, when I started to wonder: *Weren't things too good? Wasn't I too lucky? What if this were the last great day of my life?*

Then again, maybe I'd just done what I was always trying to do and lived in the present for a minute and been part of something bigger than myself. Maybe that was why I felt good. Maybe it was okay to feel good even before a doctor gave me permission. Maybe it was still okay to desperately want the doctor's permission. Maybe that pulse that went around the circle wasn't my Last Good Day *or* Proof That I'd Finally Learned To Feel Good In The Face Of Anxiety (Meaning That I Could Now Be Rewarded With A Baby). Maybe that heartbeat was its own life force, both bigger and more banal than the meaning I kept trying to fill it with. It just *was*.

CHAPTER 33: WAITING AROUND UNTIL THINGS CHANGE

The day of the student reading was not my last good day. At my appointment the following morning, Dr. Hills felt me up and beamed her encouraging smile and sent me on my way. I returned to the world of *It's barely even POSSIBLE for me to get cancer again,* though my euphoria faded when I had to get my blood drawn at a lab in Pasadena and wait for Dr. Chung to relay the results at yet another appointment.

Meanwhile, we knew this about Erica:

- She was twenty-nine.
- She lived in Southern California, talked like a Valley Girl, tossed off phrases like "Central Coast."
- She'd placed a daughter for adoption before.
- She was Latina.
- She got pregnant by an ex who was likely in Mexico.

- She called and texted when she said she would.
- She told Katie, the IAC case manager, that she didn't want to see other profiles.
- She was, possibly, a unicorn. Our unicorn?

On Saturday, my dad, Cathy, and I went to the Banning House museum. The stately white Victorian mansion, once home to a prominent Wilmington family, stood in the middle of a rolling acreage that was now a city park. Our family often toured the house when I was growing up. As a kid, I'd loved its narrow staircases, its nooks and crannies, its high beds and chamber pots and porcelain dolls. It seemed haunted and magical. It was fun to go as just us Kleins, no CC or Susan. Or, rather, it was relaxing. My original comfort zone.

My dad asked a food vendor a dozen questions about the sodium content of his soup, and asked the tour guide if he could perhaps just open the pocket door between the dining room and kitchen a little bit (he could not).

We walked from the Banning House to LA's only Civil War barracks. The suburban streets between the two historic spots were distinguished by the fact that the houses dated to all eras, and many of the yards were occupied by peacocks, who walked around on thick dinosaur legs, pecking at the grass and fluttering to the top of a cinderblock wall now and then. The street used to be part of my dad's paper route when he was in high school. "This was the nice block," he said. Some of the nearby streets weren't even paved.

It was just another SoCal day near Christmastime, with camels and peacocks. Maybe even a unicorn.

I'd been largely estranged from Piper, my friend who'd wanted queer foster teens and perfect kittens, but CC and I went to her and Lindy's annual holiday party, bickering about a possible Justine-and-Sam encounter that didn't happen. The next week, I texted Piper to say that I knew I'd been a self-centered friend, but if she ever wanted to hang out with a self-centered friend, let me know.

She had one free hour Tuesday night, which we spent eating veggie burgers in the cold, on the patio of the Oinkster. (How many times had I cried at the Oinkster? Site of the post-miscarriage taro milkshake; site of an antidepressant withdrawal meltdown.) She didn't tell me I wasn't self-centered, and we didn't talk about anything deep. Penelope was a pretty baby; in her face, you could already see the beautiful young woman she would become. She had delicate features—button nose, bow mouth, light blue eyes—and, as if to counteract all that, wore clothes that appeared to be handed down from her boy cousin.

"The adults should outnumber the kids," Piper said, re: why they had the best of all worlds, raising Penelope down the street from Lindy's brother (who was also Penelope's biological dad) and his wife and baby.

It was what annoyed me about Piper—the certainty of her opinions, even as they changed. When she'd wanted to adopt an older foster child, that had been the best choice a person could make. When she'd wanted two kids, didn't all kids deserve a sibling? I supposed it was what made her a good lawyer, too. She could argue anything, convincingly. So could I, but I always weaponized it against myself.

It was a pleasant evening, in the same way that a bunch of rubber grapes are a pleasant object but can't feed you in any way. I came home, pouted, ate cinnamon toast, resented myself for eating cinnamon toast, and cried myself to sleep.

And finally, my check-up and tumor-marker-results appointment with Dr. Chung rolled around. Afterward, I wrote a letter to myself.

Dear Terrified Self,

This is so you remember that yes, you felt this scared—maybe more—before, and it had nothing to do with your test results. Unfortunately the opposite isn't true, either. Fear does not equal health. But this is a story about how fear doesn't equal cancer, about how you are healthy now.

It rained yesterday morning, and you tried to figure out if this was a good omen. On one hand, you were a cat-like SoCal girl who feels sunny when there is sun. On the other, the weather report had predicted rain. And now it was raining. That had to bode well for the truth of statistics. All available health reports predicted no cancer for you; you just needed them to be true, even as you felt like you were throwing the triple-negative survivors and the smokers and the people who forgot to take their medicine under the bus. They were probably very nice people!

You woke up early with a knot in your stomach. You hadn't been able to buy a 2015 calendar, because would it be full of treatments or trips to the pediatrician?

"First time here?" asked the man at the front desk at City of Hope. Maybe you had that healthy body/terrified face look of the newly diagnosed.

No, you told him, and went to the third floor.

The smooth Klonopin glow of an hour ago had been trumped by your body's commitment to anxiety. The shaking, the short breath. Usually you could tip yourself over into crying at this point, and that would make you feel better, if less publicly presentable. But even that territory felt far away. You sat in the waiting room and tried to access the "anchor for calm" your hypnotherapist had taught you.

Thumbs between middle and ring fingers, mind in rainforest with Mom and T-Mec and Squeakies-as-balls-of-light. It helped a little. Not a lot.

When the nurse called your name, you tried to divine whether she seemed happy for you or sad for you. As if she even had access to your labs. As if she weren't thinking about when her next break was, or what she was getting her kid for Christmas, or maybe a funny mole she had because why shouldn't nurses be hypochondriacs, too?

As you waited for Dr. Chung, you prayed out loud. Dear God, help me remember that I am loved. That the world is for me. That those things don't hinge on whether I have cancer or not. You wanted to add Please let me not have cancer, but that always felt like breaking some rule God probably didn't care about anyway.

And then Dr. Chung came in and your labs were fine—your tumor markers were 15.1 and 1.2, your lowest ever and midrange, respectively—and you were free to ask all your other questions: about getting an endoscopic ultrasound to screen for pancreatic cancer and whether that tiny white bump on your left eyelid seemed like the beginning of a melanoma.

Every time you have an appointment coming up, it's like being visited by the Ghost of Christmas Future, all hood and scythe and low-toned bells. And every time you get good lab results, you feel like the reformed Ebeneezer on Christmas morning.

You want to fling doors open and toss handfuls of cash into the streets. Except Scrooge lived in a just world, or at least a world he could make just. The reaper comes to visit you every four months no matter how much you help people, no matter how many blueberries and chia seeds you eat.

Nevertheless, you are now free to enjoy Christmas morning. So enjoy it. You want to run and write and give people presents. Adopt a baby and hug your family. You have a kind of manic goodwill. Let it fly.

Love,
Cheryl

After Homeboy's holiday party at a stuffy old restaurant in Chinatown called Hop Louie, I left work to go to our first-ever, in-person birth mom meeting, with Erica. We were off to Santa Barbara! I promised my coworkers I'd text an update.

The plan was to pick up CC in the Valley and head up the 101 together. I pulled up to the clinic where she interned and looked at my phone. Erica's text said, *Hi ladies, can we reschedule? I had a little fall at work and want to get checked out just in case.*

I texted CC. We sat quietly in the break room at her clinic, site of all the drama that came when psychology students worked long hours together and formed watercooler cliques. Then we moved to a steampunk-themed coffee shop. Coffee shops always made me feel better, but I was starting pretty low. I felt like shopping. The coffee shop sold watches and lockets. Learning not to melt down all over CC meant that, when I felt like melting down, I needed to be apart from her. I couldn't figure out if that was healthy or not. We drank coffee and zoned out into our phones for a while. Apart and together.

I remembered a part in a YA book I'd read, *The Kid Table,* in which the narrator says that she'd learned to handle all hard stuff by just waiting around until her mood changed. That, I told CC, was what I was doing.

Erica texted and said the baby was fine, but she'd strained her back, so could we do Saturday or Sunday? That made me feel better. A little.

We got some Christmas presents at Urban Outfitters and Big Gulps at 7-Eleven. We felt better. A little. Then the movie we wanted to see—*Top Five* with Chris Rock—wasn't playing at the theater we thought it was playing at, and we drove around the Valley, lost and increasingly grouchy in December-Friday traffic, for an hour. The theater where it *was* playing had a power outage and was shut down.

CC dropped me off at my car. She went to get her hair cut, and I went home, sitting in traffic and eating our road-trip snacks.

We went to bed early, defeated by the day. I gave her a long back scratch. As always, it bugged me that when she needed the most comfort, she also acted vaguely mad at me, so that I felt like giving her a back scratch was my punishment, or the thing I was doing to coax her back into liking me. I knew she was disappointed about Erica. I knew all the driving and lack of fun in the day was possibly the bigger bummer for her. I felt like I should apologize for something. For not being able to fix the world? Birth a baby? She'd never gotten mad at me for those things, exactly. She wasn't mad at me now, exactly.

That night I dreamed I was in a small boat riding big waves. My mom was alive again after having been dead for years, and I was trying to explain that to people, that I really did know what it was like to lose my mom. And she was waiting for her cancer to come back again, to die again. I dreamed I wrote a comic book and my writing class was unimpressed.

CHAPTER 34: IMAGINING ERICA

We rescheduled. CC and I drove up the coast one sunny Sunday morning a few days before Christmas. We dissected *Top Five,* which turned out not to be very good because the joke was always on the gay dude or the ho, and rarely on Chris Rock himself in any honest way. We discussed our own top five movies of the year, a hobby we took as seriously as critics with bylines did.

We arrived in Goleta, a suburb of white stucco and tile roofs. We bought gum at CVS to mask our coffee breath. I dissolved half a Klonopin, powdery and bittersweet, under my tongue.

We waited on the same side of a booth at the local sushi chain she'd picked. So she wasn't one of those pregnant women who avoided sushi, I gleaned.

And then she showed up. And she ordered the chicken bowl.

She didn't look like the basketball-bellied pregnant woman I'd imagined. Her pregnancy wrapped itself around her ribs and wasn't all that obvious under her loose, sparkly black top. (She said she was addicted to sparkle; there were gold flecks in her eyeliner and glitter-gold Christmas trees on her black nails.) The part of my brain that was still singed by Harmony thought, *All the more proof that it's real—if she were going to fake a pregnancy, she'd make it look like every other pregnancy, right?* Even my rationalizations had rationalizations.

She was real. She was pregnant. She also happened to be beautiful, with heavy-lidded, dark hazel eyes, full lips, and long, auburn-streaked hair. She could easily pass for a relative of CC's.

Like all first dates, I dreaded the moments leading up to it, relaxed a little in the midst of it, and was glad when it was over. In the middle, we ate our chicken and sushi and talked about hobbies (hair, exercising, hiking, gambling) and Mazdas (she and CC both drove one), dead parents, doctors, her other placement, the kicking baby. About how she was godmother to her cousin's kid, how her cousin was a struggling single mom and she just didn't want to go through that. She seemed both relaxed and a little guarded. When CC took her fingers to examine her Christmas tree manicure, she gently lifted her hand away. But she also hugged us hello and goodbye.

She talked about giving birth to her daughter a little over a year and a half ago. "I had contractions in the morning, but I have a high pain tolerance, so I didn't pay much attention to them. Then when I finally went to the hospital, she came so fast."

She wanted us there for this baby's birth, she said. If she was comfortable with that, we'd be honored, I said.

The Zodiac came up and we all agreed we didn't understand astrology and then proceeded to talk about it. She was an Aries, too, and when I said I was stubborn as a ram, she hmmed in agreement.

Toward the end of the meal, I said, "So, we would love to match with you if you feel good about it." No way was I leaving the place without some clarity.

"Oh, yeah, definitely," she said. "Two thumbs."

We floated back to our car and back down the 101. We talked about maternity leave; CC had worked out a plan that sounded doable, where she took six weeks uninterrupted, then six more weeks off from the Art Center during which time she'd see patients. She would quit her extracurricular psychoanalytic program and go back to work at Art Center part time. I would work from home one day a week.

Both of our minds were blown by this intersection of The Future—a place of hoverboards and adult-like confidence—and the actual pages on our calendars.

I texted my friends, because I was enjoying the momentary grace that always came with good fortune. We spent the evening doing early Christmas Eve with my aunt and uncle, and I wanted to stay there, in that moment of warmth and gratitude and excitement, because wasn't the future the place where things got fucked up as often as they worked out?

And then, Monday afternoon, while I was in therapy telling Dr. Schmidt about my knock-on-wood good fortune, Katie—a counselor from IAC—called and I picked up. In her bubbly Valley Girl voice, she told me that Erica hadn't sent her proof of pregnancy yet. She wanted Erica to show some commitment first, she said, because she had a "feeling" about her.

Over the next two days, as my hope drooped and Erica continued to answer Katie's texts but fail to send in her proof of pregnancy—though she claimed she was trying—my annoyance at Katie and IAC increased, until one morning on the phone, I broke into tears, telling Katie it seemed like IAC had this checklist where X + Y = emotional scam.

I resented her for hinting that Erica might be running one;

I wasn't confident she'd place her baby with us, but she *wasn't* Harmony, and she'd been nothing but kind and responsive to us. If she was dragging her feet on the paperwork, maybe it was because she was having second thoughts or stalling for time or trying to get through her first Christmas without her dad. But I didn't think she wanted to hurt us, and she didn't seem like she was trying very hard to get attention.

I texted Erica to say Happy New Year, and she didn't reply. I always loved the lure of a fresh start, but 2015 dragged 2014 and 2012 and 2003 and 1980 behind it like a bag of bricks. On New Year's Day, CC and I drove to Malibu to ride horses at a ranch she'd found online. The day was cool and bright. I kept peeling my jacket off and putting it back on. I tried to listen to our guide, a ruddy-skinned, Los Angeles–grown cowboy, and not think about Erica.

"It's the first day of the year, so I'm trying not to feel bummed out," I told CC as we returned to the car, dusty and tired. Malibu was another world, or several other worlds. This part of it was all rolling hills and chaparral that turned to kindling during fire season. My own life felt far away, but not far away enough.

"Me too," CC sighed. "But who really knows what's going on for Erica right now?"

Later that night, I wrote three fictions in my journal, in which Erica said yes, no, or maybe to adoption. I could never just not imagine the answer to my questions; the best I could do was conjure a kind of multiverse. There was the one where Erica placed with us, and the one where she didn't. There was also one where I got cancer again and died childless. The one where I lived to see grandkids. The one where I lived just long enough to hold a baby who wouldn't remember me. The future I inhabited in my mind seemed to depend on whether I'd had coffee or not, whether I'd had enough sleep, what news headlines I'd stumbled across. Mood and outcome seemed so closely linked that they almost imploded.

In the center of that implosion, that black hole that bent time, lived all the possible stories.

CHAPTER 35: RECALIBRATING

By mid-January, we still had not heard from Erica. I sat on my therapist's couch airing my usual gripes and tears. My sister and I were still figuring out our weird new dynamic. That morning, I'd written a gentle, respectful, last-ditch email to Erica.

Hi Erica,

How are you? CC and I were wondering how things are going. I know that January marks the anniversary of your father's passing, and I imagine that must bring up a lot of emotions. If you need space and time to be with your family, we completely understand; we just want to let you know that we're thinking of you.

We were so excited when you said you wanted to place your baby with us. Since Katie at IAC hasn't been able to reach you, we're not sure if that's still your plan. If you've found another family or decided you want to raise your baby, those are completely valid choices, and you have our blessing. We really respect that you're trying to figure out what's best for your baby. If you just need some time to think things through, that's fine too.

If you DO still want to place with us, we will of course be thrilled and honored! We don't want to bother you during what I'm sure is an intense time, but if you could give us an update either way, we'd be really grateful.

Sending you our warmest wishes,
Cheryl and CC

I got so much nice feedback on it from CC and the moms of my Adoptive Parent Support group online that I almost didn't feel sad when I didn't hear back. Almost.

After therapy, I got my hair cut and thought only a little bit about how Erica was a hairstylist. As I walked into Coffee Bean to work on my YA novel, I checked our adoption email account, as I did periodically, because Murphy's Law dictated that if I didn't, we'd get a bite.

Lo and behold, in tiny text on my phone, was her name in just-replied bold: Erica.

Hello Ladies,

Sorry it has been a horrible start to the new year. We had a sudden tragedy in the family, my uncle passed away on 12/27 so I have been dealing with all the grief again of my father. I do want you guys to be the mothers of the baby. I will definitely be in touch with Katie tomorrow in regards to process. I hope you ladies had a wonderful new year. You guys have been on my mind constantly. The baby needs you ladies . :) I know he

or she will be happy with you guys. I will talk to you guys soon!
Take Care,
Erica

My hands shook as I reached into the deli case for a sandwich that I barely tasted when I finally sat down to eat. I texted CC a summary.

CC: *Forward it! Now!*

I did. CC wrote back, pleased but not fully convinced the uncle story was true. I agreed.

We have learned to expect anything/nothing, I wrote. *Still.*

Totally, she texted back. *Well, back in the saddle.*

I inserted a horse emoji and hit Send. We were developing a shorthand. A few words to sum up the giant hairball of hope and longing and love and frustration and faith and distrust that we were tangled in. We were like . . . parents.

CC and I took tentative steps forward. We emailed our landlord about getting new carpet. We talked about the furniture we'd need. We imagined not hearing from Erica again until she was in labor. But CC had said she would probably place, and CC had good instincts, and I had faith in CC. I clung to her words, because my own sense of reality was as shrunken and warped as a wool sweater that had been run through the dryer.

I swung wildly between being overwhelmed with gratitude for all the people propping me up, the acknowledgments page in my head growing ever longer and more gushing, and feeling like a pioneer. I didn't have a mom. I wasn't pregnant. I didn't have ovaries. There was no dad for this baby. We had just one bathroom and a spare bedroom that was neither spare nor a bedroom.

Our house looked nothing like CC's sister's new place, which we'd seen in Santa Ana on CC's birthday that Sunday. It was a three-bedroom Craftsman restored with a level of care rarely invested in rental properties. There were hardwood floors and built-in bookcases. It had a backyard with a liquid amber tree maintained by a real arborist.

I wasn't prone to house envy to nearly the degree I was prone to other envies. I had nearly terminal baby envy and advanced art envy, yet when it came to house envy, I was stage I or II.

But that day, the Craftsman house slammed up against my baby envy. It looked like a house that a child would grow up in, meaning a house that I or one of my friends had grown up in. Suburban. A yard. Space for the odds and ends that parents were supposed to have: art supplies and ace bandages, heirlooms and gravy boats.

Our house was tidy and small. I loved the funny way it was laid out, and the flow of air and cats between the living room and bedroom, and the art on the walls. But the floor was tilted, and floor lamps and bookshelves that had been standing on it for years had begun to lean. It always took us a long time to replace light bulbs. We'd never registered for anything, and most of our dishes didn't match.

In the car, CC and I caught our breath and engaged in a flurry of self-talk as rain splattered the windshield. It's okay, we assured ourselves. Our low overhead is what allows us to do so much therapy, which is what allows us to still be together and ready to adopt in the first place.

On Wednesday afternoon, Katie from IAC called: Erica had confirmed that she wanted to place with us, and then immediately sent over her proof of pregnancy. The missing piece we needed in order to set up our formal match meeting!

Her fucking POP!

After sharing with CC and the coworkers who were closest at hand, I hopped on Adoptive Parent Support. *POP!!!!!!!* I posted. They all spoke that language. They knew exactly how important proof of pregnancy was, and exactly how much could still go wrong.

A ninety-five-comment thread followed, with congratulations and loving suggestions about car seats and formula. I'd never had such a strong virtual hug.

The gratitude felt like a physical thing, rattling my nerves and bowling me over. That night I wandered, amped up and spaced out, through Target. With a baby due in three weeks or less, I kind of *needed* baby clothes, didn't I?

Just one, I told myself. *Just one.* Because too much would be greedy and presumptuous and we all knew that that led to no baby, right?

I bought an $8 set of zip-up footie pajamas with little foxes on the chest and feet. Unisex (the baby was still butt-to-camera at every ultrasound, Erica said). As adorable as some of the baby clothes were, I also felt a strange ascetic detachment that I can only ascribe to my fantasy of parenthood slowly giving way to reality. I'd mourned baby-as-status-symbol, house-as-beautiful-frame-for-my-beautiful-life. What was in its place was better and more interesting, a life that was about love and learning, but I still missed my perfectionism palpably, the way a happily sober person might miss a drug.

It was fun to watch CC get excited. Her lack of devastation over our letdowns wasn't proof she didn't want to be a mom, as I'd worried, just more proof that she wasn't me. She was up at 6:00 a.m., looking at baby gear online.

But clouds of anxiety swirled up at random, like when I was in line at Starbucks, and sometimes not at random, like when someone at IAC called and didn't leave a message, and I was sure it was Katie calling to say Erica had backed out or been exposed as the biggest scammer ever. As it turned out, it was another counselor trying to reach another Cheryl.

Anxiety is a ghost that haunts your body, and loss haunts your expectations.

We had our match meeting on a Friday afternoon in late January. Erica met us at the IAC office in a bright patterned dress, flip-flops, and her usual sparkly eye makeup and long false lashes. The "match counselor," Miriam, ushered us into IAC's blue-walled conference room and offered us water five or six times. She was tiny, young, and energetic.

She asked us easy questions (family traditions, what we were like as kids) and hard ones that she'd warned us about: What would we do if the baby was born with serious medical problems?

I said, honestly, "I've been reading Dr. Sears, and he writes about how one of his sons was born with Down syndrome. At first, it was really hard for him to see other babies because he'd always be thinking about what his son wouldn't be able to do. But later he started thinking about his son on his son's own terms—what he *could* do, and who he was, and he started to feel a lot better. I think we want to do the same for our child. But if there were medical problems that required a level of care we couldn't provide, we'd do what any loving birth mom does and work with the agency to find parents who could take care of the baby."

We talked about the termination of parental rights—the big thing that would put the ball in our court. We would still be foster parents until a court date about six months out, but at least we could control requirements like showing up to meetings with the agency.

The meeting took more than three hours; all of us were exhausted by the end. I hung out on the Westside and made a weak attempt at writing. I wandered around Ross, looking at baby things, and talked to my sister, picking up our vague, sad fight where we'd left off.

Cathy was mad at me for saying mean things to her when I was sad, for snapping bitter predictions about her "perfect" future, and she was right. I'd been awful. In my defense, Cathy exuded a level of anger and frustration that I couldn't quite wrap my head around, like some sort of ancient religious text that defied translation.

"I'm mad that I'm going to have to let all of this go when the baby comes," she said.

"That's how I felt when you decided to have surgery when I was two weeks out of treatment," I said. "Like, 'Your turn is over. Time to be mature again.' But you don't actually have to stop being mad at me, you know."

We were still arguing when Erica's call came in on the other line.

"Take the call," Cathy said. "I love you."

Erica said, "My water broke."

CHAPTER 36: SOMEONE'S MOM

There's a focus that comes with almost any crisis, where the *This is happening* part marches ahead and does what's needed, and the other part remarks on how strange it is, how it's nothing like how you imagined it, because the Vaseline lens of the imagination has fallen away. It's surreal precisely because it is real.

CC met me at home. The house was a construction zone of unopened Amazon boxes, which I'd planned to organize that evening, or maybe Saturday morning. We loaded the one containing the car seat into her car, along with the bags of baby toiletries and infant clothes friends had given us. I wasn't quite sure why we needed to bring Children's Tylenol to a hospital, and we hadn't washed any of the baby clothes or even bought baby detergent, but arguing with CC seemed like a worse idea than throwing random bags into her back seat.

We called our families from the 101. They congratulated us, said to keep them posted. We hadn't planned to get a changing table, but now CC asked me to call my sister and ask her to get one and set it up in our house. She wanted me to ask my dad to bring up my old dresser and our family rocking chair. He couldn't see why we needed those things immediately. He said what everyone said (usually right before proselytizing their favorite product): "Babies don't need much."

When we got off speakerphone, CC freaked out. "I can't believe he's making us justify what we need! I don't want to *argue* about it. Your dad's been helpful in a million ways, but this isn't one of them. I feel so unheard."

Cottage Hospital was a sprawling Spanish-style building in the middle of a sleepy and sleeping residential neighborhood. It took a long time to find the entrance and longer to find Labor and Delivery. Eventually a nurse led us to Erica's room. It was quiet and dimly lit. She was in a hospital gown and breathing a little bit heavily but otherwise not so different from how we'd left her a few hours before.

"I got home and ordered a pizza, and all of a sudden I noticed I was wet. I was like, *Did I have an accident?* But then I realized."

She'd called her cousin, called us, called her mom and told her not to come home from visiting Erica's aunt in San Diego. So it was just us and a nurse with a soothing voice, who checked Erica's cervix and asked if she felt "pushy."

The agency had given us some paperwork to bring to the hospital. I tried to give it to one of the nurses on duty, but she told us to wait for the hospital social worker, who would be there the next morning. I promptly forgot all about it.

Erica writhed on the bed, saying things like, "Oh my gosh, I'm in so much pain." She'd refused an epidural and now regretted it. When she moaned, she said, "I don't want to stress out the baby!" It seemed to me that this was going to be a stressful experience for the baby no matter what. But even while in labor, Erica was measured and controlled.

I held her hand during the contractions. CC practiced Therapy 101: "It seems like you're just really in a lot of pain."

"I *am*," Erica said, as if CC had just gleaned something very important and personal.

And then, when Erica's cervix was nine centimeters wide and "stretchy," the nurse called the doctor—a grouchy woman who'd been sleeping in the other room—and the room transformed. It was like a theatrical scene switch. The lights went up. Blue tarps were thrown down. Additional nurses appeared. The bed turned into a birthing chair with stirrups.

And then, out slid the baby—a small, red-gray pellet, coated in goo.

"It's a boy," the doctor said.

Per our birth plan, she handed him to Erica, who held him on her chest. They looked so perfect and natural together that my heart took a step back, the way it was used to doing in deference to any mother-child pair. Reverence and longing and not-for-me-ness stood side-by-side for a short, complicated moment.

Then Erica said, "You have a son."

She put the name we chose on his birth certificate, the birth certificate that would be replaced after the adoption was finalized. (This was one of many strange adoption procedures: the replacement of the original birth certificate, turning the first mother into a kind of ghost, hiding the baby's true origin story.)

Dashiell Walker Esquivel. She asked how to spell Dashiell.

Over the ensuing days, people would read the name in text announcements and reply "Congratulations, she's gorgeous!" Or they'd pronounce it Da-SHEEL. For once I was glad I hadn't talked CC into letting me give our kid a weirder name. When I put it on forms, I felt like I was getting away with something, like when I occasionally filled out a survey or signed up for a mailing list using a character's name. For a while, Samantha Netherby, heroine of a novel I'd started in grad school, was my go-to. When I told my therapist I felt like I'd made up Dashiell Walker Esquivel, he said, "Well, we're all partly creations of our parents' imaginations."

"Dash," mused one of the nurses at the hospital. "That's like one of those cool-guy names."

We thought of the name as short and quick and cute, like the kid in *The Incredibles*, not a douche name like Chad or Thad or Cash. And he quickly asserted himself as a Dash more than a Dashiell, and I felt helpless in the wake of his *him*-ness. Not a cool guy necessarily, but a relaxed and informal guy. He would be his own person.

The hospital hadn't gotten the paperwork from IAC yet, so only one of us could stay with Erica in the Mothers and Infants section. (Security was high at Cottage Hospital. Apparently a baby was abducted there a few years ago.) CC got a room at the Best Western down the street.

Erica and I camped out on either side of a cloth curtain. They made up the vinyl bench in the room into a bed for me. We took turns holding Dashiell and sleeping. We disguised the awkwardness and exhaustion as politeness. "Really, it's fine, I've got him," she said. "Get some rest."

On my side of the curtain, I deliriously texted our families and wondered if she was saying goodbye. Even now, thinking about all the pain she went through, all the marks he would leave on her body, only to hand him over to us, feels like looking at the sun—a thing I can't do directly. Like trying to figure out who my own mom is to me.

The next day, CC joined us. Doctors visited. So did nurses and the hospital social worker. Our friends Jennifer and Joel, who lived in Ojai, just happened to be in town picking up Jennifer's dad from the Santa Barbara airport. They showed up with their nice camera and a funky pillowcase that Jennifer joked was a baby sleeping bag. They did a quick photo shoot with Dash and us and Erica.

"What are you going to do when you get home?" I asked Erica.

"Probably some cardio," she said. "And have a bloody Mary."

"You've earned it."

We hugged goodbye. No tears. There are stages of joy, as well as grief. The two probably aren't as different as people think; polar opposites are always connected by an invisible axis through the Earth. I was still in shock, as giddy as when I'd woken up from my mastectomy to learn my lymph nodes were clear. This, too, was like being granted an extension on life. But it wasn't until Sunday morning, in the shower at the hospital room they gave us, that I broke down into tears.

We spent the day at what we called the Baby Spa, eating veggie breakfast burritos from the hospital cafeteria, watching instructional videos about infant CPR, and taking turns holding and feeding Dash.

I kept up my manic texting. The thank-you list for Project Baby was a huge one, and I couldn't wait for my therapist and our former couples therapist and Amy and Robin and Connee and my dad and sister and Kim Miller and Joewon to celebrate with me. And, of course, the Adoptive Parent Support moms. The people who'd helped me get through the worst were the only ones who could really understand what this moment meant. And, in a more perverse Little-Red-Hen sense, I felt like they were the only ones who deserved to.

At every step, I reminded myself Dash wasn't an accomplishment or a party. He was a person. This might be some kind of climax in *our* story, but his was just beginning. A few hours ago he'd been safe and cozy inside a uterus, and now he had ninety-nine problems.

We enjoyed Baby Spa while we could. We weren't sick. We didn't have to make use of the sit-down shower or the weird postpartum granny panties. We also didn't have to deal with maternity leave or health insurance or setting up the bottle warmer just yet. We just had to lie around in our adjustable beds and make conversation with the hospital staff, not one of whom batted an eye about gay open adoption. The jolly, semi-retired social worker was as encouraging as Santa himself might have been. A middle-aged nurse—who fretted when she nicked Dash while removing his umbilical cord clip—shut the door and told us in a quiet voice how her twenty-two-year-old son had just come out as gay. She and her husband were fully supportive, but she'd always wanted grandkids, and her son had always wanted kids, so it was inspiring for her to see us, she said.

Sunday afternoon, Dash took his first car ride, and it was a long one. But he slept through it like a champ, and over the next few days, he distinguished himself as one of those calm babies I always imagined I wasn't.

Dash cried when he was hungry. He cried when he needed a diaper change. But he never cried for no reason. Then again, maybe no one did.

ACKNOWLEDGMENTS

I'm grateful to the people who helped me live to tell this story, and those who pulled me gently back from the brink when doom was the only narrative I could hear. My dad, Chris Klein, who loves me fiercely, steadily, and unconditionally; my sister, Cathy Klein-Bedell, who never gets tired of me, or at least pretends not to, and channels our mom in all the best ways; and my spouse, CC. These events belong to her too, but she never questioned why I needed to write my version. She reminds me that the universe is as wondrous as it is unfair, and that enjoying it is a worthy pursuit. Raising Dash—that joyful, sensitive, goofy kid who sometimes slept till 7:30 and let me work on this book—with her is the delight of my life. Nicole M. made it possible, and I send her my gratitude every day.

Dr. Sam Chung at City of Hope said the exact words I needed to hear, on top of the saving-my-life part of his work. Dr. Dawn Hills, Dr. Max Lehfeldt, and Dr. Irina Jasper also encountered me at my most vulnerable and terrified, and pieced me back together. Julie Roberts Sanders, our couples therapist, got CC and me through our crisis year. My therapist, Dr. Jens Schmidt, finds a thematic arc in every session, and I would be blown away by his own work as a storyteller if I weren't so busy appreciating his role as realistic optimist and advocate of good-enough-ness.

Nicole Kristal is equal parts loyal, honest, and caring. Kim Miller is a hilarious, wonderful, and very busy person who always finds time to respond to my medical freak-outs. Keely Shaw is a fierce, funny veteran mom. Jamie FitzGerald Lahey weathered far more of my breakdowns than her job description required. Amy Gallagher is my favorite radical pragmatist, and she always lifts CC's spirits, too. Finally, the Women in the Next Bed: Joewon Yoon and Molly Kochan O. They are mirrors and windows.

Then there are the many people who helped me write this story. The IKEA Writers' Collective is my source of daily inspiration and grace: Aubrey Collins, Shea Tuttle, Debbie Weingarten, and Jennifer Young. My IRL writing group, who are as brilliant as they are kind: Elizabeth Chase, Sarah Eggers, Auzelle Epeneter, Kate Martin Rowe, and Kim Young. Dan Koeppel was the first person who saw this book as a book, and told me to write it in order. Dani Shapiro told me in the most encouraging way possible that my draft was a collection of notes, and having an eight-week-old child was just the beginning of parenthood. Meg Lemke at *MUTHA* is the best editor and advocate a writer-mom could ask for.

Wendy Thomas Russell at Brown Paper Press saw the heart of this book from the first page, and lent her considerable expertise to the process of making it stronger and taking it into the world. Good editors are word surgeons, and I'm immeasurably grateful to Wendy for applying her craft with such kindness, delicacy, and savvy.

CHERYL E. KLEIN is the author of two works of fiction, *The Commuters* (City Works Press) and *Lilac Mines* (Manic D Press). Her stories and essays have appeared in *Blunderbuss Magazine*, *The Normal School*, and several anthologies. Klein writes and edits for *MUTHA Magazine* and blogs about the intersection of life, art, and carbohydrates at breadandbread.blogspot.com. She lives in Los Angeles with her partner and son.

BROWN
PAPER
PRESS

BROWN PAPER PRESS engages readers on topics of contemporary culture through quality writing and thoughtful design. Unbound by genre, our press delivers socially relevant works that advise, guide, inspire and amuse. We champion authors with new perspectives, strong voices, and original ideas that just might change the world.

For more information about new releases, author events, and special promotions, visit brownpaperpress.com.